THROUGH THE CARIBBEAN

Through the Caribbean

The MCC Tour of the West Indies,

1959–1960

ALAN ROSS

faber and faber

This edition first published in 2012
by Faber and Faber Ltd
Bloomsbury House, 74–77 Great Russell Street
London WC1B 3DA

Printed and bound by CPI Group (UK) Ltd, Croydon, CR0 4YY

The right of Alan Ross to be identified
as author of this work has been asserted in accordance
with Section 77 of the Copyright, Designs and Patents Act 1988

A CIP record for this book is available from the British Library

ISBN 978-0-571-29614-9

CONTENTS

CONTENTS

INTRODUCTION

In 1955 Australia, having been beaten at home by England in Tyson's series, went straight to the Caribbean and demolished the West Indians 3–0, becoming in the process the first visiting side to beat the West Indians on their own pitches. In 1957 England, under Peter May, beat West Indies 3–0 at home. A mere seven years earlier John Goddard's side, with the three W's and Stollmeyer as leading batsmen, and Ramadhin and Valentine as spinners, had cleaned up England 3–1 in England. Four years later only miraculous efforts by Hutton had salvaged a draw from a series England were losing 2–0 by the time of the third Test in Georgetown, Guyana.

It was expected by most people that West Indies would do more than hold their own in 1960. They had in Wesley Hall the fastest bowler on view, they had a dazzling array of fast scoring batsmen, and they still had Ramadhin, to say nothing of the all-round skills of Worrell and Sobers.

In the event, without ever looking the more talented side, England won their first ever series in the Caribbean. Only one Test, at Port-of-Spain, was finished and, despite some time-wasting bottle-throwing, England won it by 256 runs.

For the most part it was a batsman's tour, though Hall and Watson, both warned for intimidatory bowling, gave England a rough time. There were no helmets then, nor did anyone appear to need one. But from Cowdrey and Pullar, the opening pair, all the way down the line England batted with immense determination. When May, never in good health, had to return home before the final Test, Parks came into the side and made a saving hundred.

England were lucky to win every toss, but they played as a side, and a single day of inspired bowling by Trueman and Statham won them the crucial advantage. Thereafter, Dexter, Barrington, Smith and Subba Row made sure it was never thrown away.

Looking back, that journey down the islands twenty-five years ago seems to belong to a magical period. No one can forget their first experience of cricket in the Caribbean, and the West Indies then seemed pleasure-loving and trouble-free, as well as the most beautiful place on earth.

Since then, the image has lost some of its shine, the feeling become less friendly. Although there were bouncers enough bowled by Wesley Hall in his day, there was no endless battering by relays of pace bowlers at each end, hour after hour. Ramadhin even finished top of the West Indian bowling averages, though Hall took more wickets.

Of course, it was no paradise in the Caribbean in 1960, whatever it may have seemed like superficially. But the islands were much cheaper to live in and they were less Americanised. Politics, visible though they were, intruded less. Best of all, there was the heat of the tropics, day after day of hot sun, blue skies and breaking surf, and England edging their way to memorable victory.

A. R., 1985

PREFACE

THE 1960 Test series between West Indies and England will be renowned for two things especially: for England's first victory ever in the Caribbean, and for the riot that so disfigured the Second Test at Port-of-Spain, Trinidad. The former, against most predictions, was memorable; the second will, I hope, be regarded as a signal lapse that must not be repeated.

It was a grim, ruthless, evenly contested and sometimes dramatic group of matches. Not until the final morning of the Fifth Test was the outcome certain. In such circumstances the tension was bound to hold; and for the student of the game, no less than for the partisan spectator, these Tests were of absorbing interest. I trust that this tension, as well as the technical interest, carries over into print.

Yet all was not entirely well; four draws in five matches speaks for itself. Draws can be exciting, and two of these, at least, were. But such pitches as were provided on this tour make for impossible contests, if the final result is taken to matter. Otherwise the time element would have to be scrapped and each match played to a finish. Had these been timeless Tests West Indies would probably have won, though it is doubtful if there would have been anyone there to watch. But the time element exists: and if at the end of six five-hour days, the game is barely more than half over, then something must be badly wrong. In this case, it was, of course, the pitches. In West Indies, unless a team is willing to lose, it has usually small chance of winning—except, as happened with England on this occasion, when it consistently wins the toss, or is overwhelmingly the stronger. It is not enough to settle for a steady 200 runs a day: which is more than what, once England got wise to the correct defensive tactics, West Indies were usually reduced to. The side that can miraculously achieve a break-through calls the tune thereafter. West Indies lost the tosses, fatally buckled up in the Second Test, and disappointingly failed to strike a faster scoring rate than England in the last three. In the circumstances, though they possessed brilliant individual players, they deserved as a side to lose. England were the better team, the one which showed greater determination and which developed a shrewder over-all tactical appreciation.

I don't know what can be done about West Indies pitches: they conduce to a dog-in-the-manger attitude on the part of batsmen and to slave mentality among bowlers. Considering everything, the results, especially as far as England are concerned, were remarkable. The more casual spectators often found themselves assisting at a ritual, rather than enjoying a spectacle, but this was in the nature of things—assuming the pitches, the climate, the sequence of events, and the prize at stake.

The number of overs bowled during each day was often less than one likes to see: but on discouraging wickets, in great heat, an air of urgency is a lot to expect. Speed up the wickets and you will speed up the tempo. Taking everything into consideration, there was nothing to choose between the two sides: they were both slow.

One factor, more than any other, marred this series, producing a lack of sympathy, if not actual hostility, between the two sides. That was the persistent short-pitched bowling of the two West Indian fast bowlers, Hall and Watson. Certain critics in the West Indies could see nothing untoward in three, sometimes four, balls an over being banged into the pitch so that they rose at the batsman's throat, forcing him to fend, or duck, or, if he were quick enough, to hook. They regarded this as perfectly reasonable, given the pitches and, of course, the bowlers. But if the law referring to such bowling has any meaning at all, then, not twice as actually happened, but a dozen times the bowlers should have been restrained. Unfortunately, the law, as it stands, makes impossible demands on any but the toughest, and most assured, of umpires. One must be clear about this. It is not the out-and-out bouncer that is in question: these fly harmlessly overhead and merely waste time. It is the repeated pitching, by fast bowlers, on a length of such shortness that the batsman's instinctive concern—however he may adjust and control it—must be for his physical safety. It is hard to pin down in words: in practice, what I mean is quite plain. Again, it is the wickets that are to blame, generally. But something will have to be done soon if the finer arts of batting are not to fall into desuetude, or the spectators simply to give up.

It has been suggested that one remedy against slow play by a fielding side might be the introduction of a standard number of overs, rather than of hours, for each day, any deficiencies being made up on the next day. About both this and the question of defining and remedying persistent short-pitching there will have to be careful thought. Cricket has had constantly to adapt itself to problems throughout its history and up till now it has succeeded without loss of character, if not entirely without loss of charm.

However, this book is not all about cricket. As in *Australia 55*, and as in *Cape Summer*, I have presumed some interest in places and people, in environment and local character. A tour of this kind is both a journey into colonial history and an exploration of its landscape. Cricket is as much an integral part of West Indian culture as it is of our own, and I have treated it so. It is also part of the process of learning, sometimes enjoyably, sometimes not. The non-cricket passages are quickly apparent and anyone desiring to skip is cordially invited to do so.

A number of the photographs are my own; for certain others I am indebted, as far as action pictures of the Tests are concerned, to Mr. William Alleyne in Barbados, to the *Trinidad Guardian*, to the *Daily Gleaner* of Jamaica, and the *Daily News* in Georgetown, British Guiana. I must acknowledge, too, the help of the Tourist Boards of Barbados, of Trinidad and Tobago, and of Jamaica, and of the

Government Information Service, British Guiana. In addition, I am especially grateful for the help of Mr. George Hunte in Barbados; of Mr. Ernest Burbridge, of the British Council, in Jamaica; of Lieutenant-Colonel Roy Alston, Mr. Derek Walcott and Miss Margaret Maillard in Trinidad; and of Mr. A. J. Seymour in British Guiana.

A. R.

I

DESCENT INTO BARBADOS

THE darkness that had begun at four o'clock on a gloomy, drizzling post-Christmas afternoon in London ended seventeen hours later with a thin sliver of light, like a piece of lemon skin, over Bermuda. The great wings of the Britannia cut and tilted through these growing segments of yellow as if peeling them. Fighting head-winds all the way over the Atlantic we had been forced to make for Gander to refuel, and there, at two in the morning, we had landed into a temperature seven under zero. The hardier spirits descended for coffee and to stretch their legs; John Woodcock, of *The Times*, my fellow-passenger, stumbled over me wrapped in a blanket as if emerging from an igloo. I was not among them. Behind me, Jim Swanton slumbered on his bunk, a sultan islanded in sleep. Ian Peebles, more upright of posture, nodded hopefully (for rest was not easy among airline dervishes re-stocking and cleaning), doubtless dreaming of Chalfont St. Giles, if not Inverness.

We had assembled, what seemed an age earlier, at London Airport, Jim and Anne Swanton, Rex and Elspeth Alston, Ian, John and myself, with racing honourably represented by Noel Murless, trainer of some of the Queen's horses, and his wife, and Quinton Gilbey, an old friend, racing correspondent and tipster (though I know not at what financial profit to his readers), of whom I was to see much later. Such are the differences between our respective sports that the racing fraternity (one could not, with any regard for truth, call cricket writers and players a fraternity) were paying for their own holiday, while we were being paid to come. It could be said—depending on how you look at it—that we were the more fortunate, though during the first Test Match I began to doubt it.

Friends, wives, children, with Gubby Allen, Chairman of Selectors, on hand to provide official benediction, were there to see us off, but soon they had sunk away beneath us, left to resume their enforced hibernation while we should wake to the light and the coral sea. I got out my homework, Wiseman's *Short History of the British West Indies*, and Nicole's *West Indian Cricket*, but somehow there seemed too much to talk about, or one had drunk too many whiskies at BOAC's expense, and such sentences like 'Modern history in the West Indies begins with the discovery of the islands by Columbus and the influx of Spaniards, Portuguese, Dutch, English and French, seeking trade, settlement, souls to save and bodies to enslave, strategic bases, nurseries for seamen and testing-grounds for ships, treasure and adventure' merely fuddled me, taking me back to those long hot afternoons at Haileybury, when, listening to droning discourses about the Conquistadors, I fretted impatiently to get back to the nets and to Bert Wensley's pithy admonitions about the outswinger. The history of West Indian cricket was little better, and though I returned to both with pleasure, I was contented enough now to let them drop off my lap and to doze fitfully into what seemed a disgracefully late dawn.

At Bermuda Airport, the only 'dry' airport in the world, I believe (though the idea of drink was repellent at that hour), we decanted passengers, sought coffee and attempted to freshen up. The coffee tasted like a detergent, the lavatories contained not even old newspapers, there were neither soap nor towels, nor, for those who use such things, plugs for electric irons. No wonder it was dry. A semi-intoxicated man would have broken the place up.

Three hours or so later—noon local time—we taxied in along the tarmac of Seawell Airport, Barbados, stepping out into what, after London and Gander, appeared the oven-like temperature of 82°.

Cameras flashed, we were welcomed by John Goddard,

most genial and hospitable of former West Indian captains, who was to do so much to make our stay enjoyable, and by Stanton Gittens, the Press Liaison officer. Customs, tickets, immigration, and we were bowling along the shores of the bluest bays—the eastern Mediterranean and the Great Barrier Reef not excepted—that I have ever seen. Boats were drawn bows up on the salt-white sand, coral-pink fishing nets, slung between palms and casuarinas like frail hammocks, hung out to dry, poinsettias like scarlet mops bobbed in front of squat confectionery villas and coffee-coloured weatherboard shacks. We swung through narrow roads almost overhung by tall sugar canes, the driver of our taxi, in that curious Barbadian yawny singsong drawl, with its overtone now of the Welsh valleys, now of Ireland or the west country, answering questions with great good humour. Our taxi drivers became close friends, and by the time we left, there was little of their private lives we did not know. He told us about the fish and the monkeys, about illegitimacy and the snares of marriage (the possession of a family scarcely ever implied the possession of a wife), about the delights of Harry's Niterie and the prospects for the Test.

'Are there any snakes in Barbados,' I asked. 'I de only snake in de island, Boss,' he replied, laughing hugely.

★ ★ ★

The Marine Hotel, our home for the next fortnight, is a large rambling place of coral stone weathered to pale pink, with deep eaves, verandas looking onto pleasant gardens, and a relaxed, informal air. Tussore suits and bow ties were *de rigueur* among the elderly expatriates, though occasionally American tourists, in baseball caps, plaid shirts and Bermuda shorts, outlining generally unsuitable bottoms, wandered through the palms and flamboyants, or collapsed, exhausted by sightseeing, on the Victorian white wickerwork chairs.

The Marine, by metropolitan standards, has decided drawbacks of service and cuisine, but a friendlier hotel there has never been. The brilliant sand and surf of Accra Beach are two minutes away by taxi, or a ten-minute walk through rock pools full of scuttling crabs and tiny striped fish. The rooms, each with adjoining bath, are comfortable, spacious and airy, and these at night, with the muslin mosquito nets hoisted like sails, and the tree frogs tinkling like the harness bells of Indian *garis*, returned me nostalgically to the Bengal of my childhood. I could smell my father's cigar and hear the ice tinkling in the burra pegs that succeeded each other with formidable rapidity after bad days at the office, the Legislative Assembly or, more likely, the races.

M.C.C. had preceded us by the *Camito* to Barbados, ploughing through cruel December gales by way of Guadeloupe and Grenada, and one by one, in the bar, one greeted old friends. Peter May, Colin Cowdrey, Brian Statham, with whom I had been round Australia and South Africa: but it was a shock to realize that only those three of the present fifteen had been with Hutton in that legendary series of 1954/55 or on the more disappointing one through the Union in 1956/57. No Sir Leonard in the corner, with wary eye cocked for the calculated joke or features drawn after a night of metaphysical or financial speculation; no Jim Laker, stalking the foyers with the just air of one who regarded the taking of 19 wickets in a Test against Australia as little better than a chore; no Trevor Bailey, explaining in the lift with carrying tones just how the ball had come off bat to pad, rather than vice versa; no Frank Tyson, loping and camera-hung, nor Godfrey Evans, bubbling like Veuve Clicquot with the cork half off. No Denis Compton, nor not-so-happy-go-lucky Johnny Wardle. These were the great players among more or less my own generation, and it was impossible not to miss them.

Instead there were Geoffrey 'Noddy' Pullar, of Lancashire, one of the successes of the series against India, a sturdy left-handed opening batsman of sound technique and stolid temperament; Ken Barrington, restored to his rightful place as a Test all-rounder, with infectious sparring-partner's grin; Fred Trueman, puffing on his pipe, and thinking four-letter thoughts about West Indian pitches; Ted Dexter, an aloof all-rounder whose selection had not pleased the popular pundits who saw in it a predilection for amateurs; Roy Swetman, as wicketkeeper, with Keith Andrew as deputy; Ray Illingworth, a Yorkshireman with at moments a disconcerting resemblance to Wardle, especially on the field, and Pinocchio-featured David Allen, with barely a full season for Gloucestershire behind him, as off-spinners; Tom Greenhough, as leg-spinner; Alan Moss as third pace bowler; Mike Smith, scorer of 3,000 runs during the summer, and Ramon Subba Row as batsmen. As Peter May said at a pre-sailing press conference —and was obliged to say what must have been monotonously often throughout the tour—it was 'a young experimental side'. There were two other changes. Freddie Brown, as Manager, had been succeeded by Walter Robins; and we had no longer George Duckworth, most Pickwickian of wicketkeepers, as scorer, baggageman, philosopher and friend. However it all turned out, one thing was for sure: it would not, by a long chalk, be the same.

We had scarcely settled in before the West Indies players, 13 of whom had been nominated already, began to arrive. Sonny Ramadhin from Trinidad; Rohan Kanhai from British Guiana, with that great chuckling and noble giant Clyde Walcott, now retired, over to observe. Gerry Alexander, West Indies Captain, and Frank Worrell, last of the fabulous W's, all of whom were born within a stone's throw of each other within the same year here in Barbados, flew in from Jamaica. Already the local Barbadians, Gary Sobers, mercifully recovered from the heartrending car accident that killed his friend Collie Smith, Wesley Hall and Hunte had checked in. Perhaps, had it not been for Collie Smith's death, we should not have seen Worrell, who had played no first-class cricket at all since West Indies toured England on their wretched tour of 1957.

Watching all the players arrive was like being in a concert hall with the orchestra tuning up. The full circus was present; the familiar circuit was about to begin.

★   ★   ★

I had few quarrels with the M.C.C. side when it was announced. My own choice, though, would have differed in two respects. First, likeable and technically proficient as Keith Andrew is, my second wicketkeeper would certainly have been Jim Parks. Not because he comes from my own county of Sussex, but because on a tour such as this the deputy wicketkeeper has scarcely any wicketkeeping to do and Parks would have made an extra batsman for colony matches, one moreover who would have pushed the others hard for a place in the Tests as a batsman in his own right. Parks has, in some quarters, been regarded as suspect in temperament and not exactly a placid player of the quickest bowling. This latter he is not: he cuts, drives and hooks it, and if sooner or later he pays the penalty, he has generally scored several dozen more runs against it than most of our backfoot prodders and pushers. I suggest that anyone who doubts this looks up Parks' innings over the last three seasons against Surrey (Loader), Lancashire (Statham), Yorkshire (Trueman) or any other fast bowler they fancy in preference. The real point, however, is that he is as safe and dominating a player of off-spin and leg-break bowling as any we have, and in view of the probable arrival of Tayfield with the South Africans this summer and of Benaud the year after, his presence in the Caribbean could have been only to the good. (In fact, he was to arrive there, but in the capacity of coach in Trinidad). It's true that 1959 was his first full season as a wicketkeeper and that he had no one faster than Bates or Thomson, or more ambiguous of spin than Marlar, to keep to. Yet by some extraordinary feat of sympathetic magic he induced bowlers who probably get the ball past the bat less than those of any other county to allow him the greatest number of catches in the country and to put him firmly at the head of the wicketkeepers' table. This, I know, is no test of absolute merit and Andrew, with Tyson, Tribe, Manning, Allen and Barrick to take regularly, must of course be regarded as the more experienced and correct technician. Parks' progress over the summer was astonishing to observe, and since wicketkeeping on Caribbean pitches demands less skill than anywhere else in the world, the chances are that Parks would have been more than up to it. At any rate, I, in company with the correspondents of the *Daily Telegraph*, *The Times* and the *Sunday Dispatch*—to name only three shrewd judges—considered it a risk well worth the taking.

As to temperament, Parks has consistently played magnificently for M.C.C. when under official scrutiny at Lords, and year after year he has carried the Sussex batting against every kind of attack.

It was a great pity that the West Indians, so appreciative of elegance and imagination in batting, were to be denied a view of one who, after May and Cowdrey, is our most exciting and varied stroke player. At least, denied hindsight, that was how it looked then.

What probably turned the scales against Parks was the fear that Swetman might be put out of action early on. In which case Parks' form against Statham and Greenhough— the only two likely to cause him difficulty—would have had to be taken on trust. Yet Statham is of an accuracy that makes few demands on a wicketkeeper's agility, while Greenhough, as it turned out, was not used as the striking force that had been expected.

The second change would have been Wardle. I don't propose to go into this controversy yet again—and to readers of *The Observer* my views must be familiar to the point of boredom—except to say that, overseas, he seemed to me now our only potentially match-winning bowler. I base my views on his performances in Australia in 1954/55 (when Hutton confined him largely to stock bowling), in South Africa in 1956/ 1957 (when the South Africans could make little or nothing of his chinaman) and his showing on the last tour of West Indies, about which I quote Alex Bannister, *Daily Mail* correspondent, in his book *Cricket Cauldron*: 'I thought that in the two Tests in which he played, Wardle proved to be an essential member of the team. These were the two Tests England won . . . Wardle baffled a surprising number of the West

Indies batsmen with his left-arm chinamen and googlies, probably because no one in the islands bowls this type of ball, and therefore many of the batsmen found themselves playing against it for the first time in their lives.' This still holds good.

I will add only that I regarded Wardle's quarrel with Yorkshire as a local one, that though he behaved subsequently with crazy and shortsighted impulsiveness, it was under much provocation, and that, on any of his three M.C.C. tours, he never put a foot wrong. He may not be the most genial or sociable of creatures, and I express my opinion here, not expecting it to be popular, but merely practical. I find it hard to believe that anyone could seriously dispute that England would have been a stronger and better-balanced side with him. Those who would object to him on other grounds seem to me dismally ignorant of the stresses undergone, in this day and age, by a professional cricketer, of international class and possessing unique gifts, who finds himself passed over—as were Hutton, Watson and Wardle—in favour of a comparative nonentity (as far as cricket is concerned) by their county committee.

Nevertheless, I did not regard these omissions, predictable if disappointing, as of major importance. It was possible they might not even matter at all. And at least it allowed the entry into Test cricket of Allen, of Gloucestershire, a young off-spinning all-rounder, whose bowling, fielding and batting in the First Test quickly confirmed his promise.

★　　★　　★

As to the more general context of these Tests, both for England and West Indies they were something in the nature of experiment. Though nearly every player on each side had played in a Test Match before, few had done so against each other, or against the major cricketing countries of Australia and South Africa. The West Indians had been blooded against Pakistan, the young England players against India.

This in fact was to be M.C.C.'s eighth tour of the West Indies, though not till the fourth visit, when the captain was the Hon. F. S. G. Calthorpe, was a Test Match played. The first English visit was in 1895 when R. S. Lucas led a party, and this was followed a year later by two teams, under Lord Hawke and A. Priestley, touring the islands at the same time. In 1900 West Indies, under R. S. A. Warner, came to England, and this visit was returned in 1902 when R. A. Bennett took out a side. Professionals were included for the first time under Lord Brackley, in 1905, and then, in 1911, M.C.C. lent their name to the proceedings. A. F. Somerset led the two first M.C.C. teams, the Hon. F. S. G. Calthorpe the next two, R. E. S. Wyatt the fifth, in 1935, G. O. Allen the sixth, in 1948, and L. Hutton the seventh in 1954.

Not one of these sides returned victorious in the rubber. In 1929/30 Calthorpe won one, drew two and lost one; in 1934/35 Wyatt lost two, drew one, won one; in 1947/48 Allen lost two, drew two; and in 1953/54 Hutton lost two, won two, drew one. In England, West Indies lost all three Tests in 1928, lost two and drew one in 1933, under G. C. Grant, drew two, lost one under R. S. Grant in 1939. Then, after the war, in 1950, came J. D. Goddard's great triumph. England won the first Test at Old Trafford, then lost the remaining three, including at Lords. It was the year of the three W's, of Ramadhin and Valentine, of Lord Beginner's victory calypso. 1957, when much the same stars, with the reinforcement of the young Sobers and Kanhai, came again under John Goddard, was a disastrous season for West Indies. Ramadhin ran through England in the first innings of the first Test at Edgbaston, but in the second innings May and Cowdrey, in their record-breaking stand of 411, literally hammered Ramadhin into the ground. He was never any trouble again, and West Indies, with Walcott, Weekes and Worrell never coming off together, were outplayed in each of the remaining Tests. Weekes played a legendary innings in a vain attempt to save the second Test at Lords, Walcott and Worrell batted at times with the dignity and magnificence of declining masters, but the weather, the toss and injuries were against them.

This series, then, saw the jettisoning of most of the established great on both sides. Of the West Indians, Walcott and Weekes had retired, Valentine was no longer regarded as of Test quality, Goddard and Atkinson, former Test captains, played only club cricket. In their places Hunte, Butcher, Solomon and Alexander, the new captain, had won their spurs in Pakistan. Of those who toured England in 1957 Worrell, Sobers, Kanhai, Ramadhin, Alexander and Hall remained. On paper it seemed a formidable batting side, especially on West Indian wickets. The bowling remained to be seen.

★   ★   ★

M.C.C.'s performance, in their first Colony match against Barbados, admittedly the strongest colony side, was not such as to inspire confidence. Towards the end of the second day Barbados had declared at 533 for 5, and M.C.C. were 23, with Cowdrey, Smith and May out. A comparative newcomer, Seymour Nurse, had thrashed around to the tune of 213, while Sobers, scoring 154 without apparent effort, proved that there was no psychological reaction after his accident. He batted, as he did throughout the series, with his right wrist strapped, though it's doubtful whether it would have made much difference if his whole arm had been in splints. The first thing he had done, on returning home from England, had been to go out and practise on the streets with his brothers, using an ashcan as a wicket, in order to accustom himself at once to the greater bounce and the harsh glare. He played in this innings with ominous certainty, appearing to have all the time in the world against both Statham and Trueman.

None of the M.C.C. bowlers looked up to much, and May, not yet having got the hang of the field placing, had no answer to Sobers and Nurse. Trueman looked little over medium pace, his 24 overs costing him 110 runs without reward, while Statham, who bowled 19 overs for only 34, seemed intent on conserving his energies. Illingworth rarely flighted the ball, and his aim generally was too various for May to set the 6—3 field essential to keep runs down. Barrington bowled his leg-spinners rather more reliably than Greenhough, getting greater bounce out of the pitch, and this performance, keeping Greenhough out of the first Test, finally cooked his goose once and for all.

When M.C.C. batted, the pitch, that had seemed devoid of all spirit for two days, suddenly appeared to show signs of life. At any rate Griffith, a big hulking fellow, banged the ball down on it and even managed to run the odd one away. Cowdrey was l.b.w. to him for 16, Smith was yorked first ball, and May, surviving the hat-trick, edged a lifting outswinger to slip. One way and another, but pretty laboriously all the time, M.C.C. struggled up to 238. Pullar contributed 46, Barrington a painfully tentative 79, Dexter and Swetman, the two most fluent of the lot, 33 each.

Following on, M.C.C. did rather better. Smith was again yorked by Griffith, fourth ball this time, but most of the others got between twenty and eighty. Nevertheless, eight minutes before stumps were due to be drawn, M.C.C. were out for 352. It had been agreed, before the game began, that an extra half hour could be claimed if there was any likelihood of a finish. Everton Weekes, captaining Barbados for the first time—which he did with unobtrusive subtlety and skill, as well as taking 4 for 38 with donkey-dropping leg-breaks—therefore exercised his prerogative. Barbados needed 58 runs in 28 minutes.

Weekes sent in Hunte and a hitter of great local renown, Cammie Smith. The shadows of the palm trees and of the stands had placed the pitch in total shade. The sunset, flaring behind the tamarinds, was being overhauled by storm clouds. By the time Statham began his first over the light had almost gone.

Cammie Smith at once showed himself no respecter of reputations. With a series of long-armed pulls and hits off the back foot he smote at Statham and Trueman with such biblical fury that 50 came in 19 minutes. For some of this time it was raining heavily and Statham, cartwheeling to earth in mid-delivery, pulled a muscle that subsequently put him out of the First Test Match. The ball was wet, the bowlers, unable to get a foothold, pitched short, and Smith did the rest.

To mounting and frenzied cheers Barbados finally got home with two minutes to spare. The crowds gathered outside the pavilion, chanting 'We want Weekes', 'We want Smith', until at last these two heroes appeared.

It had been a great occasion, the first time Barbados had beaten M.C.C. since Sir Harold Austin led them to victory against Calthorpe's team in 1926.

★   ★   ★

There were, of course, extenuating circumstances as far as M.C.C. were concerned. They had played on the mat in Grenada and, apart from this, the only fixture had been a two-day affair against Barbados Colts. That was scarcely enough for them to acclimatise themselves, to get used to the differences of light, of pace, of bounce. Colin Cowdrey told me how he had found that the ball seemed to hang up in the air, others appeared to find it on top of them before they got a proper sight of it. Either way, it made timing difficult and I have never seen a top-class batsman push back so many full pitches to mid-off as Barrington did in his two long painstaking innings. Another lesson that had to be learned the hard way was that it was not so much the half-volley that West Indians hammered but the ball just short of it which they hit on the rise off the back foot.

Again, the M.C.C. spin bowlers were novices in these conditions, uncertain of a suitable strategy, unaware yet of an economic field-setting.

But, even taking all this into consideration, it was plain that, unless Statham or Trueman were able to produce devastating spells, the M.C.C. bowlers were going to find it hard going. There was no left-arm bowler of any kind; no stock bowler to take Bailey's place (unless Dexter was to make marked strides); no spinner with anything like the experience or subtlety of Laker, the occasional hostility of Lock.

M.C.C., too, had shown, at a crucial point of the second innings, their old fallibility against the leg-spinner, even so kindly a one as Weekes.

Yet, curiously, this defeat did M.C.C. some good rather than harm. It quickly removed any illusions about the nature of their task in the Tests, removing too a growing scepticism and fatalism about the possibility of bowlers taking wickets. They *could* be taken, it was plain; but guile and flight rather than finger spin had to be the weapons of the spinner on so placid a pitch, while the quick bowlers, afforded so brief a honeymoon with the new ball's shine, had to rely on sheer pace and steepness of lift, or intelligent variations of pace, with discriminating use of the crease, for their wickets. Griffith, of Barbados, for instance, had used the full width to slant the ball into the batsman at an angle.

The other thing was that May, by playing on through the rain to allow Barbados victory, earned much goodwill—goodwill that, after M.C.C.'s last tour of these islands, was sadly needed. The constant on-and-off-the-field complaints about that tour—as also about M.C.C.'s tour of South Africa in 1956/57—became one of our most constant burdens when receiving hospitality. The truth was that several veteran members of those teams, Test-tour weary, affected a distant superciliousness of manner that often wounded and offended. At the same time, many people, wanting to be kind, and eager to arrange outings and entertainments, tend to forget the varying claims on a touring cricketer's time. So that, if players seem to appear offhand and unenthusiastic, they need to remember how exhausting it can be constantly to have to see new faces, however well-disposed. There are, too, the professional buttonholers who fasten on to cricketers longing only to be left alone, and who regale them with stale and tedious cricket anecdotes till death would seem a better fate. Great strength of character, tact and charm are needed to prise off such leeches, the touring cricketer's vocational hazard, and it has to be said that Test cricketers are not chosen specifically with these attributes in mind.

Kensington Oval, Bridgetown, where the Colony match and the First Test Match were played, is not among the most decorative of grounds, though it has a certain local appeal. The pavilion, with its green balconies and white bedhead back, is latched on to various stands that are both gimcrack in appearance and of contrasting and undistinguished design. The Challenor stand, where the gentry sit on the first floor, is under cover, the lower part forming a cream-coloured cement sight-screen. There are two other covered stands, also an uncovered one, but over half the ground is simply grass, wired off from the field of play so that the spectators there appear to be prisoners in a cage. There are no seats here, so people either squat on their haunches in front, or stand behind with faces peering through the wire. Down here are the fried flying-fish booths, the negroes in fabulous garish shirts, cowboy-style hats and pants, and their women in cinnamon, scarlet or turquoise dresses. Elsewhere, higher in the social scale, sit the coloured Barbadians, magnificently dressed, the lithe women moving to and from their seats with affecting and regal grace. Tall palms curve round to the south, studded here and there with flamboyants and tamarinds, and in several of these rickety private pavilions, howdah-like in opulence of decoration, had been constructed. At moments of excitement these swayed alarmingly in the north-east Trades.

On my first visit to the ground John Goddard and Gerry Gomez, both members of the West Indian Selection Committee, who had given me a lift up, described how Caribbean wickets are prepared. The pitch is completely shaved and after that watered. The cut grass is then rolled into the ground until it has almost disappeared. The result is a striated, camel-coloured wicket, like plasticine in texture, with a network of cracks, like small veins, on the surface. As the match progresses these cracks widen, sometimes chipping, though with little effect. Such life as the pitch possesses lasts for about half an hour, after its final watering; otherwise it starts slow, imperceptibly quickening up each day.

One other thing deserves recording about the Bridgetown ground. That is the daily appearance there of a gentleman variously known as King Dyall, the Count, or The Best Dressed Man in the Island. He takes his place in the open stand each day, carrying white gloves, sharkbone cane, and wearing alternately a scarlet, butterfly-yellow or white shark-skin suit. He uses two buttonholes, a rose in one, a piece of costume jewellery in the other, and as he comes through the gates the crowd rise to him, giving him prolonged applause. He doffs his white fedora in solemn recognition of his ovation, and takes his seat with the due deference and graciousness of a Governor. Sometimes he changes costume during an interval, and makes as formal a reappearance. The cricket usually has to stop for him.

Subsequently, I had several long talks with King Dyall. His full name, he told me, was Redvers Dundonald Dyall, and he was named after Sir Redvers Buller, a Boer War hero whom his father much admired. A man of about fifty-eight, gaunt and with steel-rimmed spectacles, King had inherited a certain amount of money from his father and, conducting himself in *rentier*-fashion, had scorned the servitude of employment. Instead, he strolled the streets in one natty outfit after another, or spent the time at home reading. Once launched into conversation, King soon revealed himself as a skilled monologuist on almost any topic—philosophy, haute-couture, negro culture, history, cricket, British imperialism. 'I regard myself as an Englishman,' he said, 'this may appear funny to you, since I am black, but there's no more loyal subject than me. I support England most fervently wherever they play.'

Another time, King discussed the revolution of the negro. He had written a thesis, he said, which he hoped to get published, called 'I Plead the Negro Cause'. Despite his title, however, he had little faith in the negro as a leader, and though we tried to suggest various names to him in dispute of this, he shook his head sadly. 'No, no, the negro lacks resilience, and the ability to co-operate. His history is against him. I explain all this in my book.'

I expressed admiration of one of King's suits. 'You would like one?' he asked delightedly. 'My tailor is a very old man, but I will take you to him. Of course, on a commission basis,' he added sharply. 'You see, I have squandered most of my money.'

I inquired about the cost of these suits. The answer was 100 dollars. Seeing me demur at the price, King said he would try for a special reduction, and thereafter he would come to the press box each day with further concessions. However, we failed to strike a bargain, so the King remained alone in his scarlet and canary glory. If one could not with honesty regard his taste as discreet or unerring, it was not without imagination or élan.

'I always felt myself a man of destiny,' he said once, 'even as a child I predominated and was apart from others. At football, there was wizardry in my boots, and at all sports, I was a master all-rounder. Yes, a master all-rounder,' he repeated nostalgically.

We used often to see him, striding purposefully through the streets, his white cane twirling, and a court of small boys chirping and, I fear, teasing, in his wake.

2

THE FIRST TEST MATCH

In the England camp, the suddenly revealed unfitness of Statham, the day before the Test was due to begin, came as a bombshell. Statham bowled half a dozen balls in the nets and announced that the hamstring at the back of the thigh was hurting him. He had kept quiet about this, hoping it would heal itself, but now he said he could not promise more than a few overs at full pace. It was a hopeless risk to take in a six-day Test. The only problems in the England team therefore were Greenhough or Allen as second spinner. The selectors—May, Cowdrey, Statham and Robins—decided on Allen, despite his total lack of match practice, on the grounds that Barrington could probably do all that Greenhough could, while Allen might be expected to bowl more accurately to his field. Allen, too, as the better field and batsman, would be an asset, unless a more defensive line had been taken altogether and Subba Row brought in to pack the batting.

The West Indies announced the following team, in batting order: Hunte (Barbados), McMorris (Jamaica), Kanhai (British Guiana), Sobers (Barbados), Worrell (Jamaica), Butcher (British Guiana), Alexander (Jamaica, captain), Scarlett (Jamaica), Hall (Barbados), Watson (Jamaica) and Ramadhin (Trinidad).

Of these, we hadn't yet seen McMorris, a sound, stolid opener, Butcher, a busy player who made many runs against Pakistan and India, Scarlett, an accurate off-spinner, and Watson, a fast bowler.

There were ugly murmurs among Barbadians about the absence of Nurse, and Griffith, though neither could really have expected to oust successful Test players in the first Test. But inter-island jealousies, not only in politics and economics, are ever strong, and, besides, no love is ever lost between Barbadians and Jamaicans anyway.

FIRST DAY

There is nothing quite like the first minutes on the opening day of a Test series. The weather was pleasantly warm and a fair breeze blew through the palms. May and Alexander walked out to a pitch that shone like a mirror, May called correctly, though no one on the spot could have known it, for his features never softened, and a moment later the loudspeaker announced 'England have won the toss and have chosen to bat on a lovely wicket.' It seemed true enough.

The crowd settled itself, in pavilion balconies, in covered stands, in the branches of tamarinds and flamboyants, and in private contraptions complete with sofas, deckchairs and awnings, constructed on the corrugated-iron roofs of shanties. Hall from the south end set his field for Pullar—3 slips and 2 gullies, 2 backward short legs—and his first ball lifted to some height outside the off-stump. The second Pullar played at and it went through at shoulder height. He was soon off the mark, though, with a neat turn off his legs for 4 and a flowing off-drive through the vacant extra cover spaces, both off Watson, a gangling boneless fellow with long arms. Cowdrey flicked Hall, much the quicker of the two in this first spell, for 3, and Hall rapped him on the thigh. Twice in the next over Cowdrey fended down steep ones. Not satisfied, Hall bounced two in the next over at him, and then two in succession. Cowdrey hooked one for 4, lost his cap to the second, and ducked the others. Watson tried two at Pullar, and then Alexander spoke to Hall. Whatever he said, Cowdrey took the next one on the knuckles and just got out of the way of another bouncer. When drinks came after 11 overs, over a dozen bouncers had been bowled and 19 runs scored. It had been a torrid overture, and Cowdrey, who had borne

the brunt of it, wore an expression of just distaste. Hall and
Watson had gone all out to make a dent, and only in Cowdrey's comfortable flesh had they succeeded.

Worrell, with easy loping run, replaced Watson and the
drop in pace was notable. Cowdrey swung a full toss to the
mid-wicket boundary and then pulled a long hop to the Goddard Stand at fine leg. So we had Ramadhin, rubbing the
ball and his hands in the dust, on in Worrell's place after only
two overs, and he began with a maiden. Scarlett, a Bedser-
size off-spinner, with an Oakman leisureliness of approach,
spun one past Cowdrey at the other end. Pullar, fretting at
Ramadhin, swept at a half volley and it sailed through
Worrell's outstretched hands at square leg. Cowdrey drove
Scarlett off the back foot and the 50 went up. Scarcely had
the polite applause died than an altogether greater volume of
interest and noise announced the arrival of King Dyall, resplendent in red linen suit, white gloves, cane and hat. The
latter he doffed to the crowd and took his seat. Watson, from
Hall's opening end, came back for a fling before lunch and
with Hall's length as a yardstick set about his own variations.
He at once struck lucky, for Cowdrey, instinctively putting
his bat up to a shortish flier, gloved it high to the slips where
Sobers at full stretch took it with his back to the wicket.
Cowdrey shook his knuckles in both pain and irritation. The
striped parasols opened and shut in glee.

The flying-fish booths and Coca-Cola tents had long finished their luncheon business before England got on the
move again. For twenty-five minutes Hall, Ramadhin and
Sobers denied Pullar and Barrington a run. The sun beat
down, the field was spread in a ring halfway to the boundary
and Pullar, try as he might, could not force a way through.
Barrington, taking it more philosophically, profited from an
odd full toss and when Watson came on he slashed him twice,
a shade riskily, to the third man boundary. Watson replied
with a vicious bumper that struck Barrington above the
elbow, and then another that earned England four byes over
the wicketkeeper's head. Pullar reached a fifty that was dour

rather than modish. Scarlett, whose cumbersome, Jamaican
bending in the field gave the Barbadians much malicious
pleasure, bowled a fair spell without looking awkward, and
the 100 slid quietly by in the wake. By tea England had been
levered to 131, Pullar 57, Barrington 37, a rate of 37 an hour
or just over 2 runs an over. No one could have fallen out of
a tree with excitement. Yet the few English present must
have been relieved, if not entirely content.

Alexander resumed with one fast, one slow: Hall from the
pavilion, Ramadhin with a slight breeze blowing from mid-
on. Hall demonstrated his virility with a flurry of bouncers
but these were tame little fellows compared with those of the
morning. Pullar jumped out to Ramadhin and just cleared
Hunte at midwicket. Barrington now raised the 150 and the
100 for the partnership by pulling a long hop from Scarlett
with something like enthusiasm. On 49 himself, he now hit
a full toss from Scarlett hard to Kanhai at deep mid-off,
paused and then ran. Pullar, whose habit is to follow the ball
rather than watch his partner, was late in answering and
never looked like getting in. So many comparatively easy
runs had already been missed through indolence or excessive
caution, that this seemed all the more sickening. Pullar had
been there four hours and nothing short of a typhoon looked
likely to shift him. But the calling all day was such that a
run-out always looked on the cards.

May came in, relaxed and seemingly at ease, but such an
unfamiliar sunniness of situation was not allowed to last.
May had just taken his cap off—usually a good sign—when
Hall pitched one well outside the leg stump. May got the
faintest touch and Alexander, making ground quickly, took
a low and brilliant catch.

So the last half hour, instead of seeing England stepping
up her rate of knots, was as full of anxiety as the first. Smith,
out twice to the fast bowlers in five balls against Barbados,
was greeted with howls of anticipation and the new ball to
boot. Hall began with a bumper and generally he and Watson pitched short to him, curious tactics when it is to the

yorker that Smith is most fallible at the outset. Barrington now played two grandiloquent strokes off Hall, dispatching him off the back foot fine of cover and then cutting him sternly and late to the pavilion. Hall bounced the next ball past his ear and Barrington raised his cap in reply. Smith lost a short one from Watson in flight, ducked, but mercifully took it on the wrist. Twice then he hit Watson for 4, once on either side of the wicket, and we breathed again.

There was coolness now and a smell of rain in the air. A rainbow appeared briefly over the flamboyants. The field was striped tigerishly from end to end in shadow, the coconut sellers and peanut vendors packed their wares. Barrington at least looked glad when it was over.

It had been a day of bumpers and surprisingly hostile fast bowling, of shrewd captaincy and admirable wicketkeeping by Alexander, and some determined, wary batting by Pullar and Barrington. All in all, the balance remained firmly held.

ENGLAND

First Innings

Pullar, run out	...	...	...	...	...	...	65
M. C. Cowdrey, c. Sobers, b. Watson		...	...	...	...	30
Barrington, not out	...	...	...	...	...	73
*P. B. H. May, c. Alexander, b. Hall		...	...	...	...	1
M. J. K. Smith, not out	...	...	...	...	...	9
Extras (b.4 l.b.2 n.b.4)		...	...	...	...	10
Total (for 3 wkts.)		...	...	...	...	188

E. R. Dexter, Illingworth, Swetman, Trueman, Allen and Moss to go in.

FALL OF WICKETS.—1–50, 2–153, 3–162.

BOWLING (to date)—Hall, 19–6–41–1; Watson, 16–5–44–1; Worrell, 2–0–11–0; Ramadhin, 19–9–37–0; Scarlett, 16–6–25–0; Sobers, 10–2–20–0.

WEST INDIES—*F. C. M. Alexander, C. C. Hunte, E. McMorris, B. Butcher, R. Kanhai, G. Sobers, F. M. Worrell, R. Scarlett, W. Hall, C. Watson and K. T. Ramadhin.

SECOND DAY

The first half hour would obviously be crucial. There were the last vestiges of shine on the new ball and Alexander gave Hall and Watson a long bowl with it. Neither got anything like the same lift or pace out of the wicket as on the morning before and though they managed half a dozen bouncers between them they were in the nature of ceremonial rather than declarations of war. Barrington and Smith were rarely hurried. Barrington contented himself with strokes off the back foot, taking singles here and there, and every so often flashing the ball to the third man boundary. Smith bided his time, awaiting the spinners. Ramadhin bowled a subtle and variously flighted maiden to him. Then Smith swept him off the leg stump into the palms for six and sent a no-ball skimming over extra cover. Barrington, with a string of Test fifties and seventies behind him, but no century, stuck on 97. At length Scarlett threw one up to him and Barrington smote it hard between mid-off and extra. It had been four and a half hours of concentrated grind, with few attempts at decoration, and none of the sudden rushes of blood that sometimes overturn him when apparently well set. His hundred behind him, Barrington reserved his watchdog wariness while Smith, with greater reach, swung his bat through a fuller arc. The 250 went by and then Smith, cutting at Scarlett, was caught at the wicket. Dexter arrived with the sky full of clouds behind Ramadhin and at once sent him scudding off the back foot past extra cover. At lunch England were 260 for 4, a score anyone would have settled for before the match began.

Barrington can scarcely have digested his lunch before, having cut Watson gorgeously for four, he was struck a fierce blow in the back by a bouncer that failed to get up. Having taken a boxerly count of nine or thereabouts, Barrington came back full of spirit. Yet he still seemed unable to carry the fight to the enemy. Hall and Watson bowled themselves out and it was Dexter now who kept the score moving with crisp off-drives and forces past mid-on. Ramadhin and Scar-

lett returned and this time Ramadhin, having kept both batsmen quiet by giving the ball plenty of air and setting mid-off
and mid-on deep, broke the stand. Barrington tried to turn
one outside the leg stump round the corner, Alexander took
the ball and both he and Ramadhin appealed. Barrington,
seemingly unable to believe his eyes, saw the umpire's hand
go up. With many a dire look in the offending direction, he
walked slowly away. This was an unhappy end to so much
vigilance and control. Illingworth, looking the soul of confidence, went down the pitch to drive Ramadhin, the ball
drifted away from him a shade, and he was bowled hitting
well inside it.

Once again West Indies were back in the hunt. And a brilliant left-handed pick-up and throw by Hall all but ran
Dexter out for the third time in four innings a moment later.
Swetman pulled a long hop from Ramadhin and it looked all
over a boundary. Dexter was halfway down the pitch when
Hall, putting down an arm that seemed to be both retract-
able and extendable, picked up on the run, changed hands
and prepared to throw. Swetman sent Dexter back and
Dexter, skidding to a stop, just made his ground. Swetman
could make little sense of either Ramadhin or Sobers. He was
repeatedly hit on the pads moving down the pitch and an
occasional tickle off the inside edge was about all he managed in the hour before tea. He tried with cap on, then with
cap off, but it was no good either way. Dexter drove the first
ball of each over for a long single and Swetman then had to
fathom out the rest. Once Sobers beat him in the air, draw-
ing him well out, but Alexander missed the stumps.

At tea Dexter was 48, and soon after he drove Worrell for
two fours, one through the covers, one straight, and both
times off the back foot. Hall came back but he was palpably
done for, trudging back to his mark with the expression of
one who had just learnt that his house, with his entire savings
under the floorboards, had gone up in smoke. Scarlett too
had the air of a man who would have settled for the rest of
the day in the canefields. Dexter savagely pulled Sobers to

long-on and hit the next ball with old-world grace through the covers. So at 382 Hall and Watson were summoned back for the new ball. They put the best face on it they could, though once Dexter had flicked Watson high over slips and then slashed him square to the off, he cut his losses and bowled off shortened run. Swetman earned five in overthrows and began to tuck the fast bowlers off his legs with the busyness of a squirrel storing up nuts for the winter. Dexter now flashed his bat at anything within reach. He cut Watson for another four, then bisected cover and extra with a stroke that cannoned the ball back off the picket to mid-off. The first of these raised the hundred for the partnership, and also saw England past the 400 and into safe waters. Hall found astonishing reserves of pace, but first Ramadhin, then Worrell were called back. Swetman cut Ramadhin, Dexter hit him back so swiftly that Ramadhin took his hand away as if he'd been stung. The batsmen at last were in full and happy command. Dexter went to 99 and then Swetman, trying to force Worrell, was caught at the wicket. Trueman, disguised as night watchman, entered with appropriate solemnity of tread and just in time to shake Dexter's hand as the latter struck Hall, back yet again, through the covers. This was Dexter's sixteenth boundary, and once only, at 28 when he hit Sobers firmly but low back at him, did he make the slightest error of judgment.

West Indies had stuck to it well, and once again Alexander, quick to set as hostile a field as his bowlers earned, had used them shrewdly. Swetman should have been caught at slip when only 11, it is true, but scores of runs were saved along the boundary edge and there were some thrilling pickups. Yet England, through Barrington's tenacity, the enterprise of Smith and finally the commanding power of Dexter, were now in a position to dictate.

ENGLAND

First Innings

Pullar, run out	...	...	...	...	...	...	65
M. C. Cowdrey, c. Sobers, b. Watson	...	...	...	...		30
Barrington, c. Alexander, b. Ramadhin	...	...	...	...		128
*P. B. H. May, c. Alexander, b. Hall	...	...	...	...		1
M. J. K. Smith, c. Alexander, b. Scarlett	...	...	...		39
E. R. Dexter, not out	...	...	...	...	...	...	103
Illingworth, b. Ramadhin	...	...	...	...	...	5
Swetman, c. Alexander, b. Worrell	...	...	...	...		45
Trueman, not out	...	...	...	...	...	...	0
Extras	...	...	...	...	...	...	14
Total (for 7 wkts.)	...	...	...	...	...	430

Allen and Moss to go in.

FALL OF WICKETS—1–50, 2–153, 3–162, 4–251, 5–291, 6–317, 7–426.
BOWLING (to date)—Hall, 35–8–88–1; Watson, 28–5–100–1; Worrell, 12–2–33–1; Ramadhin, 47–20–96–2; Scarlett, 26–9–46–1; Sobers, 21–3–53–0.

THIRD DAY

Dexter started off the day by hitting a ball barely short of a length from Watson high over extra cover to the fence. Trueman at the other end played Hall with exaggerated care, as if he fancied himself to take Pullar's place at No. 1. Pullar, we learned, was hit on the toe by a yorker during his innings and would not field, nor possibly bat again in this match. Having survived Hall for half an hour, Trueman against Ramadhin was as a rabbit to a stoat, and Alexander soon took his fifth catch of the innings. Allen cut a neat single and then Dexter, moving out to Ramadhin, hit him to long on for six. Next he sent up 450 with a powerful scoop off Hall that left extra cover groping. A shower sweetened the air, giving the bowlers ten minutes' rest. King Dyall, again in double-breasted red sharkskin, made his appearance, and Dexter greeted him with a lavish square cut off Watson. Worrell had bowled several accurate, containing overs, and

Ramadhin began to make the odd one squat. Allen, after a compact useful innings, was l.b.w. to Watson at 478. Moss took four off the underside of his bat first ball and then, shifting his bottom rapidly to the off as if avoiding the closing doors of a tube train, looked back to see his leg stump flying.

So Dexter, who'd scored 33 out of the 52 added, was left high and dry for 136.

No sooner had England taken the field than there was high drama. Trueman bowled a no-ball to Hunte who hit it back fine of mid-on and started to run. Allen chased across, and Hunte, seeing him go, sent McMorris back. Allen, almost with his back to the wicket, made an underhand flick and hit the stumps with McMorris well out. It was a brilliant piece of opportunism to which England have not accustomed us.

Trueman and Moss both opened without mid-offs and Kanhai and Hunte, leaning on half-volleys, fed juicily on them. Trueman, adjusting his field, bowled to five men on the leg—wide mid-on, mid-wicket, square leg, long leg and backward short leg—and two slips, cover and extra. Moss had four to the on in an evenly spaced ring, from backward short to mid-on, slip, gully, cover, extra, and, eventually, mid-off. Kanhai was quick to drive anything overpitched but Trueman and Moss several times found the edge of both his and Hunte's bats. There was a brisk keenness to the fielding and May, setting his men deeper for the drive, showed that he had learned something from Weekes in the Colony match and from Alexander. Dexter opened with two maidens, during the second of which he beat Hunte thrice in succession. Swetman whipped the bails off the first time but failed on the third which was a cruelly difficult chance on the leg side. Kanhai now cut and pulled Dexter for fours, and when Illingworth came on, swung a no-ball clean out of the ground. Allen replaced Dexter, keeping the ball well up outside the off-stump and he was not easy to get away. Trueman returned just before tea and Kanhai, driving at a ball that was altogether slower, found himself bowled off his pads. This was a wicket for which there had been no encouragement, since Kanhai looked safer than most of the houses on this island.

Trueman after tea bowled several excellent overs to Hunte while at the other end Illingworth, with six men on the off, attacked Sobers off-stump from round the wicket. Runs had grown scarce as fresh vegetables. Sobers, down at Trueman's end, drove back a full toss and though Trueman was off-balance, it very nearly stuck. Trueman looked crestfallen, though he did well to get a hand anywhere near it. King Dyall went off past the Press Box for a quick change, re-appearing this time in yellow blazer, with K.D. embroidered on the pocket and brown edging, pale blue trousers and mauve tie, fresh buttonholes and white fedora. He had looked better.

Allen had a go in place of Trueman, with a similar field to Illingworth, and he was scarcely less accurate. At a quarter to five Barrington came on, the first ball of his second over popped and Hunte, long silent at the crease, was snapped up by Swetman. Barrington gets unusual bounce from his rollicking matelot's action and this was a shrewd move by May.

The great Worrell, last of his generation, made his slow, meditative way out. May brought back Moss, Barrington bowled two maidens, Moss two, and Sobers, for all his scarlet bat-handle and the extravagance of his power, had small opportunity to wield either.

ENGLAND

First Innings

Pullar, run out		65
M. C. Cowdrey, c. Sobers, b. Watson		30
Barrington, c. Alexander, b. Ramadhin		128
*P. B. H. May, c. Alexander, b. Hall		1
M. J. K. Smith, c. Alexander, b. Scarlett		39
E. R. Dexter, not out		136
Illingworth, b. Ramadhin		5
Swetman, c. Alexander, b. Worrell		45
Trueman, c. Alexander, b. Ramadhin		3
Allen, l.b.w., b. Watson		10
Moss, b. Watson		4
Extras (b.4 l.b.6 n.b.6)		16
Total		482

FALL OF WICKETS—1–50, 2–153, 3–162, 4–251, 5–291, 6–317, 7–426, 8–439, 9–478, 10–482.

BOWLING—Hall, 40–9–98–1; Watson, 32.4–6–121–3; Worrell, 15–2–39–1; Ramadhin, 54–22–109–3; Scarlett, 26–9–46–1; Sobers, 21–3–53–0.

WEST INDIES

First Innings

C. C. Hunte, c. Swetman, b. Barrington		42
E. McMorris, run out		0
R. Kanhai, b. Trueman		40
G. Sobers, not out		21
F. M. Worrell, not out		8
Extras (n.b.3)		3
Total (for 3 wkts.)		114

*F. C. M. Alexander, B. Butcher, R. Scarlett, W. Hall, C. Watson and K. T. Ramadhin to go in.

FALL OF WICKETS—1–6, 2–68, 3–102.

BOWLING (to date)—Trueman, 13–5–24–1; Moss, 11–5–19–0; Dexter, 4–2–14–0; Illingworth, 13–2–28–0; Allen, 13–5–15–0; Barrington 6–2–11–1.

FOURTH DAY

The break-through we hoped for with the new ball did not come. It should, in fact, have taken place before the new ball was due. At 143, with Sobers forty, he pulled Allen straight to Trueman at mid-wicket. It came low, though at no great pace, but Trueman back on his heels and feeling somewhat out of sorts, was slow in starting. He got both hands on the ball but he was off-balance and dropped it. This, with the new ball ahead and Butcher yet to play in a Test against England, was little short of tragic. Then Moss in his next over brought one back at Worrell to hit him on the pads and it must have been a matter of centimetres. These were England's only glimpses during the day into subtropical paradise. Barrington, Illingworth and Allen had bowled contemplative and accurate overs early on but once the new ball was taken Worrell, last surviving member of the most famous black triumvirate since Toussaint L'Ouverture, Christophe and Dessalines founded the republic of Haiti a century and a half ago, cut loose. A Barbadian renegade now in Jamaica, Worrell, who had appeared somewhat apprehensive of his reception here, had played no serious first-class cricket since the Tests of 1957 in England. He began cagily but suddenly he flashed successive balls from Moss gorgeously past cover and, restored now to proper eminence, crashed Trueman to the sight-screen. Trueman grew less quick and with Sobers patiently content to remain Worrell's aide the chance of a wicket slipped steadily away. At lunch West Indies were 180, Sobers 52, Worrell 42.

In great heat, with a stiff breeze reaching only one wicket, Worrell and Sobers took their partnership to 150. Sobers every so often pulled and cut with the savagery of one who sees a sudden way out of captivity. The bowling was never untidy, Allen in particular making Sobers chafe at the leash. Somehow, though, the feeling spread that the crucial chance had been allowed to go begging and Worrell and Sobers, contained but ruthless, looked in no mood to offer another. A shower sweetened the air but an evening dip on one of Barbados' coral beaches was really all that the English fielders had to look forward to. Sobers, after five hours at the wicket, had just time to reach his hundred before the shower thickened into a cloudburst that soon had the palm trees mirrored in water. The final hour was lost, so West Indies, at 279 for 3, were still 203 behind.

ENGLAND
First Innings

Pullar, run out	...	...	...	...	...	...	65
M. C. Cowdrey, c. Sobers, b. Watson	...	...	...	...	30
Barrington, c. Alexander, b. Ramadhin	...	...	...	...	128
*P. B. H. May, c. Alexander, b. Hall	...	...	...	...	1
M. J. K. Smith, c. Alexander, b. Scarlett	...	...	...	39
E. R. Dexter, not out	...	...	...	...	...	...	136
Illingworth, b. Ramadhin	...	...	...	...	...	5
Swetman, c. Alexander, b. Worrell	...	...	...	...	45
Trueman, c. Alexander, b. Ramadhin	...	...	...	...	3
Allen, l.b.w., b. Watson	...	...	...	...	...	10
Moss, b. Watson	...	...	...	...	...	...	4
Extras (b.4 l.b.6 n.b.6)	...	...	...	...	...	16
Total	...	...	...	...	...	...	482

FALL OF WICKETS—1–50, 2–153, 3–162, 4–251, 5–291, 6–317, 7–426, 8–439, 9–478, 10–482.

BOWLING—Hall, 40–9–98–1; Watson, 32.4–6–121–3; Worrell, 15–2–39–1; Ramadhin, 54–22–109–3; Scarlett, 26–9–46–1; Sobers, 21–3–53–0.

WEST INDIES
First Innings

C. C. Hunte, c. Swetman, b. Barrington	...	...	...	...	42
E. McMorris, run out	...	...	...	...	...	0
R. Kanhai, b. Trueman	...	...	...	...	...	40
G. Sobers, not out	...	...	...	...	...	...	100
F. M. Worrell, not out	...	...	...	...	...	91
Extras (l.b.2 n.b.4)	...	...	...	...	...	6
Total (for 3 wkts.)	...	...	...	...	...	279

*F. C. M. Alexander, B. Butcher, R. Scarlett, W. Hall, C. Watson and K. T. Ramadhin to go in.

FALL OF WICKETS—1–6, 2–68, 3–102.

BOWLING (to date)—Trueman, 21–7–44–1; Moss, 21–7–53–0; Dexter, 10–3–28–0; Illingworth, 31–7–72–0; Allen, 28–7–42–0; Barrington, 13–3–34–1.

FIFTH DAY

What with the hour lost in the cloudburst of Saturday and one thing and another the match seemed to have died a natural death over the weekend. After a Sunday of sailing and water-ski-ing and picnicking under the casuarinas of Sandy Beach the return to cricket for everyone was something of an anticlimax. With Worrell on 91 and Sobers 100 the only means of reviving the corpse looked to be an immediate splitting of the partnership followed by a deep inroad into the West Indian tail. Or, alternatively, opulent and harsh attack by Sobers and Worrell.

May, on a cloudy morning with a more cooling breeze than usual, set Trueman with the breeze and Allen into it. Trueman was pretty much on the target, without really looking dangerous, but Allen at once found a spot. He spun one sharply away to beat Sobers' forward stroke and Worrell twice had to jab down hurriedly as the ball both turned and squatted. Both batsmen had some shaky moments and the crowd, hepped up to cheer Worrell's century, were silent as mourners. At last Worrell got Allen away to the cover boundary but his features remained as woeful as ever. Allen bowled seven overs for 8 runs and they were good overs. Illingworth replaced him but never managed to get the same turn. Moss kept Sobers tediously quiet, to a degree that West Indies scored only 34 runs in the hour and a half before lunch. The fielding again was alert, with May redeeming several misfields on Saturday with some spectacular stops.

The afternoon was scarcely any more exhilarating. Dexter bowled four accurate overs downwind, Illingworth dug the ball in rather than flighted it, a strange policy against such a breeze, but Barrington, performing remarkable feats of agility at extra cover, kept Sobers runless.

Cowdrey at mid-on once failed to hang on to a firm hit back by Sobers off Illingworth. The new ball became due, but May kept the spinners going for 15 overs more, Allen from the pavilion, Barrington with the breeze to help along his leg-break. Suddenly Worrell sprang out on Allen, hitting him to the pavilion and into the stand at mid-wicket off successive balls. Sobers swept Barrington twice to where King Dyall, all in white, was just taking his seat. At 386 Trueman took the new ball and the old record for this wicket, 283 by Weekes and Worrell, soon went west. There was something automatic and dream-like about the batting: these were sleep-players on a feather-bed who every now and then woke up and fired off a couple of rounds at flies on the ceiling. Now Sobers crashed Moss for two successive fours, taking West Indies into the fourth hundred, their partnership into its third.

The general leisureliness of the batting, nevertheless, meant that West Indies were depriving themselves of any excitement on the final afternoon. The extra hundred runs that should have come during this partnership would have given Ramadhin, for example, three or four hours' bowling at England with perhaps 200 runs up his sleeve. Instead of which Sobers and Worrell remained content to cruise gently along, first Worrell to his 150, then Sobers to his 200. In the last over of the day West Indies pushed their noses in front. It had all the inevitability about it of a long sea voyage and about the same element of drama.

ENGLAND

First Innings

Pullar, run out	65
M. C. Cowdrey, c. Sobers, b. Watson	30
Barrington, c. Alexander, b. Ramadhin	128
*P. B. H. May, c. Alexander, b. Hall	1
M. J. K. Smith, c. Alexander, b. Scarlett	39
E. R. Dexter, not out	136
Illingworth, b. Ramadhin	5
Swetman, c. Alexander, b. Worrell	45
Trueman, c. Alexander, b. Ramadhin	3
Allen, l.b.w., b. Watson	10
Moss, b. Watson	4
Extras (b.4 l.b.6 n.b.6)	16
Total	482

FALL OF WICKETS—1–50, 2–153, 3–162, 4–251, 5–291, 6–317, 7–426, 8–439, 9–478, 10–482.

BOWLING—Hall, 40–9–98–1; Watson, 32.4–6–121–3; Worrell, 15–2–39–1; Ramadhin, 54–22–109–3; Scarlett, 26–9–46–1; Sobers, 21–3–53–0.

WEST INDIES

First Innings

C. C. Hunte, c. Swetman, b. Barrington	42
E. McMorris, run out	0
R. Kanhai, b. Trueman	40
G. Sobers, not out	216
F. M. Worrell, not out	177
Extras (b.1 l.b.4 w.1 n.b.5)	11
Total (for 3 wkts.)	486

*F. C. M. Alexander, B. Butcher, R. Scarlett, W. Hall, C. Watson and K. T. Ramadhin to go in.

FALL OF WICKETS—1–6, 2–68, 3–102.

BOWLING (to date)—Trueman, 37–13–69–1; Moss, 36–11–88–0; Dexter, 28–9–70–0; Illingworth, 47–9–106–0; Allen, 43–12–82–0; Barrington, 18–3–60–1.

SIXTH DAY

The records continued to be broken at snail's pace and with depressing pointlessness. Finally Sobers, 10 hours and 47 minutes at the wicket, lost his off-stump to a ball from Trueman that pitched on his middle stump and kept low. He and Worrell had scored, during their two and a half days' communion, 399 runs, twelve less than May and Cowdrey (who now smiled darkly to each other) made together at Edgbaston when West Indies were last in England. Butcher, whose pads must have been in danger of growing into a second skin, made immediate but sketchy attempts to compensate for Worrell's almost total immobility at the other end. Alexander several times signalled to Worrell for more action but Worrell, off on some pipedream of his own, chose to ignore him. Nelson at the Nile could not have been more disdainful. After an hour of sterling effort by Moss, Trueman and Dexter, West Indies were 32 runs further on the road to perdition. Worrell was responsible for eight of them. Butcher at length hit Dexter quietly to Trueman at deep mid-off, and Hall was l.b.w. to Trueman. Alexander, doubtless thinking black thoughts about Worrell's rate of progress, struck out and was snapped up by Smith at short mid-on. Justice was ever thus. Worrell remained at 197 for so long that Alexander was able to declare without evidence of malice. Worrell's innings, of golden origin, grew baser in metal as it proceeded and long since had depreciated out of recognition.

England, 81 behind, had three hours to fill in. Hall whistled several about both batsmen's ears and again his pace was astonishing to see. Ramadhin, bland and dissimulating, wheeled his arm over but the current wasn't on. Scarlett bowled a high wide that nearly knocked the square leg umpire's hat off. Cowdrey, in deeply ironic and mimicking mood, applauded the many bowlers, encouraging them to bowl maidens. After nearly two hours he had scored 12 and he made it plain that even these were pure self-indulgence.

So the match, once full of promise, petered wretchedly

out. It had become increasingly futile since the weekend. What was going on in Worrell's mind that he could bat two hours for 10 runs with West Indies ahead and his own score past 150? No one seemed to know. Yet excuses were made for him, palpably thin though they were. He was tired; he wanted to deny England further batting practice and knew there to be no prospect of a finish; he was carrying on a personal vendetta against the Barbados members for a long-standing social slight. Which was it? Perhaps none of these. Yet those who explained that Worrell was a front-foot player and that by setting a deep defensive field and getting his bowlers to pitch short May made it impossible for him, merely insulted Worrell's intelligence and skill. In any case, the bowling was never particularly short; if Worrell was so tired he should have got himself out; and, most evident of all, if Worrell found it difficult to force a way through, there was a single off nearly every ball for the asking.

Whatever the explanation, the result was bad cricket. Bad in the context of the match, bad in itself. Worrell perhaps was less to blame than the pitch, six-day Tests, and the whole economics of the system. Yet this kind of game, as demoralizing and painful as the water torture, could only have sent people away vowing 'Never again'.

At least, one could take comfort from England's all-round performance. Since the week before, the whole team seemed to have undergone a psychological transformation. It was most noticeable in the field, in the general air of alertness, in the cleanness of the picking up and straighter throwing. In this Barrington and Allen had constantly taken the eye. May looked altogether more at home, and he sealed the gaps very capably. The bowlers now concentrated their attack on one side of the wicket at a time, so that May was generally able to avoid splitting the field.

It had been a long time since England, with May and Cowdrey both out cheaply, had scored over 400 runs abroad. Not since the Second Test at Capetown in 1957—eight overseas Test matches back—had England approached such a total. Now it was the newcomers who had made the runs, giving the batting greater depth, a more even distribution of burden.

And here were the century makers, Barrington and Dexter, playing a useful part in the attack, and the spinners, Illingworth and Allen, with batting techniques enabling them to more than hold their own. This was something quite new.

We hoped it would last.

ENGLAND

First Innings		Second Innings	
Pullar, run out	65	not out	46
M. C. Cowdrey, c Sobers, b. Watson	30	not out	16
Barrington, c. Alexander, b. Ramadhin	128		
*P. B. H. May, c. Alexander, b. Hall	1		
M. J. K. Smith, c. Alexander, b. Scarlett	39		
E. R. Dexter, not out	136		
Illingworth, b. Ramadhin ...	5		
Swetman, c. Alexander, b. Worrell	45		
Trueman, c. Alexander, b. Ramadhin	3		
Allen, l.b.w., b. Watson	10		
Moss, b. Watson	4		
Extras (b.4 l.b.6 n.b.6) ...	16	Extras (b.7 l.b.1 w.1) ..	9
Total	482	Total (for 0 wkt.) ...	71

FALL OF WICKETS—*First Innings*—1–50, 2–153, 3–162, 4–251, 5–291, 6–317, 7–426, 8–439, 9–478, 10–482.

BOWLING—*First Innings*—Hall, 40–9–98–1; Watson, 32.4–6–121–3; Worrell, 15–2–39–1; Ramadhin, 54–22–109–3; Scarlett, 26–9–46–1; Sobers, 21–3–53–0. *Second Innings*—Hall, 6–2–9–0; Watson, 8–1–19–0; Ramadhin, 7–2–11–0; Scarlett, 10–4–12–0; Hunte, 7–2–9–0; Kanhai, 4–3–2–0.

WEST INDIES

First Innings

C. C. Hunte, c. Swetman, b. Barrington	...	...	...		...	...	42
E. McMorris, run out	...	...	...	...	...	...	0
R. Kanhai, b. Trueman	...	...	...	...	...	...	40
G. Sobers, b. Trueman	...	...	...	...	...	...	226
F. M. Worrell, not out	...	...	...	...	...	...	197
B. Butcher, c. Trueman, b. Dexter		...	...	...	...	...	13
W. Hall, l.b.w., b. Trueman	...	...	...	...	...	14
*F. C. M. Alexander, c. Smith, b. Trueman		...	...	...	3
R. Scarlett, l.b.w., b. Dexter	...	...	...	...	...	7
Extras (b.8 l.b.7 w.1 n.b.5)	...	...	...	...	...	21
Total (for 8 wkts. dec.)	...	...	...	...	...	563

C. Watson and K. T. Ramadhin did not go in.

FALL OF WICKETS—1-6, 2-68, 3-102, 4-501, 5-521, 6-544, 7-556, 8-563.

BOWLING—Trueman, 47-15-93-4; Moss, 47-14-116-0; Dexter, 37.4-11-85-2; Illingworth, 47-9-106-0; Allen, 43-12-82-0; Barrington, 18-3-60-1.

By the time the Test Match was over, I suppose I had driven to and from the Kensington Oval a dozen times—almost as many times as I go to Lords in a summer. I grew increasingly fond of the journey. Often we would bathe first at Accra Beach, the surf unrolling out of a sea of unreal blue, driving then through the beach houses, pink and green concrete under umbrellas of poinsettia or trailed with bougainvillaea, past the Garrison buildings overlooking the wide green circle of the racecourse and the savannah—with troops drilling among numberless private games of pick-up cricket—towards the Carenage. Here the twin-masted sloops that trade between the islands cluster under the eye of Nelson on his Trafalgar Square plinth among Bernini-style fountains and the vinous, gold-turning tendrils of the cannonball tree. Along the handsome, pink wharfside warehouses of DaCosta's, and up past the sugary but elegant lacework of the Colonnade shops—a Colonial adaptation of an arcade from Tunbridge Wells or Bath—and then suddenly one is bogged down in the cricket traffic. But Bridgetown, alone among the bigger colony capitals, has a certain grace, even despite the uneasy amalgam of architectural styles, and the eye is constantly caught by a beautiful weather-boarded house, with its white jalousies glittering between hibiscus, poinsettia and stephanotis, and the palms scratching at the sky. Nearer the Oval the houses move up in the social scale; growing heavier and more ornate, with surrounding galleries and lush, strident front gardens.

In the evening it would be different. Often the air would have been rinsed by a sharp shower. We would nose our way through swarming narrow streets, with a dozen or so children peering out of the tiny wooden chattel houses—doll-like wood constructions, neatly designed with shutters balancing the central door and a tiny veranda—and skirting the town centre, emerge into Fountain Gardens, the Carenage heavy with the smell of rope and sacking, of ship's chandlers and stale spices. The sky behind the tall cabbage palms alongside the Yacht and Aquatic clubs turns from the colour of a tea-rose to a sulphurous yellow, an electric green, as you watch it, and the small sailing boats in Carlisle Bay blacken in the lee of gaunt cargo ships with the occasional cruise liner, the white *Colombey* or the *Antilles*, high in the water.

Further along, where peeling fishing boats are drawn up behind the sailors' dives on spits of sand, housewives crowd round the flying-fish sellers, the catch freshly in. Before we had passed the rows of rum-shops with the Coca-Cola signs and blaring juke-boxes, the chocolate romanesque of the Methodist church and the endless massage and nature cure establishments, the sun had slipped over the horizon in its final green flare. At Accra the sea was a deep mauve, and judging the rollers, curling in high overhead before crashing over you, was as difficult as it must be picking out Statham in bad light at Old Trafford.

3

AROUND BARBADOS

BARBADOS, the size of the Isle of Wight and about as flat as Sussex, with a ridge of hills stretching along the north-east coast to the height of the South Downs, differs from most islands of the British Caribbean in that it is coral, not volcanic, and was settled peacefully rather than conquered. Among the conquered islands are Jamaica (1655), Virgin Islands (1672), St. Lucia (1803), Grenada (1762) and Trinidad (1797). British Guiana was ceded in 1803, while Barbados, like Antigua, Montserrat and St. Kitts, was quietly occupied, with little more than a few swine and perhaps a handful of Indians, who made an undetected escape, to disturb.

It is not an exotic island. You can drive round it in a long day and most of the time you will find such view as there is obscured by the tall sugar cane that gives each road simply the appearance of a forest clearing. There are few trees, except palms and mahogany, and birds are sadly rare. At Nicholas Abbey, a handsome house in the Cape Dutch manner, with triple white gables, a pair of monkeys swung repeatedly from the branches over my car, as if practising for the circus. Otherwise, except in the Museum with its gorgeous array of local fish—angel fish and whiprays, groupers, parrot fish, barracudas, and snappers of fabulous beauty—I scarcely saw an animal, living or dead, either on the coast or inland. There are half a dozen species of endemic birds—sparrows, sugarbirds, yellow birds and grackles, a kind of blackbird, are most common—and we saw a few imported ones, like humming birds, or winter migrants, like belted kingfishers and blue herons, from time to time. But the birds of passage, the snipes, the plovers, the avocets and stilts, had long since arrived in their South American resorts.

We were unlucky, too, with the flowering trees, the yellow cassias, the pink and yellow pouis, the frangipani and cordias, all of which reach their peak during the summer.

But there are compensations in Barbados for the absence of dramatic physical features, of lush tropic vegetation and exotic fauna. The beaches, for example—those of the Coral Reef and Colony clubs, and in front of the swish beach-houses on the 'platinum' St. James' coast, the dazzling sweep of the Crane, of Paradise Beach and Accra—are among the finest in the world. Blue linked lagoons as smooth as milk, with casuarinas and manchineels acting as dense, feathery wind-breaks, the sand salt-white, or else fresh thundering surf, with the long breakers spilling in over the coral reefs—they stretch round the coast in miraculous profusion. Not even in the coral cays of the Great Barrier Reef off the Queensland coast, certainly nowhere in the Mediterranean, have I seen sea of quite this blue or sand of such purity.

Notable, too, are the handsome 'tropical gothic' parish churches, islanded in the canefields, or among the palms and paw-paws hunted by the ceaseless north-east Trades, with the sea swirling at the reefs far below them. Each of the eleven parishes into which the island is divided has churches which rarely fail to give pleasure, nearly always for their setting, always for their harmonious proportions. The battle-mented towers, castellated early gothic naves and local varia-tions like fan-topped windows, corbels or pulpits, such as the one in St. John's, made from five separate woods—mahogany, ebony, manchineel, locust and pine—may seem to the purist uneasy conjunctions, but though these churches were nearly all rebuilt after the 1831 hurricane that practically de-molished Barbados, the resulting style, held together by the weathered coffee-pink of the stone, has curious distinction.

The most celebrated, and justly, is St. John's, perched high over Martins Bay, with a view of the lighthouse at Ragged Point and of the Atlantic breaking up on the huge circular rocks, like giant cannonballs, of Bathsheba and Cattlewash. In the churchyard here, not many yards from the cliff sundial, a headstone of pink Portland stone carries these words: *Here lyeth ye body of Ferdinando Paleologus, descended from ye Imperial lyne of ye last Christian Emperor of Greece. Churchwarden of this parish 1655–1656. Vestryman twentye years. Died Oct. 3, 1679.*

A long haul, one might think, from Byzantium 1453 and the death in action, defending his capital against the Turks in one of the bloodiest of all battles, of the Emperor Constantine XI Paleologus. From Gibbon this last heroic stand of the besieged Greeks, with the Turkish Janissaries surging over the battlements of Byzantium by way of the heaped-up bodies of their own dead, drew forth a grandiloquent passage; and Patrick Leigh-Fermor, after one of the many imaginative historical reconstructions in *The Traveller's Tree*, tracing the breaking-up of the imperial dynasty and the scattering of the Paleologus family, affectingly sums up the 'brief epitaph' of Ferdinando, son of Theodoro Paleologus, of Saltash, Cornwall: 'Such, then, was the destiny that scattered the bones of those exiled princes in Tuscany, Cornwall, London, Barbados, Wapping, and Corunna; a strange and rather inappropriate story. And rather sad. For nothing, after all, could be more remote in distance, or in feeling more alien to this little coral island, than the waters of the Golden Horn: waters that once reflected the vanished palace of Blachernae, the home of the purple-born; or the cypresses of Mystra, whose Byzantine parapets look down from the Taygetus towards the plain of Sparta and the wide valley where the Eurotas meanders through the olive groves of Lacedaemon to the mountains of the Peloponnese.'

An incongruous end to a great dynasty, certainly, this quiet death on a pineapple plantation in Barbados, of the last but one of the Paleologues (Ferdinando's son returned to England to serve in Charles II's navy before dying at Corunna), but other royal familes have perished in straiter circumstances or through more sudden and violent means. And

leaving this wind-buffeted church—with its fine wooden
stairways and galleries, its chancel tablet commemorative of
the first rector, the Rev. William Leslie (1653–76), grandson
of the fifth laird of Kincraigie, great-great-grandson of John
Leslie, eighth Baron of Balquhain—one could not but feel, in
face of the sudden blueness of sea and sky, the sun warm on
the walls of the Georgian rectory low among the rustling
grey arrows of the cane, that there were, after all, worse
places even for the descendants of Emperors to die.

After the parish churches—perhaps even before them on
grounds of architectural merit—come the planters' houses of
Barbados. Jamaica has some few that can compare with
them (the French and American islands none), but, these
apart, nowhere else in the British West Indies has the taste
and manner of life in England under Queen Anne or the first
of the Georges been so faithfully or so elegantly reproduced.

There are, I suppose, a score or more of these houses, each
the size of a small manor house, dotted around the island,
usually on a slight eminence at the end of a long avenue of
mahogany or cabbage palm. To reach them you turn off the
main highways, curving through the cane and twisting up
short but steep hills that dip down over thin river beds, with
sturdy stone bridges taking the mottle of the water on their
parapets.

I visited about half a dozen of them. First Canefields, again
the home, after various changes of owner, of Mrs. Anne
Drayton, with its airy, hansomely-furnished rooms, finely
moulded and corniced, its surrounding open galleries, ex-
pendable in hurricanes (the house itself has huge protecting
shutters that bar behind the entrance), over which the cabbage palms and flowering trees throw their shadows. The
cooling Atlantic breeze, never quiet for long, beats on the
columned portico of the apricot windward façade, stirring
the water-hyacinths in their pool and funnelling through the
splayed white spokes of the fanlights.

Northwards, beyond Mount Hillaby (the highest point of
the island, at 1,100 feet some 300 feet higher than Ditchling

Beacon) lies Farley Hill, to my taste the most beautiful of
them all, though now empty and slowly rotting away in the
absence of a buyer. Here, in the garden, I saw for the first
time a specimen of the Traveller's Tree, with its astonishing
fan of long-stalked leaves, each of which contains at its base
a waterproof hollow that holds the rain—hence the name.

Farley Hill, used for the Fleury homestead during the
shooting of the film *Island in the Sun,* must be saved soon or
it will have gone for ever, its splendid interior gnawed away,
inch by inch, by the white ant. Yet outside, in its clearing
hacked from the undergrowth, with the tall masts of the
palms scraping the blue and the clouds building up white
and fleecy over Gay's Cove and the headland of Pico Tene-
riffe, it retains an air of nobility, the aloofness of a deserted
galleon riding the Caribbean. It is the kind of place that at
once sets one dreaming. If one were to do this and this, perhaps pull down that and replace those, could one—possibly
—at a pinch—make a go of it? And, supposing one could,
how much time would one spend there, how much money
in getting to it? No, Farley Hill, where Froude, the historian,
stayed in 1887, and where the Princes Alfred, Albert Victor
and George (before he became King George V) planted trees,
needs some spectacular bit of luck—a crusading eccentric
millionaire, a man of taste for whom money is no object and
who wanted to live there and there only—if it is to survive in
anything like its original form and as a private house, rather
than as a school or an institution. I hope it gets it.

Colleton, on the St. Peter coast, just north of Six Men's
Bay, is another house, with its beautiful stabling, that would
be an ornament to any English county. In the centre of the
island, about halfway between Bridgetown and Bathsheba,
stands Drax Hall, scarcely inferior to any, while a mile or
two to the east, set back behind its large artificial lake and
barely visible at the end of an imposing palm avenue, lies
Codrington College, the most ambitious building, as well as
one of the most beautiful, in the colony.

An oblong Palladian construction of grey stone, its eastward balustrades looking over lawns to the surf of Conset Bay, its front façade, with triple pediments, doubling itself in the fish-fluttering lake, Codrington College has undergone the vicissitudes common to most buildings of any age in Barbados. The original mansion, built in the mid-seventeenth century, was destroyed by the hurricane of 1780, and then, within a year of the College being opened in 1830, by another one. Parts of both buildings remain, but to all intents and purposes Codrington College belongs, like the planters' houses, to the post-hurricane late 1830's.

The founder, Christopher Codrington, Governor-General of the Leeward Islands, was the descendant of a similarly named ancestor who made a fortune in the island around 1640. The younger son of this Codrington was Treasurer of Barbados in 1684, before becoming a Colonel of the Life Guards. An elder son, Deputy-Governor of Barbados in 1668 and Captain-General of the Leeward Islands twenty years later, was father of the Governor-General who founded the college.

Codrington's idea, according to a letter written by a Rev. Gordon in 1710, was the 'maintenance of monks and missionaries to be employed in the conversion of negroes and indians, which design he took from the conversations of a learned Jesuit of St. Christophers between whom and him there passed several letters upon the antiquity, usefulness and excellence of a monastic life'. Codrington's own will, made in 1702, stated 'my desire is to have the plantation (in Barbados) contained intire and 300 negroes at least always kept there and a convenient number of Professors and scholars maintained there, all of them to be under vows of poverty and chastity and obedience who shall be obliged to study and practise Physic and Chirurgery as well as Divinity, that by the apparent usefulness of the former to all mankind they may both endear themselves to the people and have the better opportunities of doing good, to men's souls whilst they are taking care of the body's'.

This austere but valuable scheme was put into operation

and an Anglican theological college, affiliated since 1875 to Durham University, admitted its first students in 1745.

Wandering alone about the Library and Chapel, which together flank the triple-arched entrance, it was possible to believe that the desires of the flesh and the pleasures of riches could be more easily forgone here than in many places. The students were not yet in residence, and an old woolly-headed negro, wicker hat over his face and fast asleep under a cabbage palm, was the only sign, and not much of one at that, that human life ever intruded here at all.

★　　★　　★

Between the Colony match and the First Test I made many drives around and through the island. Sometimes with Quinney Gilbey, whose hired Volkswagen developed pronounced Left-Wing tendencies, to the extent that whenever I, as map-reader, said turn right, it did just the opposite. There are horses, I believe, which can only perform on left-hand tracks, so I suppose Quinney's racecourse instinct had transmitted itself to his car. Quinney, a regular visitor to Barbados, was to show me the sights: but though we had a lot of fun and saw many things they were rarely the things Quinney intended. Indeed, had I not, with my superior skill in navigation, developed over years at sea, guided us home by the stars we should probably be driving among the cane-fields still.

We set out for Oistins Bay and arrived at the airport; looking for the lighthouse we discovered Codrington College; in search of The Potteries at Chalky Mount we pulled up at St. Joseph's police station. We arrived too early to see the flying-fish fleet make their way through the reefs at Bathsheba, and at The Crane Quinney was involved in so complex an anecdote while swimming that both of us were all but swept out to the Azores. But we lunched lazily on the sands at Cattlewash and bathed in the late afternoon off Romie and Naps Brinckman's house on that magical coral curve that stretches between the Miramar and the Coral

Reef Club, and among whose casuarinas are such imaginative and surprising buildings as Ronald Tree's grandiose Palladian villa and Sir Edward Cunard's lovely house in the Cape Colonial style, both with elegant Italianate beach pavilions standing at the very edge of the coral.

This leeward strip, as perfect as anywhere in the Mediterranean, is being developed now at a fabulous rate. By the time this book appears, the scaffolding will be going up for a luxury hotel. The casuarinas are already being chopped below Holetown to make way for a kind of millionaire's building estate that will stretch up the hill towards Sir Edward Cunard's other house. Monthly, the value of land, like a bad fever, climbs on up its steep graph, so that even Montego Bay in Jamaica (which has no comparable area of beach) may soon be exceeded.

Meanwhile, the rafts and yachts bob at their moorings, the speed-boats swerve their water-skiers among the floating heads of bathers, the afternoons glitter out into the softness of turquoise, and the water takes on the bloom of a grape. At night you can see the flares of the fishermen hunting out lobsters on the rocks (which they pull out with gloved hands), the cha-cha-chas begin in the clubs, and for a few days, a few weeks, a few months—even a few years—according to temperament (and income), there can be little more enticing and romantic this side of paradise.

With George Hunte of the Carib Publicity Company, as informative and as helpful a guide as one could wish, I made other, more orderly trips. Round Cherry Tree Hill, for example, where you look over the thick woods of the region known as Scotland, and at the settlements of the surviving Redlegs, poor whites who through generations of keeping to themselves and inbreeding have retained, at some cost in social development, their racial purity. These wretched communities, founded when shiploads of British convicts were added to those already deported to Barbados by Judge Jeffreys at the Bloody Assizes, at last show signs of breaking up. Intermarriage with coloureds, unknown even a few years ago, is increasing, though who may be the loser in these unions is another matter. For the Redlegs, if never slaves, had no great resources, and whereas every other racial group in Barbados contributes now to the life of the community, these anachronistically Nordic creatures—as curious in aspect as albino negroes—have merely lived on in total squalor, perpetuating themselves in isolation, as though the great Quaker families—the Sturges, Gurneys and Frys, with whom I am proud to be connected by marriage—had never succeeded with Wilberforce in achieving the abolition of slavery throughout the British Empire.

We lunched one day at Sam Lord's Castle, in Long Bay, St. Philip. This castellated white mansion, vaguely Regency in feeling, with jutting verandas looking over wide lawns to the sea, is one of the genuine curiosities of Barbados. Legends about it are many, some of them well founded: that, for example, Sam Lord kept his wife in a dungeon, exhibiting her with uncut hair and long fingernails, to friends after drunken orgies. Certainly he was a professional shipwrecker, hanging lanterns in the swaying branches of coconut trees at the cliff edge so that passing vessels, imagining ships riding at anchor in a safe anchorage, made for the rocks, there breaking up and providing Lord rich plunder. Having made his fortune, Lord spent his money in riotous living in England, dying in Jermyn Street in 1844. He left, together with his castle, built by slave labour in 1820, a herd of deer that was sold in Bridgetown on his death. The most interesting thing about the building is its interior, now mistakenly painted overall in white, so that the superb detail of the ceilings, thought to have been done by an Italian specially brought over for the purpose, is largely lost.

With George Hunte I made various sorties round 'Garrison' Bridgetown. Even now, when most of the original buildings have quite different functions, parts of Bridgetown retain a strongly garrison air. The pink, Italianate clock tower of the present Savannah Club once housed a guard-room; the Barbados Museum was the military prison;

the red buildings on the south side of the Savannah, where my British Council friends of Brussels and Venice, Michael and Elsa Combe Martin, live, were officers' and sergeants messes. The offices of the Barbados Electricity Supply Corporation occupy the former Army Commisariat, while the Royal Barbados Yacht Club was the house of the Chief Engineer. And so on. You can still see, on the leeward coast, ruins of the old forts.

The Barbados Museum repays many visits. Admirably displayed showcases illustrate the teeming fish, coral and animal life of the island; the pottery and implements of the Arawak Indians, among the earliest colonists; the story of cane and sea island cotton; the gay zouave uniforms of the original Barbados Yeomanry. Here, too, one can see fascinating marine pictures, made around 1800, with embroidered fish and birds or in the form of Valentines with arrowed hearts and 'I love you' picked out in shells, which the troops sent home to wives or mistresses.

While I was in Barbados, I sought out the works of Ivan Payne, the foremost Barbadian painter, now in his midthirties, who practises as a carpenter or as a painter of antique furniture at the rate of $1 an hour. Completely self-taught, Payne made such strides that in 1956 he won a Unesco scholarship to England, where he spent seven months looking at pictures. Whether this has been of any lasting benefit or not remains to be seen, but the two pictures which I brought back with me show some of his qualities—an unusual ability to organize sharp architectural planes into a firm composition, and a feeling for the light and landscape of Barbados. Payne, who has sold over a hundred paintings, admires Constable more than any other painter, and if his ambition to be a West Indian Constable seems faintly incongruous when you think of how the Caribbean light compares with that of Suffolk, he has enough honest respect for accuracy in representation and truth of feeling, for Barbados, at least, to be glad of him.

A more ebullient, if less controlled painter, is Ralph

FIRST TEST, BRIDGE-
TOWN. E. R. Dexter bat-
ting during his innings of
136 not out. In the back-
ground are the chattel-
houses, little bigger than
sentry boxes, in which
many Barbadians live.

below : K. F. Barrington,
who made 128, playing
all off the back foot.
Hall, who used an arc of
five men between first
slip and gully, bowled on
a length that rarely
allowed the batsman to
play forward.

SECOND TEST, PORT OF SPAIN. These six pictures show various stages of the riot that took place during the West Indian collapse on the third day. It began, after Charan Singh had been run out, with an astonishing deluge of bottle throwing and by an invasion of the field. The first picture shows Dexter surrounded, the second an arrest taking place, the third Sir Edward Beetham, Governor of Trinidad and Tobago, during his brave but unsuccessful attempt to restore order.

e of many
vate fights
breaks out.

inforcements
arrive.

nally, mop-
ng-up opera-
ns begin. But
y had to be
andoned for
 day an hour
early.

Dexter, coming in at 57 for 3, played
a brilliant, aggressive innings of 77.

Watson, who took six wickets in tł
match, was a fiery partner to Ha

Kanhai, with a second innings of 110, almost saved the match for
West Indies.

DaCosta Gibbs, a garage hand at the Shell Station opposite Eaglehall Market. His pictures, mostly portraits of passing itinerant vendors, have a vitality and freshness that make them of more than passing interest. A non-stop discourser on his own art, Gibbs, from his cubby-hole at the station, gave George Hunte the full treatment one afternoon. 'Anything I can do. A born painter. Masterpieces. Genius. I paint flying-fish as they really are. Not like the fellow who painted a flying-fish and it looked like a mullet.'

Payne and Gibbs may not yet have the *réclame* or be part of so fertile a movement as their Haitian colleagues, but they have made a start in the process of recording the life of their time that every people with any regard for a culture and art of their own must sooner or later make.

★   ★   ★

I made a mild but unsuccessful attempt—in case M.C.C., faltering, became in need of sympathetic magic—at finding an Obeah. However, I made a number of inquiries and the notes that follow are based on what I learned from these, and from two articles on the subject by the Rev. C. Jesse, FMI and Mr. G. Barratt.

F. N. Bayley, in *Four Years in the West Indies*, published in 1831, wrote 'Obeah is now fast disappearing and, I have no doubt, will shortly be extinct.' A hundred and thirty years later, this is, despite increased education, quite obviously not the case, neither in the larger islands like Jamaica and Trinidad nor in smaller ones like St. Lucia and Dominica. 'Obeah remains popular and prevalent in every stratum of society in Trinidad,' writes Barratt, 'many are those people in Trinidad today, in every walk of life, who would tremble at the sight of a miniature coffin found lying on their doorstep, and many are the people whose opened purse or wallet would reveal a small green lime and three grains of rice.'

How did Obeah—the corruption of an African religion into the superstitious practice of sorcery and magic ritual—reach these islands? Whatever the correct derivation of the word (Captain Rattray in *Ashanti Proverbs* suggests that it comes from the Ashanti word Obayifo, meaning sorcerer or wizard) there is no doubt that its practice in the West Indies coincided with the arrival of slaves from the Ashanti country in West Africa. An eighteenth-century writer in Barbados asserted that no slave born in the island was able to practise Obeah, 'only those that are brought from the coast of Africa and chiefly the Calamale negroes'. A century later Mrs. Carmichael, describing social conditions in the West Indies, wrote, 'There is not perhaps a single West Indian estate upon which there is not one or more Obeah men or women: the negroes know who they are, but it is very difficult for white people to find them out. . . . I know of an instance where fifteen people in the course of a few months, died from no other cause. It is in vain to reason with them—"Missis, I'm obeahed—I know I'll go dead", is all you can obtain from them.'

The Obeah-men, feeding on the fears and credulousness latent in most human beings, often acquire great riches. In our own age which, if it has shed certain of the more absurd superstitions of the past, is one in which people still like to have disagreeable things done for them at secondhand, the Obeah-man is the universal fixer-up. 'He can', writes Barratt, 'effect a response to a hitherto unrequited love affair, he can create hate where love once bloomed, he can make you rich and he can make you poor, he can give you health and he can strike you down in sickness—he can do all these things as long as you believe in his power and meet his price.' He can also provide amulets or charms for racegoers and football pool enthusiasts.

The Obeah-man operates partly by means of incantation and partly by means of charms and evil objects. To put a curse on an enemy you must leave a bundle of coloured rags, a few strands of human hair, or a dead frog lying on his doorstep. A good-luck charm consists of a small green lime and three grains of rice carried in one's purse or wallet. Garlic, sweet broom and money bush are other potent objects. Salt sprinkled over the floor of a living-room is a useful agent of household discord; so is a grain of clove.

If you're after a job and consult an Obeah, the Obeah writes down the name of your prospective employer on a piece of paper and places it near a candle which burns on your behalf. Next you must take a 'bush-bath' in a solution which contains, among dozens of ingredients, red lavender, rum and olive-oil. After this the Obeah-man gives you a massage while uttering certain incantations. Finally, you make for your appointment, taking care never to look backwards, certain that you will be offered the vacant post.

Apart from a straightforward cash payment to the Obeah-man, the transaction may require sacrifices of one sort or another. The easier problems can be disposed of by a white cock, though it must be one that has never crowed; the more difficult ones need a white goat.

Often the Obeah-man is sought out by people due to appear in court. The procedure then is that the examining magistrate's head must be 'cooled off'. The Obeah-man writes his name down, puts the piece of paper into a hole bored in ice, and places a burning candle beside it. The theory is that the magistrate's head will be so 'cool' at the trial that he will simply dismiss the case.

A serious case, one that will be heard before a judge, correspondingly deserves more obscure methods. Into the mouth of a male frog, which must be caught only in the act of jumping, a sheet of paper with the names of the judge and principal witnesses has to be inserted. Holes are bored in the frog's mouth which is then padlocked.

A sportsman having a poor run of luck mounts a silver coin on a cartridge. This, should he be a batsman, will counteract any Obeah worked on him by opposing bowlers.

The Obeah-man often carries out his incantations in the shade of cannonball or silk-cotton trees, though his favourite place for spirit invocation is a graveyard, especially when an executed criminal has recently been buried. Froude, writing in 1888 about Jamaica, observed that the silk-cotton tree was 'the temple of Jumbi', the proper home of Obeah, and 'to cut down such a tree it was necessary to dose the men with plenty of rum to give them courage to defy the devil'. This belief, probably because the silk-cotton tree is often found in graveyards, still exists in Barbados.

The most dreaded objects connected with Obeah in Barbados are Obeah coffins and dead lizards. An Obeah coffin in the Barbados Museum, about four inches long, is made of reddish wood, the sides painted black, the bottom left unpainted. The brass lid bears a cross, under which are the words In Memory with the age in figures of the person to whom harm is intended. Beneath this a cat, emblematic of a duppy or jumbie, stretches over a setting sun, denoting the decline of life. At the bottom are the letters R.I.P., which seem in the circumstances unnecessarily hypocritical. It is believed that the Obeah-man can cast a shadow over the victim by means of this symbolic coffin, causing him to die.

A similar practice is the depositing of a matchbox containing a dead lizard on the victim's premises. Blue is a colour particularly associated with Obeah, and houses with blue curtains or with blue candles are supposed to be the abodes of Obeah men or women.

Father Jesse records that a priest entering the hut of a dead Obeah-man in St. Lucia found the following things: rags, feathers, cat-bones, parrots' beaks, dogs' teeth, grave-dirt, and bones from a rattlesnake's tail. He also found human bones and flesh dug out of graves.

Father Jesse distinguishes between the various categories of 'zombie' active in St. Lucia. *Ca qui Ka voler*, those who fly, and can transport themselves through the air like a flame of fire; *Les Diablesses*, the She-devils, who can take on visible shape; and *Gens Gagés*, who make a pact with the devil, and in return for sacrilegious favours, are enabled to fly or turn temporarily into animals, in fact do what they want for any private purposes.

In St. Lucia there have been cases of people, at the point of death, making public confession of indulgence in Obeah.

The St. Lucians call this 'deparler', to unload the conscience. But even against this the *Chemboiseurs* (the term for Obeah-men in St. Lucia) have a remedy: by utterance of a spell they can seal the lips of any dying initiate.

I was told in Bridgetown of a case that came before the courts only a year or two ago. A woman, fearing to have lost the love of her husband, consulted an Obeah-man. She was given a medicine to mix into her husband's food, being assured that it would stimulate his desire for her. This she did, but soon the husband sickened and died. An autopsy was performed and the wife was charged with murder. Her fear of the Obeah-man was so much greater than her fear of the law that she preferred to be convicted and hung rather than tell the truth.

What usually happened when a woman requested a love-potion from an Obeah-man was that she was given something to make the man slightly ill and therefore the more dependent on her. In this case the Obeah-man must have given an overdose. But such is the fear of reprisals that few Obeah-men are ever denounced, let alone brought to justice. And though the practice of Obeah remains a criminal offence, for the consulter as well as the consultant, it is not one that figures much in the day-to-day affairs of the courts.

The Barbadian accent, immediately recognizable once one has grown accustomed to it, is common, in greater or lesser degree, to all local-born inhabitants, whether white, coloured or negro. It is an accent almost impossible to describe, though Frank Collymore, in his absorbing *Glossary of Words and Phrases of Barbadian Dialect*, emphasizes certain basic attributes. For example, the accentuation of the first syllable in disyllabic words, or the former of two monosyllabic words (*Pe*-ter, you got *cold*-feet), the drawling out of vowels (boat becomes bo-aht), the use even among the educated of 'de' for 'the', the tendency to omit final consonants (hopin' for 'hoping'), the Irish intonation of the diphthong I, and the general use of the sound UH for any short vowel sound (Give it tuh muh (to me)). The result is a curious amalgam of accents, basically delivered in a slow sing-song that can have a deceptive element of servility about it.

I pick out at random some of the more typical or pleasing phrases liked by Collymore. *I see you're asked out* means that your trousers are torn in the seat (an evident pun, Collymore notes, when you consider that the final consonant in *ask* is omitted), *bellyologist*, a facetious word for glutton, *biscuit* means knee-cap, *blue-duppy*, a bruise from a cricket ball, *busylickum*, a busybody, *chinky*, miserly, *skinning cuffins*, turning somersaults, *But what you dog-dancing me for?*, why are you following me?

A shooter in cricket is a *grounder*, narrow trousers are *gun-mouts*, bowling wide is *hidin' the ball*, to have a private income is to rely on a *hind claw*. About hurricanes there is a common saying:

> June, too soon;
> July, stand by;
> August, you must;
> September, remember;
> October, all over.

A *keep-miss* is a kept woman. Collymore notes various malapropisms such as *costive*, for costly, and *swivelled* for shrivelled. *Mauby* is a drink made from boiled bark, diluted with sugar and vanilla, and well iced. *Molly* refers to hair worn bun-fashion, *moses* covers all kinds of small dinghy (from the seventeenth-century Thames lighters shipped to the Caribbean for carrying sugar to the ships. The original boats have gone, but the name survives), *much* means to caress (She was muching me all night). It is always *Old Year Night*, not New Year's Eve; a *piss-to-windward* is a clumsy fellow; a *poppit* means a laughing stock (She look a regular poppit in that dress, though, nuh?).

Rice is the verb for support. Thus a woman might say *Think I taking any orders from you! You does rice me?* A

Scotland Johnny is a red-leg (because Scotland is the region of Barbados where red-legs mostly settled). You refer to your close friend as your *second*. *He went down the road shelling* means he ran like hell. A caller who has outstayed his welcome is referred to as a *sitting breeches*. A Casanova earns the name of a *skinsman*, long underpants are called *sliders*, and a *white missy* means a glass of cheap white (uncoloured) rum.

Finally, if the crowd at a cricket match want a batsman to hit out, they shout, *Wet him! Wet him!*

★   ★   ★

Though social hierarchies based on colour are more clearly marked in Barbados—'little England' (or Bimshire, after the dashing Royalist leader Byam, who, having urged the colonists to declare for King Charles, led them in their defence of the island against the blockading fleet of the Commonwealth) —than in other West Indian islands, here too they are rapidly breaking down. White Barbadian society has earned many harsh words from visiting English writers, but that strict segregation so violently condemned by Patrick Leigh-Fermor and James Pope-Hennessy, among others, scarcely exists any more. And where it may survive—in places like the Yacht Club and Savannah Bridge Club (where only the cards and stewards are black)—it is of small consequence, for no coloured Barbadian of intelligence could seriously crave membership of such obsolescent institutions.

Certainly in the hotels, from the Marine downwards, there is no vestige of a colour bar. And in the residential beach hotels on the 'platinum coast', like the Colony and Coral Reef, that affect the term 'club' the qualifications are financial rather than racial. (At £100 a week they would need to be.) In any case, these are holiday places, for northerners fleeing the winter, and what coloured Barbadian takes a holiday, at that price, in his own island?

One could say, more accurately, that the various communities—white planters or business people, educated or uneducated coloureds and negroes—tend to move socially among their own kind, because that is where they are likely to find a community of interests, and that only the English intelligentsia — masters at Harrison College or Lodge and the few cultivated exiles — and those coloureds or negroes who move in the worlds of politics and the arts, the higher realms of government service and the law, mix freely together, out of preference and as a matter of course, after official hours.

There are exceptions to this, on both sides regrettable, but it is much more likely that Leigh-Fermor's contemptuous reference to Barbados as being characterized by 'those twin orbs of Empire, the cricket ball and the black ball' will have, in a decade or so, to be rephrased to the 'cricket ball and the white ball'.

The cricket ball, at any rate, seems certain to survive. Throughout the British Caribbean it is impossible not to be made aware, in back streets and beach, on the vast savannahs or in rough village squares, of the West Indians' surging affection for cricket, their astonishing natural skill. Stop the car anywhere at a haphazard pick-up game and you will see boys of all shapes and sizes hitting through the covers with joyous lack of inhibition and, moreover, surprising correctness of technique. 'They can pick them off the trees,' it is said, and one begins to suspect that if a monkey from Cherry Tree Hill came upon a cricket bat he too would drive off the back foot as a matter of course.

West Indians at net practice apply themselves to the business with an enchanting gleefulness that never masks the essential seriousness of their preoccupation. When the first act on returning home of a player like Garfield Sobers is to get out in the street with his brothers and get them to hurl the ball down at him with an ashcan for a wicket, so as to accustom himself to the greater bounce and harsher glare, there can be no mistaking the gravity of the art. No *torero* devoted himself with greater sense of responsibility to the perfecting of a technique on which his life depends. The background to the West Indian cricketer may be waving cabbage palms and the hypnotic beat of the steel bands, his normally irrepressible and bubbling good humour may suddenly collapse in adversity into total dejection, but what remains consistent is that, on any and every level, cricket is his natural means of expression.

★   ★   ★

Barbadians, compared with other Caribbean islanders, are generally regarded as a dour and unresponsive lot. I cannot say they struck me as such, though living as they do in a strict matriarchal society, in the heavy shadow of the Protestant Church, they are probably the most orderly. They do not dress with quite the dash of the Saga-Boys of Port-of-Spain, they have the small-islander's provinciality and *petit bourgeois* propriety, but no one could call them gloomy.

Dependent on a one-crop economy, with few other agricultural resources, they must watch the weather and the prevailing winds with a sailor's non-committal cunning. They stand or fall by the sugar crop, and it may be that, because of this, their features display a certain wariness less common in the more sophisticated Trinidadian.

But my memories will be of driving through the country villages on Sundays, with the whole island in its Sunday-best and the pavements floating with elderly matrons and young girls in white muslin or pink lace, gloved and hatted, all of them laundry-fresh and immaculate, no matter how humble or overcrowded their own shacks. The children, thin-legged and pig-tailed, stick together like gaily-wrapped chocolates, the whole awful solemnity of life in their huge rolling eyes.

At night sometimes we'd pass into range of more fervent worshippers, Holy Rollers and Shakers, Evangelists, Seventh Day Adventists and other revivalists. The croaking air would thump with tambourines and the self-induced ecstasies of the faithful, and even the steel band in Harry's Niterie would have to work hard to keep the forces of conversion at bay.

Harry's Drive-in Niterie, off Carlisle Bay, must be one of the more eccentric nightspots in the tropics. Harry Wills, the powerfully-built negro proprietor, ex-merchant seaman, ex-boxer, among other more robust activities, runs the place with a mixture of genial tolerance towards every whim of his clients and pastor-like decorum. Eschewing the drunks and more violent below-deck customers off the ships, he sets his sights at officers and gentlemen. The walls of his dark one-room establishment, which has a kind of canteen appearance, with space for a steel band, half a dozen tables, and a small dance floor, are plastered up with notices denouncing careless talk (about what goes on in the premises), bad manners, undue familiarity and lewd behaviour. Before Eleanor, one of the two resident hostesses, begins her Bath Tub dance, or Strip Tease (all strip and no tease), Harry solemnly orders the doors to be locked and then delivers a little homily: 'What you see here, savour and keep to yourselves. Enjoy yourselves, but keep your lips tight-shut when you leave the premises.'

Sometimes we would drop in late for a final nightcap, and a talk with Harry, or Eleanor and Stella, whose stories of Barbadian upbringing and domestic custom were more instructive than any learned social study. The steel band would play, Eleanor would shed her last garment, and Harry would whisper huskily anecdotes of Bridgetown life or his days at sea, or of how to run a high-class joint.

'I smell the girls' breath when they come in to see it's sweet and I sniff them from head to toe to see they're fit for my guests.'

★ ★ ★

So 1960 came in with Elsa the Bombshell dancing with vestry-like daintiness at the Coconut Creek, with the bar for the Limbo being lowered until the dancers went under it, heads almost back on the floor, and with English, coloured and negro couples revolving to the cha-cha-cha on the string of open-air dance floors that glitter above the sea all along the leeward shore of Barbados.

4

TRINIDAD:
BEFORE THE SECOND TEST

THE two Colony matches against Trinidad, at Port-of-Spain
Oval, and Guaracara Park, Pointe à Pierre, both resulted in
victories for M.C.C. During these ten days we saw M.C.C.
at their worst and at something like their best.

The worst came first. Trinidad, at Port-of-Spain, declared
at 301 for 9, Carew, a young left-hander of frail physique,
scoring 102 not out. The wicket looked little, if at all, quicker
than at Bridgetown, and Carew, always ready to throw his
bat at anything up to him, batted with dash and a surprising
power. The first Trinidad pair, Corneal, another left-hander,
and Davis, had put on 88, without ever really looking like
getting out. Corneal spanked the ball through the covers,
though he rarely moved into the correct position to do so
until he had finished his shot.

A cloudburst had taken an hour from the first day's play
and the match looked all over a draw. But within the space
of a morning's and afternoon's cricket M.C.C. had been spun
out for 171. It has become a commonplace over recent M.C.C.
tours that any local left-handed or leg-break bowler who cares
to give the ball some air can have the English batsmen
dithering at the crease like dowagers caught in heavy traffic.
So it turned out here. Charan Singh, from San Juan, a
twenty-one-year-old messenger on the Aranguez Estates,
with little experience of Colony cricket, bowled 37 overs on
a perfect batting pitch to take 5 for 57. A slow left-arm
bowler, Singh has a gently curving flight with some late dip,
though no evident sharpness of spin. But he kept a fine length
on or about the off-stump and M.C.C. made increasingly
heavy weather of him. Subba Row battled through to a

rather laboured 49, May made 24. Scarcely less impressive than Singh was Corbie, a tall off-spinner who showed much guile and accuracy in a spell of 3 for 34 in 19 overs.

May, declaring at 171 for 9, made an effort to give the last day's play some meaning. Rodriguez, Trinidad's captain, accepting the challenge on the last morning, himself declared at 131 for 6.

M.C.C. therefore were set to make 262 in 205 minutes. The batting this time was of a different nature altogether. Pullar and Subba Row, the first M.C.C. batsmen on the tour to make use of Richardson's old tactic of a single for each defensive jab, took 30 off five overs from the new ball. Pullar left at 44, Barrington was stumped off Singh at 73, and May, again in his twenties, skied Asgarali to mid-on at 121. Not long after, at 156, Subba Row, who had been lofting and lapping the spinners with rare self-indulgence, was caught hooking at one of the pace bowlers for 73.

But now Dexter joined Smith and these two, with Dexter producing some astonishing strokes off the back foot, raced to victory with eleven minutes of the extra half-hour to spare. Dexter scored his 69 in just over the hour, Smith, 80 minutes over his 47, showed his usual leg-side strength but a familiar lack of power on the off.

This, due to excellently timed declarations, ended by being an entertaining game of cricket after all.

The Port-of-Spain ground, in any case, must rank with Newlands, Cape Town, and Adelaide as having one of the three most spectacular settings in the world. The enclosing mountains, densely wooded, of the Northern Range curve round ahead of the pavilion. The various stands are shaded by vast, scarlet-flowering tulip trees or overhung by the top-heavy filigree spread of samans, always, on account of their shallow roots and bulging superstructure, the first to be bowled over by heavy winds. An enormous, all-informing scoreboard, with COCA-COLA picked out in large letters above it, dominates the mountain end of the ground. But since the sponsors of Coca-Cola, at a reputed cost of $8,000, built the board and maintain it, who could demur at the disfigurement of natural beauties?

Towards close of play here, when the air sweetens, flocks of white pigeons endlessly circle behind the tulip trees, keeping perfect formation like aircraft on display.

Ramadhin had been hidden from M.C.C. at Port-of-Spain and at Pointe à Pierre he was kept out of sight too. Singh was withdrawn for Test Match practice at the last minute so that, with both Trinidad fast bowlers being replaced, their side for the second match was scarcely at full strength. It seemed, as things turned out, going a little too far.

The Guaracara Park ground, an hour's drive from Port-of-Spain through the flat canefields and rickety Indian settlements that flank the Princess Margaret highway, is in the middle of the Texaco (once Trinidad Leaseholds) oil refinery. The smell hits you two miles out and stays with you. The perpetually burning flambeau towers over the shiny aluminium containers like an Olympic emblem.

May won the toss this time and Cowdrey, at the expense of moderate bowling and disastrous catching, helped himself to 173. This indeed was a juicy snack out of the blue. Pullar made 69, but none of the others came off and May declared at 337 for 9. He himself, with his fourth successive score of twenty or under, still looked disconcertingly tentative.

The pitch had shown signs of taking spin on the first evening, but with Illingworth and Greenhough being rested, there was only Allen to make use of it. He was quite enough. Keeping the ball right up, so that the batsman had to play forward, his length and direction were so admirable that no Trinidad batsman could get him away. Though he obviously still lacked Laker's variousness of flight he got surprisingly sharp turn with his off-break. Trinidad were all out for 166, Allen taking 7 for 33, and following on, were out a second time for 172. Allen's pickings were 10 for 63 in the match. Carew again batted with imagination for 70. He made little of Statham, who worked up something like his real pace, but again hit eagerly through the covers. Barrington, the only

other M.C.C. spin bowler on view, showed his limitations
and was unduly expensive.

★   ★   ★

During the first Colony match at Port-of-Spain, I bowled
most afternoons in the nets at those not playing, Cowdrey,
Andrew, Greenhough and Swetman, before going up to the
Governor-General's house for a swim in the blue pool under
the great awning of the nut-loaded coolie pistache tree. The
Governor-General's House, twenty minutes' walk across the
Savannah from the Queen's Park Hotel, lies among exotic
gardens under the ridge of hills that cuts off Port-of-Spain
from the interior.

Port-of-Spain, though it insidiously grows on one, is, at
first glance, cruelly disappointing. In situation, it has affini-
ties with Adelaide: that is to say, it consists of a dead-flat
area, built upon in the grid fashion, bounded by mountains
on the one hand and a wide, virtually landlocked bay on the
other. The sense of living in a port is negligible, if one excepts
the view from the hills at night and the sailors' clipjoints on
the Gaza Strip in Wrightson Road. There is nothing left of
the old Spanish encampment at San Jose, so wantonly fired
by Raleigh in 1595, when, out of pique at finding that the
Spanish Governor Antonio de Berio was either unable or un-
willing to help him in his search for Eldorado, he set alight
the tapia houses built by Domingo de Vera only three years
before. Not that Raleigh's spiteful act mattered, architecturally, in the long run, for in 1808 Port-of-Spain was totally
destroyed by one of the many fires that have dogged the city.
The atmosphere, as one feels it now, is essentially Victorian,
though Victorian with almost every embellishment that the
nostalgia of expatriates could conceivably devise.

'Anyone approaching the Island by sea must be struck by
its scenic beauty: As the steamer glides through the Bocas,
how can you help admiring the dipping verdure-covered
hills and the seaside resorts clinging to or nestling beneath
them. Under us is the swiftly-moving current and here and

there bobbing porpoises. We round the island and then the town of Port-of-Spain, with spires and domes towering above the rooftops that shine with the dazzling brightness in the morning sun, bursts upon our view?'

So writes De Suze in his generally helpful guide to the island, first published a quarter of a century ago. And perhaps from the sea it does in fact strike one like this.

But landing, as we did, at Piarco airport and driving in under the mountains, it is Port-of-Spain's eccentricity, not its exoticism that strikes one.

There are three, perhaps four, Ports-of-Spain. First, the Queen's Park Savannah: a vast, spilling common of rough grass, three miles in circumference and 200 acres in area, that contains a racecourse and enough room for several dozen matting cricket pitches. Any time of the day you can see hundreds of white-flannelled figures hurling themselves up to the wicket like frenetic scenes from a ballet by Katherine Dunham; racehorses being slowly led round by patient stable lads; dusky girls in gym tunics or white pleated skirts banging a hockey ball about and sadistically hacking each other's ankles.

To the north of this stands Governor-General's house, re-built after the fire of 1867, a white, airy building, half Colonial-Palladian, half Scottish baronial, that adjoins the Botanic Gardens. (Since Federation, the Governor of Trinidad has been removed to a smaller building at the back, almost making him an inmate of the newly founded zoo.)

Round the rim of the Savannah, in Maraval Road and Queen's Park West especially, stand the astonishing houses and villas that constitute Port-of-Spain's claim to architectural originality. Colin Laird, an English architect practising in Port-of-Spain, has described these houses of the 1880's in a fascinating article called 'Trinidad Town House': 'A period that showed the logical culmination of a marriage between indigenous peasant building and imported European architecture. . . . The Amerindian peasant house of tapia and clay from the Main, though more numerous in number and though a very strong ancestor of the present-day peasant house, played the minor role in the evolution. It supplied the local colour, the use of local materials. The white settlers' houses with their European background and traditions were the main influence. The most colourful characteristics of the houses of these vagabonds, adventurers, rebels and colonists were mimicked, copied and embraced by all, and by the turn of the twentieth century became one of the most clearcut idioms of the Trinidad vernacular. Near in time to the standards of their homelands and with leisure and money to repeat these standards, we clearly see the personalities of the men mirrored in their houses: vulgarity, gayness, boldness, daring, all mixed with a dash of nostalgia for England, France, Scotland, Spain, Holland, Ireland, Corsica.'

To this list I would add India, China and Switzerland, for if the Spanish, Scottish and French influences are the most usual, it is the kind of grandiose pagoda-chalet, the Bavarian-bred mosque that immediately draw one's unbelieving eye.

A few circuits of the Savannah and of St. Clair Avenue and one has seen every style, sometimes in the same house, that late nineteenth-century European and oriental architecture had to offer. In a morning one can peer into almost as many types of building—with consequent subtleties of detail—as Phineas Fogg saw in the whole of his eighty days.

These 'sugar' houses, built during a period of wild extravagance, social ambition and real, though precarious wealth, put everything on public show. The most casual passer-by had to be made devastatingly aware of each owner's affluence, taste and every whim. 'Filigree enrichments, *porte cochère*, glass, it is only in the front that the glass window is used in its own rights. In other places it is just a single panel in a long line of jalousies. In the front it is featured. Bay windows. Even the roof dormers are glazed. The single-storied houses gain importance from this apparent second story. Marble steps up to the front entrance, the entrance itself with quite an elaborate door and possibly a large lamp. The gate posts and cast-iron gates, magnificent gate lamps, private street lights, the sweeping driveway, the romantic figured ornamental fountains and the aviaries.

'Despite all this however the houses are eminently suited to climatic conditions. The gallery surround, sheltering the painted wall from the sun and rain and providing extra external living space and breaking down the glare of the bright sky. The lightness and low heat conduction of the timber, the exposure of underfloors and the jalousied walls to the breeze, the painting of the roof and the many other features described, make these houses far superior for comfortable living than the mass of houses that have since been built.'

The business and shopping centre of Port-of-Spain, an oblong area between Savanah and waterfront, has lost almost any charm it might once have had. Fires, earth tremors, tasteless modern, concrete blocks, have created a series of crude, incongruous skylines, in which both perspective and detail are hopelessly obscured. The eyes may pause here on an original piece of Spanish gabling, there on the low, galleried storehouses of the Chinese merchants, or on the stanchion-shaded openings of rumshops with seamstresses working on the verandas overhead. But generally even these are hidden by the vast American cars, with their sharp occluding fins, that block the view down any street.

Probably this central area will simply evolve over the years, in a rather behindhand modern manner—concrete and chromium—until it becomes indistinguishable from any European provincial commercial suburb. Oases will remain: Woodford Square, open-air forum of political speechmakers and tub-thumpers, with its fountaining sea-nymphs and canopy of tropical trees; Harris Square, with the shade-splashed features of Lord Harris, one of Trinidad's more notable governors (who married a local girl), gazing towards Laventille Hill; Marine Square, with its shipping agents and banks, it tamarinds, warehouses and disused lighthouse; the wharfsides with the masts of the island sloops—each bearing the name of one of the Grenadines, St. Lucia or St. Kitts on its stern—thick beyond Columbus' statue; the Catholic and Anglican Cathedrals, curious structures both of them, and the huge cosmopolitan cemetery of La Peyrouse; and finally the few imposing public buildings—the sprawling red colonnades of the Law Courts and government offices, the handsome St. James barracks, built in 1824 and now the Police Depot, the green-and-white onion domes of the Jami Masjid mosque—curious enough and sturdy enough to withstand the demolition squads.

These will afford moments of respite to the atom-age visitor, scuttling out of the way of pursuing automobiles, or seeking shade from the sun that splinters off corrugated-iron and rubbery tarmac. And under the dappled leaves of a saman he may muse on how twentieth-century man sets about, unheeding and unwitting, the wholesale destruction of his urban origins.

Outside this rectangle lie the residential areas, high bourgeois to semi-slum, that through tapering social levels reach their base in the shanty town inland of the Beetham Highway. The arc of social decline curves from Maraval, St. Clair and Tranquillity to the north-west, through St. Anns, north of the Savannah, to Belmont, East Dry River and Laventille in the east. Architecturally, the drop is from large-roomed, galleried houses with vivid gardens decently spaced in leafy avenues, to fragile, one-roomed wooden shacks wedged in tiers up Laventille Hill. East of the street called Piccadilly, at the seaward end of East Dry River—scene of Errol John's *Moon on a Rainbow Shawl*—the battered hulks of the refuse-coated shanty huts smoke among the city sewers and debris. The shanty towns of the Transvaal are more orderly than this. The cynical like to say that the shambling figures you see pottering among their discarded tins and vegetable rubbish own refrigerators and radios; this may be so, though I doubt it, but if it is, it merely represents the natural order of priorities that operates even at the bottom of the human scale.

✳   ✳   ✳

Few cities of the tropics, no matter how dilapidated, can
escape a sunset beauty, be it only for ten minutes. Port-of-
Spain is no exception. At six o'clock the Savannah swoons in
a melting honeyed light, the tall palmistes sharpen like cut-
out black paper against a green sky, the hooting of taxis, the
melancholy bleat of ships' sirens acquire a muted and plain-
tive nostalgia. The lights come out on Laventille Hill, and the
decks of the sloops along Queen's Wharf turn into a series of
illuminated stage sets. High above the Savannah, off the
steeply winding Lady Chancellor's Road, the Belvedere
Restaurant, neon-lit pink, blue and white, hangs in the dark
like a kind of birdcage made of ice-cream.

The nocturnal pleasures of Port of Spain are few but posi-
tive. Gastronomically, they scarcely exist. You can eat toler-
ably at the Belvedere, its owner an Austrian who distils
Strauss waltzes while you eat Wiener Schnitzel on the terrace and gaze at the heart-shaped, flickering bay—like a
Dali jewel—far beneath you. At the Tavern on the Green a
copper-haired soprano sings *I Could Have Danced All Night*
as you toy with the tiny oysters, tomato-sauced out of recognition, that grow in the roots of the mangrove swamps. But in
Trinidad, as in most other islands of the Caribbean, the meat
has been so long and so many times frozen that it never sheds
its tasteless donkey-coloured toughness. You settle in the end
for oysters, omelettes, and an occasional chicken. The best
restaurants are certainly the Chinese, which rate here in reverse order to their squalidness. But, for most people, one
dose of bamboo-shoots, sweet and sour pork, and crispy
noodles a week is ample.

What then has a night in Port-of-Spain to offer? For the
bourgeois, it must be said, practically nothing. You can
dance at the Yacht Club, among the lapping waves and the
proxy sailors; or drink at the Normandie Bar among Carlyle
Chang's murals. If you have a taste for railway-station
gloom, then the huge drinking saloon of the Queen's Park
Hotel is the place for you. But each and every one of these
places (on their quiet days, not without odd charms for the

sympathetic) is liable to be inundated with sudden influxes of tourists off the American cruise-ships that twice or three times weekly turn Port-of-Spain into an annexe of Miami. The microphone is taken over by a prattling tourist entertainment officer, who cracks sycophantic jokes and introduces an endless series of unwanted cabaret turns and hastily improvised calypsos. Dining out then becomes akin to being present at a boring private party at which, mercifully, one has not been introduced to any of the guests.

The real life goes on elsewhere. At the Miramar, for example, a dockside dance hall with almost the dimensions of a *palais*. As you climb the bare stone stairs a smell of dust and sickly sweat greets you like an anaesthetic. Inside, dozens of wooden tables are crammed together round a square space cleared for dancing. A steel band, the best in Trinidad, with a fabulous drummer, throbs away under the smoke and orange lights. Lord 'Groundhog' Melody, the huge, gold-smiling doyen of Calypsonians, gets up and sings *Crazy Love*, which is his own composition. The drums go off on a crazy, compulsive adventure of their own.

The tables are packed. Round them, barely distinguishable in the smoking dark, circulate negresses, Chinese, Chinese-negroes, Anglo-negresses, negro-Indians, American and British sailors, Spaniards and Portuguese-negroes, the majority being something of everything—a 'salad of racial genes' to use the narrator of *Lolita*'s phrase about his own antecedents. A tall lovely girl—half Indian, half negress—in slinky tiger-skin dress of sheathlike tightness dances with a small Chinese gentleman with pebble glasses and black-and-canary striped velvet cap. They go through the shunting motions of the calypso rhythm without word or change of expression, his tiny nose pressed between her beckoning breasts. A half-drunk Norwegian lumbers onto the floor with a vast smiling negress spilling out of her black blouse and emerald skirt. After a few moments of bear-like gyration they seek more comfortable positions at the back of the establishment. A saga-boy, with tight black jeans, leather belt and

pink silk shirt, puffs at his cigarette while condescendingly
guiding a doe-eyed Chinese girl in turquoise cheongsam.
Saga-boys are the Trinidadian equivalent of the Ted, dolled-
up exquisites (American style) who smoke and drink and idle
the daylight away. Sometimes they get themselves taken on
as 'sweet men', that's to say the kept lovers of moneyed or
working women who prefer this sort of relationship to marriage or like it as a change between marriages. The 'sweet
man', for all the work-free favour of his position, is not a
ponce; the earnings he lives off are rarely immoral ones.

A roll of drums and the cabaret begins. First, the Limbo,
that acrobatic dance which no matter how often you see it
never fails to astonish. The bar is lowered by stages from five
feet to eight inches and the leaping, cavorting figure with
his flat hips and tight jeans edges his way miraculously under.
He dances back to his mark on spring-heeled feet. Next
might come any one of those frenetic dances of mourning,
the Bongo or the Shango, that make the long Caribbean
wakes both an exorcising and a cartharsis. The drums throb,
the maracas shake, and the taut brown legs of the dancers
stamp and tense as the spirit quickens into orgasmic climax.

Finally, the Bottle dance. A piece of sacking is spread over
the centre of the floor. Empty beer bottles are collected off
the tables, the tops are knocked off and the jagged re-
mainders are flung together to form a glistening green pile on
the sacking. The dancer, with bare torso and baggy black silk
trousers held in with a scarlet cummerbund, leaps onto the
floor and works his way round the edge. The drums grow
louder and more passionate, his bare feet pound, the sweat
begins to pour. Now he turns inwards, lost and self-absorbed,
but thudding, thudding all the time. Suddenly, as if unable
to bear it any longer—like a swimmer on the blue pool's edge
—he leaps onto the broken glass, leaps in, then out, gyrates,
leaps again, this time staying to trample and crunch. Then
out and round the edge before, without warning, cartwheeling through it, handstanding back into it, and just as suddenly disappearing from sight.

The lights dim, the broken glass is gathered up, the ship's engineer unseats the complaisant negress he has been fondling on his lap.

Fresh rounds of Carib lager are ordered, the band goes into a mambo, the Chinese in his canary-striped cap resumes his bosom-embedded and hypnotic shunting.

Outside the paper moon is upside down, the bay is aglow with gently tilting masthead lights. Where to now? The open-air haunts of the 'Gaza Strip', the Oasis, or the Flamingo? The floozies are more importunate, the clientele tougher and further gone. Perhaps not.

But at Le Cupidon, Grace of the doubly voluptuous figure and gleaming teeth that would illuminate the plushy darkness on their own is still swaying at the microphone in her moonlight-on-sea sequins. '*So Many Beautiful Men, So Little Time*,' she breathes huskily, her eyes roaming the room, and one had better get up, pay the bill and get out while one can.

★   ★   ★

Trinidad, it could truthfully be said, lives on its perpetual dream of carnival. The precursors of carnival, which is celebrated on the two days before Ash Wednesday, are the calypso 'tents', pitched each year towards the end of January, along the quays. This year there were four tents, bearing such names as the Big Bamboo and the Young Brigade. Nowadays the 'tents' are sheds, seating several hundred people at anything from one to five dollars a head. Originally, when the slaves who brought the calypso from West Africa first arrived, the tents were thatched bamboo structures on the sugar estates. The songs sung by the slaves—either about their homeland or as they worked—became known as 'canne-boulay', patois for burning canes, because they were sung more often than not while the slaves helped to put out the fires they had often themselves started. The forerunners of the calypsonians, the West African Tai-Tai, were jesters in the courts of the African kings. They travelled from village to village, singing on market day in the squares, and improvising words according to what was required of them. They praised their employers, welcomed the slave-traders and commented generally on the times they lived in.

The leading calypsonians of today—Lord Melody, the Mighty Sparrow, Christo, Spoiler—are commercial troubadours who perform all over the world, returning annually like migrant birds when the tents are set up.

The Young Brigade Tent at ten o'clock: a sour-sweet smell, the hall packed, the band on stage, hidden by a waist-high board that leaves only their bobbing heads visible. The calypsonians come to the microphone one after the other and fire off their verses like machine-guns: each sally is greeted with stampings and roars of approving laughter.

Not long ago the Mighty Sparrow, a good-looking charmer in a wide-lapelled pearl-grey suit, was concerned in an incident outside the Miramar; a woman was the cause of it and Sparrow used a gun. Much of the patter between Lord Melody and Sparrow devolves round this affray on the one hand and on Melody's rhinoceros-like appearance on the other.

Melody begins a calypso, *Cowboy Sparrow*:

> Sparrow you should use your head
> The mister could have fall down dead
> Slinger you should use your head
> The mister could have fall down dead
> You were in love with the man wife
> And so the man pull out a knife
> If he had done the same to you
> It is the same blasted thing you would do.

Chorus:
> Attention, listen everyone
> Beware, Sparrow got a gun
> And he shooting like a madman all over Town
> Ay! Sparrow got a gun.

Sparrow takes over the microphone, saying, 'Out of the way Groundhog, out of the way now.'

'You calling me brown hog?'

'*Ground*hog, *Ground*hog, boy. I wouldn't be calling you *brown* hog, if I was calling you *brown* hog, I'd call you *black* hog.'

Sparrow sings, his three gold rings flashing, his intimate eyes probing the hall:

> Aye little boy let me tell you this
> Don't be afraid I'm not the police
> You wouldn't know me but I want you to show me
> A girl round here they call Mildred
> When I tell the Mister Mildred is me Sister
> He jumps up and then he said

Chorus:
> Tell you sister to come down quick I have something
>   here for she
> Tell she its Mr. Benwood Dick the man from Sangre
>   Grande
> She know me well ah give she already
> She must remember me
> Go on go on just tell she Mr. Benwood come.

And so on. Sparrow is succeeded by Christo, an energetic Belafonte-type in a scarlet sweatshirt:

> A smart man named Jonothan
> Make his wife Lilian
> Take out two policy
> Was to fool the Insurance Company
> So she make him go to lie down in bed
> And paid a quack Doctor to say he dead
> In the wake she drink rum and whisky
> And start to blast out this melody

> Doctor say you dead Jonothan
> Sleep, close your eyes Jonothan
> Don't raise up the sheet Jonothan
> Sleep, close your eyes Jonothan.

Melody and Sparrow reappear, insult one another, disappear. Melody returns to introduce, one by one, the rest of the team: Spoiler, a weaving, inspired Sid Fieldish figure with an endless calypso about locusts; then Chiang Kai Shek, Bomber, Mr. Action, a genius in blue zoot suit and dark glasses who accompanies his singing with an astonishing series of epileptic convulsions, and finally a rum-happy old-timer who allegedly just happened to be passing by. At eleven o'clock punctually Melody calls a halt. The bobbing maroon-capped bass drummers, guitarists, and sax players pack up their instruments.

So it goes on, six nights a week until the end of February. Carnival is on its way. All round the town, on Laventille Hill or in Warner Street, in the shanties of East Dry River or in San Juan, the amateur steel bands are practising their theme songs, *Annie Laurie* or *The Blue Danube*, *Waltzing Matilda* or *Night and Day*, each to calypso rhythms.

In rooms throughout Port-of-Spain the elaborate costumes of the marauding bands, each one of which costs anything from fifty to five hundred dollars, are being sewn together. For at carnival time everyone, from the highest to the lowest, joins a band and 'plays mas(que)'. These masques follow certain traditional themes, allowing the Trinidadian gift for mimicry and self-embellishment full expression. They range from Bad Behaviour Sailors to Wild Indians, from Jab-Jabs (coolie Devils) to Burraquitas (little donkeys or jennies), from Tennessee Cowboys to Bats. The most elaborate of all, though, are the historical bands which play, with extraordinary attention to detail, such subjects as Ancient Greece, Rome under Nero or Egypt under the Pharaohs, the Viking Invasion of Britain, Robin Hood, the Trojan Horse, the Serpent of the Nile. The band accompanying these historical masques must avoid being anachronistic; thus it should be composed of stringed and wind instruments. The steel band is out.

February is the month of fermentation. Increasing numbers of small parties are given to help the carnival spirit along, to prepare for the great explosive jump-up, the prolonged ecstatic shuffle. Those two days of impersonation and wish-fulfilment, of power and glory, of cathartic strut and omnipotence, glow in the mind like nearing intimations of paradise.

5

THE SECOND TEST

WHILE M.C.C. were disporting themselves among the oil refineries at Pointe à Pierre, West Indies were having an open practice at Port-of-Spain.

Two places were in doubt: those of McMorris, who had been run out for nought at Bridgetown, and Scarlett, the off-spinner, whom Singh's success had put in jeopardy. Mc-Morris failed in each innings of the trial, so that virtually put paid to him. Nurse of Barbados was summoned at a few hours' notice, but in the event the selectors plumped for Solomon, one of the successes of the India-Pakistan tour, to open with Hunte. Singh, as we expected, replaced Scarlett. This was a justified gamble on the lines of the Ramadhin-Valentine gamble in 1950, for Singh was virtually without first-class experience.

This meant that two Jamaicans were rejected. McMorris and Scarlett, both complaining of the hostile atmosphere of the crowd, even during net practice, flew home before the Test.

In this instance, the changes seemed common sense. But throughout the time we were in the Caribbean we heard criticism of the 'horses for courses' or 'proportional representation' policy of West Indian selection committees. The home player, it was repeated, stood at an overwhelming advantage when a Test was due to be played in his island. Many were those who regretted the Chauvinism that showed itself equally in attitudes to the concept of Federation as to picking the best Test team.

Yet an atmosphere of mutual trust and confidence among the players is not always helped by the Press. On the second day of the Port-of-Spain Test the following paragraph appeared in *The Nation* (formerly *P.N.M. Weekly*):

'I want to say clearly beforehand that the idea of Alexander captaining a side on which Frank Worrell is playing is to me quite revolting. Whatever the result of this series I shall mobilize everything I can so that Frank should captain the team to Australia. In 1957 during the tour in England I endured the long days of misery which need not have been. To send to Australia as captain in 1960 a man who has never been there before would be a betrayal. Show me one single individual who will come out and say "I believe Alexander will be a better captain than Worrell for such and such reasons". No one will dare. . . . If Frank is not appointed it will be over wide and public protest. . . . That Worrell was not captain in 1957 in England was a scandal known to everybody. I shall go into detail as to the mischief this kind of thing causes. I have kept silence for 25 years. I shall do so no longer.'

The article was signed C. L. R. James, the name of a locally-known literary critic, cricket enthusiast and political editor.

Now whatever the rights and wrongs relating to John Goddard's reluctant acceptance of captaining the unfortunate 1957 touring side, Mr. James must know that Worrell was offered the captaincy of the side that went to India and Pakistan. At that time Worrell was studying in England and for perfectly sound reasons he felt it impossible to interrupt his work. In face of Worrell's refusal Alexander was appointed and, generally speaking, did a good job. He never made any secret of the fact that he was the second choice.

It was not therefore surprising—especially in view of the fact that he is a resident of Jamaica while Worrell is a bird of passage with annual commitments in England—that Alexander was reappointed. The fact that he had been to Cambridge and was lighter in colour than some does not affect his genuine qualifications for the job. At Bridgetown he showed himself a much improved wicketkeeper and batsman, and a shrewd, determined captain on the field.

Who but a malicious xenophobe could write, during a Test match, 'that the idea of Alexander captaining a side on which Frank Worrell is playing is to me quite revolting'? *Revolting* is the parlance of the irresponsible agitator. Worrell's great gifts as a player, his intelligence and charm, and no doubt his capacity for leadership, cannot benefit from such advocacy.

The English selectors had no problems. Statham was again fit, so that only Moss of the Bridgetown team stood down. Again one felt that the advantages, if the match were to produce a result, must lie overwhelmingly with the side winning the toss. Much, as far as England's chances were concerned, seemed to depend on Statham's recapturing of pace, and, if the wicket should take spin on the last two days, on Allen. On the evidence before us—with memories of Hall's fire and Watson's pace at Bridgetown, of Sobers' power and Worrell's relaxed certainty, of Singh's dipping flight and Ramadhin's accuracy—an English victory was a lot to expect.

FIRST DAY

The toss again to May, the promise of a pitch with 'pace like fire', from Edgar ('Man') Borde the groundsman, and long fretting queues outside the turnstiles. The samans were motionless in the heat: a few clouds like gunbursts lay above the hills.

Pullar leaned out to Hall's first ball and it was chased to the boundary edge and stopped. Cowdrey guided the next, short and sharply rising, into the grass squatters at third man and the pace of the outfield was apparent to all. A bouncer came next, then three through the short legs by Cowdrey, a couple to Pullar. An eventful opening over, which Watson, bowling to four slips, gully, and two backward short legs, balanced with a maiden to Pullar. Hall carried on with a wide and a no-ball, and the runs ticked up generously. But it was the feast before the fast.

Both bowlers, with their long arms and loose slinging actions, settled on a length—short and uppish—and the batsmen were kept back on their stumps fending the ball down. If they did not exactly hide the ball, they were not showing it any earlier than essential. After 35 minutes of such sparring Worrell bowled an over for Watson and Hall to change ends. Cowdrey cut him square for four, and the opening shift was resumed in different harness. Watson's fifth ball was well down the leg-side, Pullar followed it and Alexander was nicely across to take the catch.

If Hall and Watson looked quick at the start, they became positively ferocious now. Watson soon was in such a lather of sweat and dust that he might have come out of a coal mine. Barrington gave them any encouragement they might have needed. He felt blindly outside the off-stump, he scooped the ball dangerously near the short legs. Cowdrey, still digesting as it were, was kept on a diet of bouncers and short ones to the off. A nasty one off the seam took him amidships. Scarcely had he recovered breath when, trying to push down a rising ball from Hall, he deflected it off the inside edge. His off-stump cartwheeled over like a shot rabbit. They were dancing around now under the tulip tree.

May, kept permanently on the back foot, pottered for twenty minutes without scoring and one felt that the huge Coca-Cola sign announcing BATSMEN AT WICKET should have read BATSMEN AT WORK. Watson bowled the last over before lunch and May, having played at the fourth ball and missed, pushed tentatively at the next, pitched outside the off-stump and leaving him. The ball flew to Kanhai at second slip, knee-high, and that was that. May looked understandably sick. The score was 57 for 3.

Few fast bowlers could have kept up such pace over a whole morning. It was an onslaught much the same as they had produced at Bridgetown, and even more successful.

But Dexter wasn't having any of it. He drove Hall in

his first over through mid-on and crashed him on the rise past cover. He appeared as cool and detached as a De Rezke cigarette advertisement. At 77 Singh bowled his first over in a Test match and it drew forth applause. Dexter picked his quicker one and beat the outstretched hand of mid-off. Next he placed Sobers under the saman at mid-wicket.

Barrington, whose answer to all this had hitherto been a streaky four between the shoulders of second and third slip, at last began to make headway. He swept Sobers repeatedly down to long leg, and lay back to carve him through the covers. Dexter having pushed the field out, short singles were there for the taking. Barrington hustled to his fifty, Dexter at his heels. Watson came back and Dexter lashed a short ball past extra cover for his own fifty. Next ball he flicked a half-volley off his legs that sped like lightning to the fence. At tea England were 170, Barrington 68, Dexter 61. Together they had scored a hundred in 105 minutes, and the West Indians this time were glad of the break.

Watson returned full of fire and Dexter, rapped on the knuckles, was soon in need of binding. Harold Dalton, M.C.C.'s masseur, bounded out and bound. Ramadhin bowled again, to five off-side fielders, and he pitched too consistently wide for anyone to be able to exercise them.

Solomon trundled up some crafty overs of leg spin, full of good-natured guile, until eventually Singh replaced him. In his first over Dexter, grown weary and frustrated at this enforced idleness, hit a shade early and half-heartedly at one well up to him and Singh pounced to his left, surprised at the gentleness of the offering. Again Dexter had dominated England's innings. He had, eschewing even the calculated risk, driven the fast bowlers off and the slow bowlers had become scared to attack him.

So Smith entered with the new ball due after one run; it was twenty-seven minutes later, with the new ball only two overs old, that he got off the mark. Barrington, ducking into a Hall bouncer, must have got the seam indelibly imprinted on his skull. He went down, looked as if he might stay down, but doggedly got to his feet.

Hall kept at it with a gusto wonderful to behold. Barrington, exhausted as well as stunned, no longer looked for runs. Smith, wisely, contented himself with seeing out the day. Since tea only 50 runs had been scored in 90 minutes, so it could be said that the batting rather than the bowling had lost its energy.

Yet it had been a notable recovery. From 57 for 3 to 220 for 4 speaks for itself. Barrington, with a great lump behind the ear, could lie back and take his ease, legs crossed as honourably as any Crusader's.

The attendance, 22,000, and the receipts, $19,000, were both records for the ground.

ENGLAND

First Innings

Pullar, c. Alexander, b. Watson	...	...	...	...	17
M. C. Cowdrey, b. Hall	...	...	...	...	18
Barrington, not out	...	...	...	...	93
*P. B. H. May, c. Kanhai, b. Watson	...	...	...	...	0
E. R. Dexter, c. and b. Singh	...	...	...	...	77
M. J. K. Smith, not out	...	...	...	...	9
Extras	...	...	...	...	6
Total (for 4 wkts.)	...	...	...	...	220

Illingworth, Swetman, Trueman, Allen and Statham to go in.

FALL OF WICKETS — 1–37, 2–42, 3–57, 4–199.

BOWLING (to date)—Hall, 17–5–50–1; Watson, 19–4–60–2; Worrell, 1–0–6–0; Singh, 14–5–27–1; Ramadhin, 17–6–36–0; Sobers, 3–0–16–0; Solomon, 7–0–19–0.

WEST INDIES—*F. C. M. Alexander, C. C. Hunte, J. Solomon, R. Kanhai, G. Sobers, F. M. Worrell, B. Butcher, K. T. Ramadhin, W. Hall, C. Watson and C. Singh.

SECOND DAY

The morning papers, in Trinidad and England, were full of the bouncer war. The news transpired that Hall had been spoken to by the umpires on the previous day and now Watson, after 2 bouncers in 4 balls, was cautioned in this second over. Barrington turned Hall off his legs to reach his hundred —'Crash-helmets will be worn,' he said at breakfast—then was twice on his back ducking out of the way. Hall brought up a forward short leg and this was evidence of intention. Smith steered Watson between second and third slip, and Barrington, flinging his bat at a bouncer from Hall, scored four past gully. Hall and Watson were as fast as anything I have ever seen. When Smith faced Hall the forward short leg was joined by three others, fine of the umpire. Smith looked to have time in hand. Barrington got a slower full pitch from Hall and he spooned it just out of square leg's reach. He wasted full pitches woefully, as if suspicious of some late and latent devilry in them.

Hall, after three-quarters of an hour of assault, was spent, so Watson changed ends and Worrell, lazily lovely in action but quicker this time than usual, bowled over the wicket from the pavilion. The wind was behind him. He beat first Barrington, then Smith, both playing down the wrong line as the ball swung diagonally across them. The picking-up was brilliant, the throwing had the stumps going down at all angles. The opening hour moved England along by only 34. Ramadhin had an exploratory bowl, rather with the air of a mining geologist carrying out an unpromising survey, but England went in, intact, at 275 for 4, Barrington 121, Smith 35.

Barrington was out immediately afterwards. He flicked at a good-length ball outside the off-stump from Hall and Alexander took a fine diving catch in front of first slip.

Smith began to drive Hall wide of mid-on, which meant that either Hall was slowing down or else that Smith was getting into focus. Illingworth sent up 300 with a no-nonsense square cut; Smith pulled a sudden long hop from Singh into a crowd of English sailors to reach 50. So Ramadhin bowled again, and Illingworth, having snicked him past slip for two, came too far out and across to the next ball, was beaten by the flight, and was bowled off his pads. Swetman went back to a half-volley from Watson and was only too plainly l.b.w., Trueman arrived and the Fast Bowlers' Union came into operation: Watson produced four slowish full tosses for him. Ramadhin threw them up on a teasing length and Trueman refused the bait with the obligatory self-denial of a Moslem during Ramadan.

Singh returned and Smith, with Worrell at silly mid-off looking into his eyes with an oculist's intensity, hit him straight back for six. Trueman, not to be outdone, followed suit next over. The stout lady selling cachou nuts all but dropped her load. Ramadhin changed ends and Smith at once pulled him into the stand at mid-wicket. It was becoming a question of six or nothing. After this, it was nothing for the best part of half an hour. Then Trueman, trying to turn Ramadhin, found himself l.b.w. But 35 useful runs had been added all the same.

Hall found enough energy to bounce one at Smith but was then savagely hooked under the pagoda-chalet at square leg. Ramadhin brought up three short legs for Allen and spun one between bat and pad.

Smith was 91 at tea, England 355 for 8. Smith, farming the bowling and scoring long singles, reached his 100 with a sizzling drive past mid-off. He had batted four and a half hours, baring his teeth at every ball, but building up his innings in a way Hutton would have approved. Once past fifty, his assurance had been complete.

Ramadhin, owing much to Worrell, finally got him. Smith drove hard to leg, we looked for the ball at long-on, but there was Worrell, his arms up at short mid-on, the ball in his hands. An over or two later Worrell knocked back Statham's off-stump. So England were all out 382, leaving Statham and Trueman 35 minutes' attack in the comparative cool.

No wicket fell. Trueman, much the quicker of the two, had Hunte weaving like a lightweight. But both Solomon and Hunte played Statham firmly in the middle of the bat. One had the feeling that Trueman, at least, with his opening spate of bouncers, had made his point. It seemed unlikely, not to say bad politics, that he would continue. But he had shown his hand and it had not been a bad one. No one could possibly criticize him for that.

ENGLAND

First Innings

Pullar, c. Alexander, b. Watson ...	...	...	...	...	17
M. C. Cowdrey, b. Hall ...	...	...	...	...	18
Barrington, c. Alexander, b. Hall ...	...	...	...	...	121
*P. B. H. May, c. Kanhai, b. Watson	...	...	...	...	0
E. R. Dexter, c. and b. Singh ...	...	...	...	...	77
M. J. K. Smith, c. Worrell, b. Ramadhin	...	...	...	108
Illingworth, b. Ramadhin	...	...	...	...	...	10
Swetman, l.b.w., b. Watson	...	...	...	...	1
Trueman, l.b.w., b. Ramadhin	...	...	...	...	7
Allen, not out	...	...	...	...	...	...	10
Statham, b. Worrell	...	...	...	...	...	1
Extras (l.b.3 w.1 n.b.8)	...	...	...	...	12
Total	...	...	...	...	...	...	382

FALL OF WICKETS—1–37, 2–42, 3–57, 4–199, 5–276, 6–307, 7–308, 8–343, 9–378, 10–382.

BOWLING—Hall, 33–9–92–2; Watson, 31–5–100–3; Worrell, 11.5–3–23–1; Singh, 23–6–59–1; Ramadhin, 35–12–61–3; Sobers, 3–0–16–0; Solomon, 7–0–19–0.

WEST INDIES

First Innings

C. C. Hunte, not out	...	...	...	...	...	8
J. Solomon, not out	...	...	...	...	...	14
Total (for 0 wkt.) ...	...	...	...	...	...	22

*F. C. M. Alexander, R. Kanhai, G. Sobers, F. Worrell, B. Butcher, K. T. Ramadhin, W. Hall, C. Watson and C. Singh to go in.

BOWLING (to date)—Statham, 4–1–11–0; Trueman, 5–2–10–0; Allen, 1–0–1–0.

THIRD DAY

It was immediately obvious this morning that whatever else Hall and Watson had done they had put Trueman and Statham properly on their mettle. Both kept the ball well up, varying their pace, and every now and then whipping in a really quick one. This was the intelligent tactic in the circumstances and it resulted in an immediate break-through. Statham, in his second over, had Hunte pushing forward on the leg-stump and the ball skidded off bat and pad to Trueman at backward short leg. Kanhai tried to drive a swinging full toss from Trueman three overs later; missed and was painfully l.b.w. Now this vast excitable crowd, 25,000 strong and like a spilled paintbox under the saman trees, was really humming. Sobers drove his first ball firmly to cover and the relief was audible. He tried then to crack a slightly wider one, the ball flying off the edge at decapitatory pace to third slip. May shot out a hand, the ball went almost vertically up and Barrington, at first slip, stood under it, caught it and threw it as high as the tulip tree. Not even Olivier before his Agincourt speech achieved as total a silence or suspension of emotion as existed while that ball was in the air. The bowlers stuck to it marvellously. Some of the magic green essences of youth seemed to well up in both, and Solomon, time after time, was left groping at Statham. The first hour produced 18 runs: three bouncers, as opposed to around 15 by Hall and Watson during the comparable period, had been bowled. Worrell, too, was beaten off the seam more than once. Pullar at forward short leg made three point-blank stops in a row off powerful drives. Trueman's field at this stage was four short legs, four slips and only cover point in front of the wicket on the off-side. Statham's was roughly the same.

Ten minutes before lunch May gave Barrington a turn at Statham's end. Solomon slashed the last ball of the first over hard to Allen at cover and called. Worrell sent him back and Solomon, caught on the turn, was beautifully thrown out. He had struggled two hours for 23. Worrell now flung his bat at a ball well up to him from Trueman, got a thickish edge and Swetman scooped the ball up an inch from the ground. Worrell never even waited for the umpire's hand. West Indies were 45 for 5: Trueman's figures were 8 overs, 5 maidens, 12 runs, 3 wickets. It had been a fabulous morning's cricket, to which Statham, bowling with little luck, had contributed more than a fair share. He had not, compared with Hall, achieved anything like lethal pace, but he had moved the ball off the seam, he had made the batsmen feel for the ball outside the off-stump, and sometimes he brought one back to make them stab down at the last second. It was a model of controlled fast bowling. Trueman, to whom most of the wickets had gone, had varied his attack more, trying out swinging half-volleys and slower yorkers, using the crease and keeping the bouncer up his sleeve.

During lunch, pirate ladders were hoisted at strategic points outside the ground and admittance for the nippy became possible at ten cents a climb. The more orthodox rushed the gates or swarmed up the trees which quickly became festooned with blue trousers.

The afternoon in contrast was almost devoid of incident. Barrington, most valuably, bowled 12 overs of his leg-spinners for 3 runs and he will never do that again. Illingworth, taking over from Trueman after Alexander had turned him twice to the fine leg boundary, bowled 7 overs for 8 runs. Butcher was an hour over 3. At 65 Statham came back at Trueman's end and Butcher gave a sharp chance to Trueman at backward short leg. He had been hurried all the time by the quick bowlers and soon, shuffling back to Statham, he was l.b.w.

May used Trueman and Allen after tea, Trueman bowling into a shifting wind. Alexander, who had batted stout-heartedly for over two hours without much trouble, suddenly left one alone on the off-stump from Trueman and was l.b.w. Four runs later Ramadhin called Singh for a sharp single to cover, the return from Dexter was quick to the top of the stumps, and Singh, not grounding his bat, and a yard short besides, was given out.

Hardly had umpire Lee Kow's finger gone up than it started. First an ugly, growing roar of protest, then a storm of boos, finally, from far back in the open stand to the right of the pavilion, the bottles.

Lobbed like hand-grenades the opening volleys bounced separately along the boundary edge. Within seconds these had grown into thick showers, not from this stand only, but from all round the ground. May called his boundary fielders in, and in no time at all only a tiny island round the pitch was free of bottles.

Gerry Alexander ran out through swarms of people who had now jumped the boundaries and were advancing menacingly on the middle. He talked briefly with May who had no alternative but to lead his players off the field. Flanked by police officers and with Trueman and Statham holding a stump each they managed to get safely through, the umpires, also with police escort, just behind them. A ricocheting stone struck Pullar on the elbow: otherwise they miraculously got through unscathed.

On the field it was another matter. The whole playing area was a confusion of darting figures, of gesticulating mobs, of isolated but brutal fights which the pathetically few police present—there were fifteen of them—could do nothing to break up.

Into all this the Governor of Trinidad and Tobago, Sir Edward Beetham, a bronzed, cool figure in a fawn suit, made his way, with Learie Constantine, now Minister of Works, at his side. Somewhere there, too, were the Premier, Dr. Eric Williams and Sir Errol dos Santos, President of the West Indian Cricket Board, the man who more than any other put the Queen's Park Club on its feet.

But it was no good. The bottles, many of them deliberately broken beforehand, continued to rain and any one of these could have been nastily struck.

Blood was flowing now. In the middle of it a fire hose was

hauled onto the field and trained on groups of bottle-throwers. The pressure was low and it merely sputtered out in pools at the firemen's feet like an elephant urinating. But it brought retribution. The bottles, which had shown signs of running out, descended with renewed force and this time the broadcasting box of Radio Trinidad on its glass-fronted perch came under fire. The glass was splintered and inside it the son of Sandy Lloyd, one of the umpires, was mildly hurt. Colonel Eric Beadon, Police Commissioner, who was on the field trying to marshal his miserably inadequate forces, got cut about the legs by flying glass. A policeman, almost impaled on the pavilion railings by a rum-crazed hooligan, had a great strip torn from his thighs.

Now, three-quarters of an hour after the first bottle had been thrown, a dozen mounted policemen, with a squad of tin-hatted reinforcements, appeared on the scene. Behind the wire-nettings of the stands the bottle-throwers, devoid of ammunition, scattered. On the field the brawlers gradually dispersed.

It was all over now, bar the shouting. The hospital cases, of which there were thirty, were removed; the sirens of the ambulances died away. The sixty who had been treated for cuts and wounds were given lifts home.

The flocks of white pigeons, on their endless, undeterred circuits, took the late sun on their wings as they dipped against the hills.

Darkness was falling as the players of both teams, who had been drinking fraternally together in the dressing-rooms, drove off back to the Queen's Park Hotel under police escort.

It had been a sorry, tragic and sadly shaming business.

★　　★　　★

In the bar of the Queen's Park pavilion there was the feeling of a national disaster—as indeed in its trivial way it had been. The members were stunned, shocked and ashamed. Such a thing had never before happened in Trinidad, an island renowned for its impartiality and sporting spirit. None of them had believed that, even under provocation—which there wasn't—it would have been possible. The general distress was touching to see, for a more well-meaning and hospitable group of members it would be difficult to find. After cabling to our papers, Woodcock, Roberts and I, plied with conciliatory whiskies, discussed the sad events with Gerry Gomez, Keith Edgehill, our admirable Press Liaison officer, and others of our Trinidad friends.

What had caused it? Pique, disappointment, totally irresponsible resentment at decisions by umpires who were respectively of British and Chinese origin? Or was it pre-planned, deep-lying racial prejudices, and political bitterness, finding, and seeking, a convenient outlet? Perhaps simply it was overcrowding, with irritation at West Indian failure boiling up in the packed stands that were hot as pressure cookers, sun, rum and whisky playing their part (dozens of bottles of spirits were discovered later among the piles of Coca-Cola and Seven-Up)? Added to this, gambling on every aspect of the play, as well as on mobile roulette tables, helps to create an atmosphere of fevered apprehension and excitement, sometimes bearing no relation to the state of the game.

Probably it was something of all these things. Mob reactions are hard to predict. But once the first bottles had been thrown (and there were too many of these, despite it being immediately after an interval, for it to have been quite spontaneous) anything could have happened. Unintentional killing and lynching, under the demon rum, were not out of the question. Women, many of whom had cowered with children under parasols, could have been disfigured for life.

Some five hundred people, out of 30,000 (the biggest crowd ever to witness a sporting event in the West Indies) had, I imagine, actually fought or thrown, though several thousand had invaded the field. Yet the instigators may have been a mere couple of dozen.

That evening R. W. V. Robins, wearing the chocolate, pale-blue-striped tie of the Queen's Park Club (an inspired touch of chivalry), issued this statement:

'It has come to my notice that rumours are being circulated that the M.C.C. intend to discontinue the Test match and go back to England.

'Such a suggestion never entered any of our minds at all. We intend to go on with the game.

'Our sympathies are entirely with the good people of Trinidad who have been let down by a few hooligans.'

It could not have been more conciliatorily put.

That night Sir Edward Beetham, the Governor, spoke on Radio Trinidad. He said:

'I may not be an active cricketer, but I am an extremely keen follower and indeed a real lover of the game. Before I ever arrived in the West Indies nearly seven years ago, after watching and enjoying cricket in many places in the world, I was always told that the West Indies was the real place to watch and enjoy cricket as cricket should be watched and enjoyed: a place where cricket was really considered to be what it is—the best game in the world.

'The West Indies had a tradition and an enviable reputation for sportsmanship and love of the game for the game's sake by both players and spectators, unsurpassed anywhere in the world where cricket is played. So far as the players are concerned, that reputation remains completely untarnished.

'This evening I have, however, witnessed a scene—I need not describe it, indeed it defies description—which would have been to me unbelievable—had I not seen it with my own eyes.

'As Governor of Trinidad, I wish to try somehow to convey to the M.C.C. team and also to the members of the West Indies team from other Territories, the apologies—which those who know me will know to be abject and completely sincere—of practically every single person in Trinidad for the most disgraceful behaviour which occurred amongst a certain section of the spectators this evening at the Queen's Park Oval.

'Members of both teams, I can only ask you to believe

what I myself believe to be true—and that is that except for perhaps one person in a thousand, every man and woman, and any child old enough to understand, will condemn, as I do, the perpetrators of the disgraceful behaviour which we saw this afternoon.

'I sincerely hope that Mr. Peter May and Mr. Robins and Mr. Alexander will accept that apology from Trinidad.

'To the guilty persons, I would say this: In a few reckless minutes you have not only disgraced yourselves, but disgraced the whole of Trinidad. You have thrown away Trinidad's good name for sportsmanship and, believe me, it will take many, many years to regain it.

'Tomorrow morning the whole world will read in the newspapers of your outrageous behaviour for which we all in Trinidad shall stand condemned.

'I have been with you in Trinidad for four and a half years. Until now I have been proud to have been your Governor. Tonight I am bitterly ashamed, more bitterly ashamed than you can imagine, for I can find no excuse whatever for your disgraceful acts.'

The Premier, Dr. Eric Williams, who followed him, said: 'Ladies and gentlemen,

'After discussion with two of my colleagues—Dr. Solomon and Mr. Constantine—I have just sent off the following telegram:

"President M.C.C., Lord's, London, England.

"On behalf of the Government and people of Trinidad and Tobago, I send my deepest regrets and apologies for incidents which caused disruption of the second Test Match today here in Port-of-Spain.

"I am happy to inform you that there has not been the slightest hostility directed against the M.C.C. as a team or any individual player. We shall do our best to ensure that the happy connections on the field of cricket and other fields of sport which have always existed between us and you will not in any way be prejudiced by this occurrence.

"Learie Constantine, my Minister of Works and Transport, asks to be personally associated with this message. He and I have already expressed our personal apologies to Mr. Peter May, Captain of the M.C.C., and Mr. R. W. V. Robins, Manager, and I am most glad to say that our regrets and apologies were most graciously received."

'Ladies and gentlemen,

'This afternoon I was a witness of one of the most disgraceful episodes I have ever seen or heard of on a cricket field. From as far back as I can remember, teams from England have come here to play. In recent years we have had visits from Australia, India and Pakistan, and I have no doubt that sooner or later New Zealand will come to us. The whole cricketing world in which we have played so great a part will be shocked, and rightly so, at what happened this afternoon.

'I have apologized to the captain and the manager of the M.C.C. team and also to the captain of the West Indies team, Mr. Alexander.

'I understand that tomorrow the decision will be taken as to the future of this match. I can only express the hope, and I have reason to believe, that the decision will be in favour of continuation. In my view, the game must go on.

'Despite incidents over the last sixty years, the interchange of cricket visits between ourselves and the English people has given us such pleasure and has helped to form such deep and important ties that I do not think that, disgraceful as this incident is, it should be allowed to cut short a Test Match and thus affect a whole series and the relations which have been so securely established.

'I must ask each and every one of you, wherever you have the opportunity, to make it clear to all your friends and to all with whom you may come in contact that this incident has done the people of Trinidad and Tobago a great amount of harm and that we shall all have to do all we can to ensure that nothing of the kind ever takes place again.'

Mr. Learie Constantine, the third to speak, said:

'I have played cricket in the five Continents and I have met sportsmen and gentlemen everywhere. I have played under circumstances and conditions which have not been always favourable.

'Never before have I seen nor did I believe it was possible to see the deplorable spectacle which blotted out the match and smeared our reputation as sportsmen as occurred at the Queen's Park Oval today.

'I have coached and played in India, Ceylon, Australia, England, Ireland and Wales. There are youngsters in those countries who have worked hard at their lessons. In their efforts, many have tried to emulate me in my attitude and approach to the game.

'There are others, too, who have come after me—Headley, Achong, the three W's, Ramadhin, Valentine and the late, lamented Collie Smith, and they have exemplified West Indian sportsmanship wherever they have played in their own inimitable way.

'All this is now threatened by this irresponsible behaviour that we witnessed at the Queen's Park Oval today.'

After describing the Singh run-out, Constantine continued:

'The umpire's decision is final. Without that there is no cricket. What I want to do tonight is to appeal to my countrymen as sportsmen to accept the decisions of the umpires, to behave well during play, in victory and defeat, so that visitors to our country will realize that it matters not that we won or lost but that we played the game.'

The following report, under the by-line of J. S. Barker, cricket writer and an Assistant Editor, appeared in next morning's *Sunday Guardian*:

'There is no way of adequately describing the disgraceful conduct of certain sections of yesterday's record crowd at Queen's Park Oval. How is it possible to convey the sense of defilement of the thousands of decent Trinidadians who watched with horror, and many through their tears, hundreds of their countrymen establishing an all-time low in sportsmanship?

'The principal targets of the mob's fury were Umpires Lee Kow and "Sandy" Lloyd. They were subjected to every descriptive obscenity the cess-pit minds of these "sportsmen" could conceive.

'In the dressing-room, Singh, shaken for once out of his customary impassivity, agreed that he was most certainly out. I put that on record, just in case any of the thugs who disagreed can read.

'The bottle-stones-and-sticks throwing, however, was only the disgusting climax. Umpire Lloyd had been booed from the moment he gave his decision against Conrad Hunte at the beginning of the day. When the players went into the pavilion at lunch, the booing and catcalling reached ominous proportions.

'There were rumours that the whole thing had been planned. I do not believe this, but it is a fact that a Mr. W. Matthews, of Belmont, sold fifty cases of sweet drinks during the day—and did not get back a single bottle until he started to collect them from the ground.

'The nastiest aspect of the whole business was that many of the bottles hurled over had been broken before being thrown. But perhaps the sporting prize of the day should go to the goon who was chased off the wicket by the police whilst trying to mark the surface with the heel of his boot.'

The *Sunday Guardian* printed further statements, by the Deputy Commissioner of Police, by Sir Errol Dos Santos, and by former West Indian Test cricketers.

Major Sonny Carr, Deputy Commissioner of Police, said:

'It is the most disgraceful exhibition I have ever seen in my life. I do not speak of the attacks on the police as such, for policemen have been attacked already.

'But apart from the disgrace attached to Trinidad, the worst aspect of the incident is the fact that many innocent people, including one of Trinidad's leading sportsmen, Babsie Daniel, have been injured.'

In the Queen's Park Pavilion, where officials, sportsmen and spectators were discussing the afternoon's riots, Sir Errol Dos Santos sat, his head bowed, in one of the ante-rooms. He told the *Sunday Guardian*:

'I bow my head with shame. I never thought that I would live to the ripe old age of seventy to see my countrymen behave so disgracefully.'

Fears were also expressed that the incident might do untold harm to West Indian cricket. Two popular Trinidad cricketers, who have played for the West Indies in England, Australia, India, Pakistan and at home, commented:

Prior Jones: 'The West Indies is now emerging on the international cricket scene, and this incident might affect all future tours. It is a setback to cricket in Trinidad and the West Indies. Worse than that is the fact that it might be impossible to find umpires willing to stand in matches again.'

Gerry Gomez, a Trinidad and West Indian captain, had this to say: 'It is the blackest day in the history of Trinidad's sporting life. It is something that should make every self-respecting Trinidadian hang his head in shame. The effect can well be that the M.C.C. may ban Trinidad from all their future tours, and, in my opinion, should they decide to do so, they would be justified.'

One way and another, it had been quite a day.

ENGLAND

First Innings

Pullar, c. Alexander, b. Watson 17
M. C. Cowdrey, b. Hall 18
Barrington, c. Alexander, b. Hall 121
*P. B. H. May, c. Kanhai, b. Watson 0
E. R. Dexter, c. and b. Singh 77
M. J. K. Smith, c. Worrell, b. Ramadhin 108
Illingworth, b. Ramadhin 10
Swetman, l.b.w., b. Watson 1
Trueman, l.b.w., b. Ramadhin 7
Allen, not out 10
Statham, b. Worrell 1
Extras (l.b.3 w.1 n.b.8) 12
Total 382

FALL OF WICKETS—1–37, 2–42, 3–57, 4–199, 5–276, 6–307, 7–308, 8–343, 9–378, 10–382.
BOWLING—Hall, 33–9–92–2; Watson, 31–5–100–3; Worrell, 11.5–3–23–1; Singh, 23–6–59–1; Ramadhin, 35–12–61–3; Sobers, 3–0–16–0; Solomon, 7–0–19–0.

WEST INDIES

First Innings

C. C. Hunte, c. Trueman, b. Statham 8
J. Solomon, run out 23
R. Kanhai, l.b.w., b. Trueman 5
G. Sobers, c. Barrington, b. Trueman 0
F. Worrell, c. Swetman, b. Trueman 9
B. Butcher, l.b.w., b. Statham 9
*F. C. M. Alexander, l.b.w., b. Trueman 28
K. T. Ramadhin, not out 13
C. Singh, run out 0
Extras (l.b.2 w1) 3
Total (for 8 wkts.) 98

W. Hall and C. Watson to go in.

FALL OF WICKETS—1–22, 2–31, 3–31, 4–45, 5–45, 6–73, 7–94, 8–98.
BOWLING (to date)—Statham, 18–8–31–2; Trueman, 19–10–32–4; Allen, 5–0–9–0; Barrington, 16–10–15–0; Illingworth, 7–3–8–0.

FOURTH DAY

After the long, long weekend, back to cricket. The day was hotter, the crowd appreciably less. Ramadhin, transformed nowadays into a neat batsman, formal as an outfitter's dummy, sent up the hundred and continued to cut with aplomb. But Trueman, with the first ball of his second over, a yorker, sent his middle stump spinning down to Swetman. Statham, in his next over, deposited Hall's off-stump like a bouquet at the feet of first slip. It had taken just twenty minutes. Trueman's figures were 21–11–35–5; Statham's 19·3–8–42–3.

So England, with a lead of 270, batted again. There were those who thought May should have done otherwise; but it was an even money gamble and I should have done the same. Pullar at once produced several lovely strokes off his legs and through the covers, and with Cowdrey making him run as if he'd taken a dose of salts England were quickly on the move. At 18, though, Cowdrey, looking for runs, dabbed at Watson, giving Alexander an easy catch. A few balls earlier he had cut at Watson and the ball, coming back at him, had shot over the off-stump. Alexander nearly took an astonishing catch a moment later. Pullar went to glance a ball on the leg-stump from Hall, imagining presumably that it would go with the arm. Instead it whipped in off the seam, Pullar got an outside edge, and Alexander, changing direction and flying at it, juggled, fell and finally dropped it.

Barrington was soon taking his familiar recumbent position under exploratory bouncers as Hall and Watson worked up a better pace.

The grass slope where all the trouble had started on Saturday gradually filled up. In front of the Press Box a woman, determined to take no chances, sported a parachutist's camouflaged helmet.

Alexander, concerned mainly with keeping the batsmen as quiet as possible, set defensive fields, only slip, gully and one backward short leg for the fast bowlers as against rings of four on either side in the first innings. Ramadhin and Worrell took over before lunch, damming the runs to less than a trickle.

Then Barrington, with that curious leaning-away stroke to the off—rather like waving away a footman and avoiding a fly at the same time—turned his attention to Watson. He took ten off his first over and, getting to Worrell's end, drove him past mid-off. Next he cut Watson very late for his fourth boundary in five minutes.

Ramadhin came back and again the stream dried up completely. The covers were set deep but Pullar, with somnambulist regularity, drove hard to them. The sun seemed very heavy. Heads were nodding like black tulips when suddenly Barrington swung cross-batted at Ramadhin and the ball bounced among them.

Pullar, seemingly unable to contrive such diversions, merely remained in occupation: until, after two and a quarter hours, he made a vaguish attempt to lift a flighted one from Ramadhin and was comfortably caught by Worrell at extra cover.

May, greeted with a warmth that must have touched his heart, received an immediate bonus of four when Sobers, with no run being even contemplated, flung hard and wide of Alexander. Barrington now got unaccountably stuck on 49. For twenty minutes he lingered, a man on the springboard pondering the nature of his dive. Then, flashing carelessly at Hall, he was safely gobbled up by Alexander. Hall, as always after a wicket, found sudden reserves of pace and a ball of tremendous speed quickly flattened Dexter's off-stump.

Alexander continued with Ramadhin after tea, Watson at length relieving the pounding Hall who had begun to pitch short again. Smith, having pulled Ramadhin from outside the off-stump high over mid-wicket, tried to force a straight one from Watson wide of mid-on. It kept lowish, he missed, and England were 122 for 5.

May, meanwhile, had been picking his way along, mostly in singles. He did not exactly look like getting out; at the same time his timing, whenever he went to drive, was such that one became conscious of an element of risk. So it turned out. For Singh, holding up the last ball of an over, had May driving the ball acquiescently back to him. In just such a way had he taken Dexter's wicket in the first innings.

To the first ball of Singh's next over, well up to him, Swetman shuffled back, missed and was l.b.w., 133 for 7, England 403 ahead, but with an air of unmistakable apprehension abroad.

Enter Jolly Jack Trueman, with rollicking gait, to face Singh. A highly-tossed one comes up, Trueman lunges, and the ball clears long-on standing by the boundary. The next two Trueman sweeps for four and two down to the desert areas at long leg. The last ball is on a length and this time Trueman, catching it on the rise, lands it in the last tier of spectators under the Radio Trinidad broadcasting box. The lead is 421, Singh looks chastened.

Illingworth, observing this, emerged from his deep interior conflict about Ramadhin and pulled him for four.

At 169, after exactly 75 overs, Alexander gave Hall the new ball. Trueman by now couldn't have cared less whether it was a golf ball. He played Watson firmly past the short legs three times in succession, then got a whisker-thin edge to the third man boundary. Worrell replaced the flagging Hall, and Illingworth, playing the two best strokes of the day, drove him twice in succession gorgeously through the covers. Sixty runs had flowed in thirty-five minutes.

So, at the last, England, who had appeared half an hour earlier to be intent on frittering the day away, finished 466 ahead.

West Indies, with Alexander again proving himself the quickest thing in pads—at least as far as chasing was concerned—had regained much ground, only to lose it again. Both Hall and Watson had once more flung themselves into battle, and Ramadhin, over a long, burning afternoon, with no help from the wicket, made of every ball a problem after his fashion.

ENGLAND

First Innings		Second Innings	
Pullar, c. Alexander, b. Watson ...	17	c. Worrell b. Ramadhin	28
M. C. Cowdrey, b. Hall	18	c. Alexander, b. Watson	5
Barrington, c. Alexander, b. Hall	121	c. Alexander, b. Hall	49
*P. B. H. May, c. Kanhai, b. Watson	0	c. and b. Singh ...	28
E. R. Dexter, c. and b. Singh ...	77	b. Hall	0
M. J. K. Smith, c. Worrell, b. Ramadhin	108	l.b.w., b. Watson ...	12
Illingworth, b. Ramadhin ...	10	not out	28
Swetman, l.b.w., b. Watson ...	1	l.b.w., b. Singh ...	0
Trueman, l.b.w., b. Ramadhin ...	7	not out	32
Allen, not out	10		
Statham, b. Worrell	1		
Extras (l.b.3 w.1 n.b.8) ...	12	Extras	14
Total	382	Total (for 7 wkts.) ...	196

FALL OF WICKETS—*First Innings*—1–37, 2–42, 3–57, 4–199, 5–276, 6–307, 7–308, 8–343, 9–378, 10–382. *Second Innings*—1–18, 2–79, 3–97, 4–101, 5–122, 6–133, 7–133.

BOWLING—*First Innings*—Hall, 33–9–92–2; Watson, 31–5–100–3; Worrell, 11.5–3–23–1; Singh, 23–6–59–1; Ramadhin, 35–12–61–3; Sobers, 3–0–16–0; Solomon, 7–0–19–0. *Second Innings*—Hall, 18–3–34–2; Watson, 14–6–39–2; Worrell, 12–5–27–0; Ramadhin, 28–8–54–1; Singh, 8–3–28–2.

WEST INDIES

First Innings

C. C. Hunte, c. Trueman, b. Statham	...	...	...	...		8
J. Solomon, run out	...	...	...	...	...	23
R. Kanhai, l.b.w., b. Trueman	...	...	...	...	...	5
G. Sobers, c. Barrington, b. Trueman	...	...	...	...		0
F. Worrell, c. Swetman, b. Trueman	...	...	...	...		9
B. Butcher, l.b.w., b. Statham	...	...	...	...		9
*F. C. M. Alexander, l.b.w., b. Trueman		...	...	...		28
K. T. Ramadhin, b. Trueman	...	...	...	...	...	23
C. Singh, run out	...	...	...	...	...	0
W. Hall, b. Statham	...	...	...	...	...	4
C. Watson, not out	...	...	...	...	...	0
Extras (l.b.2 w.1)	...	...	...	...	...	3
Total	...	...	...	...	...	112

FALL OF WICKETS — 1–22, 2–31, 3–31, 4–45, 5–45, 6–73, 7–94, 8–98, 9–108, 10–112.

BOWLING — Trueman, 21–11–35–5; Statham, 19.3–8–42–3; Allen, 5–0–9–0; Barrington, 16–10–15–0; Illingworth, 7–3–8–0.

FIFTH DAY

England batted on for another three-quarters of an hour; no one exactly threw their bats at the ball, but thirty-five fairly orderly runs, few of them off the edge, boosted England's lead to 500.

Trueman turned Watson off his legs to the square leg boundary, then was caught at the wicket. Illingworth, who tends to expose his leg-stump when pushing the fast bowlers to the on, scored prettily in the long-leg area. Allen, dropped at slip off Hall, snicked four fine of gully, glanced Hall to the boundary, and was caught next ball at the wicket. Alexander's four catches took his total to 11 in three innings.

May now called it a day, which meant that the West Indies had ten hours' batting to save the game. It also allowed the fast bowlers, each of whom bowled to four slips, and four short legs (one of the latter at silly mid-on), fifty minutes' attack before lunch.

Strangely, and rather sinisterly, Solomon managed to avoid Statham for the whole of this period. Hunte, who did the bulk of the scoring, was lucky more than once, but he saw the lifting one quickly and generally looked neat and compact. Allen bowled two overs before the interval and succeeded in keeping the short legs from thinking about food.

His first over of the afternoon did more. Solomon flashed at him and missed; he flashed again and this time Swetman held the ball aloft and screeched, successfully.

Illingworth bowled at the other end and Kanhai, quick to force anything a centimetre or two short, played him away for boundaries around square leg. Then he swept Allen first bounce to the scoreboard. Allen spun one past Hunte's off-stump and was late cut in retribution. Fifty came and went.

Illingworth gave way to Statham. Kanhai continued on the rampage for a while, but gradually Statham and Allen shut him up. Allen, keeping a full length, had Trueman at leg slip, Cowdrey at short mid-on. Statham whistled one over Hunte's middle stump, had him flicking vainly at others. It was spirited, subtle bowling at both ends, the batsmen at full stretch.

The pitch was holding up; from England's point of view only too well. Statham, having bowled four desperately unlucky maidens in five, retired to nurse his grievances and Barrington had a spin. The middle hour of the afternoon produced ten runs. Hunte was stagnant and fallible, Kanhai cannily flawless. Barrington tossed them up and silly mid-off threw it back to him over after over. West Indies at tea were 76 for 1.

So it went on: Barrington at one end, Illingworth, now flighting it more, at the other. The ball hit the middle of the bat with predictable monotony. Then, within the space of ten minutes, Hunte gave short mid-on two brutal chances. First, he drove Barrington hard and low to Trueman's left. Trueman just got a hand to it. Then, with Allen on at Barrington's end, he drove no less hard through Cowdrey's outstretched hands.

Kanhai, long becalmed, contorted suddenly as if he'd been stung and the ball, from Allen, bounced off the corrugated-iron roof at mid-wicket. Allen, bowling round the wicket now, threw one up, widish, and Hunte, jumping out, got an inside edge which Swetman safely gathered. 107–2–47.

Kanhai, springing again with both feet off the ground, landed Allen a second time to mid-wicket. This second half of his fifty had taken three times as long as the first half.

Trueman came back after a rest of two hours and Sobers drove him with princely beauty through the covers. The new ball was six overs off, there was half an hour left of the day. Trueman bowled only one over, though, before Barrington returned in his place. Allen pitched one in the rough outside Sobers' off-stump and Sobers, visibly startled, went out to take soundings. This was something new.

Illingworth tried his luck there and made one jump ludicrously. Sobers lashed back a full toss and Illingworth, going for the catch, grazed his knuckles. He bowled one more ball then, wringing his hand, left for attention. An over later West Indies were safe for the night.

It had been a disappointing afternoon and evening. Few strokes, too few wickets. For three and a half hours Kanhai, with bat at forty-five degrees on the forward stroke against the spinners, had dropped the ball at his feet with the dutifulness of a gun-dog with a dead bird. Through him, mainly, the odds against West Indies saving the game had shortened to about evens. The new ball and the first hour of the morning would probably tell.

Allen had bowled well and threateningly: Illingworth and Barrington had been merely economical where economy had little meaning. Apart from that one rough spot outside the left-hander's off-stump the wicket had played with disarming ease. Or perhaps simply we lacked a spinner of sufficient violence.

ENGLAND

First Innings			*Second Innings*		
Pullar, c. Alexander, b. Watson ...	17	c. Worrell b. Rama- dhin	28
M. C. Cowdrey, b. Hall	18	c. Alexander, b. Wat- son	5
Barrington, c. Alexander, b. Hall	121	c. Alexander, b. Hall	49
*P. B. H. May, c. Kanhai, b. Watson	0	c. and b. Singh ...	28
E. R. Dexter, c. and b. Singh ...	77	b. Hall	0
M. J. K. Smith, c. Worrell, b. Ramadhin	108	l.b.w., b. Watson ...	12
Illingworth, b. Ramadhin ...	10	not out	41
Swetman, l.b.w., b. Watson ...	1	l.b.w., b. Singh ...	0
Trueman, l.b.w., b. Ramadhin ...	7	c. Alexander, b. Wat- son	37
Allen, not out	10	c. Alexander, b. Hall	16
Statham, b. Worrell	1		
Extras (l.b.3 w.1 n.b.8) ...	12	Extras (b.6 l.b.2 w.4 n.b.2)	14
Total	382	Total (for 9 wkts. dec.)	230

FALL OF WICKETS—*First Innings*—1–37, 2–42, 3–57, 4–199, 5–276, 6–307, 7–308, 8–343, 9–378, 10–382. *Second Innings*—1–18, 2–79, 3–97, 4–101, 5–122, 6–133, 7–133, 8–201, 9–230.

BOWLING—*First Innings*—Hall, 33–9–92–2; Watson, 31–5–100–3; Worrell, 11.5–3–23–1; Singh, 23–6–59–1; Ramadhin, 35–12–61–3; Sobers, 3–0–16–0; Solomon, 7–0–19–0. *Second Innings*—Hall, 23.4–4–50–3; Watson, 19–6–57–3; Worrell, 12–5–27–0; Ramadhin, 28–8–54–1; Singh, 8–3–28–2.

WEST INDIES

First Innings		*Second Innings*	
C. C. Hunte, c. Trueman, b. Statham	8	c. Swetman, b. Allen	47
J. Solomon, run out	23	c. Swetman, b. Allen	9
R. Kanhai, l.b.w., b. Trueman ...	5	not out	55
G. Sobers, c. Barrington, b. Trueman	0	not out	19
F. Worrell, c. Swetman, b. Trueman	9		
B. Butcher, l.b.w., b. Statham ...	9		
*F. C. M. Alexander, l.b.w., b. Trueman	28		
K. T. Ramadhin, b. Trueman ...	23		
C. Singh, run out	0		
W. Hall, b. Statham	4		
C. Watson, not out	0		
Extras (l.b.2 w.1)	3	Extras	4
Total	112	Total (for 2 wkts.) ...	134

FALL OF WICKETS—*First Innings*—1-22, 2-31, 3-31, 4-45, 5-45, 6-73, 7-94, 8-98, 9-108, 10-112. *Second Innings*—1-29, 2-107.

BOWLING—*First Innings*—Trueman, 21-11-35-5; Statham, 19.3-8-42-3; Allen, 5-0-9-0; Barrington, 16-10-15-0; Illingworth, 7-3-8-0. *Second Innings* (to date)—Statham, 12-4-23-0; Trueman, 8-3-18-0; Allen, 21-8-46-2; Illingworth, 21-11-28-0; Barrington, 18-12-15-0.

SIXTH DAY

Statham took the new ball almost at once, but as sometimes happens neither he nor Trueman worked up much pace with it. Sobers and Kanhai, far from being put on the defensive, took twenty runs off its first five overs. Sobers played Statham away off his legs and hooked a short one from Trueman with primitive savagery. He was, it seemed, already in purring mood. So Trueman went round the wicket to him and now, twice in an over, he hit him on the pads with ones that kept low. The first must have been preciously near; the second had Sobers walking. Statham and Trueman had picked up the scent. Statham flipped Worrell's pad in the next over and Worrell was out.

Butcher, arriving with a runner, jabbed his first ball down past the leg-stump: he pushed one just short of forward short leg; edged one inches over Smith's reach at backward short. Then Statham, in a marvellous series of deliveries, had him play and miss at seven in a row. The bowler looked pityingly forbearing.

May, after an hour of pace—Statham bowled seven overs —switched to Allen and Barrington. Illingworth, having shed most of a nail on one of his bowling fingers, was out of action. Allen was accurate, if not menacing. It became plain that the fast bowlers would have to do the work and, if England were to win, take the wickets.

At lunch West Indies were 184 for 4; three and three-quarter hours left.

Butcher was quite properly out to Statham, who'd changed ends, immediately afterwards. He played across the line and was almost rudely l.b.w.

Trueman, at a great pace for three overs, used a barrier of three short mid-ons—one more than Tayfield carries, and an unusual sight for a fast bowler. Two short legs were fine of the batsman's hip, and again only cover was forward of the bat on the off.

Suddenly, without warning, Kanhai struck back at Trueman. He crashed him off the back foot to the long-off boundary, drove the next ball to the sight-screen, pulled him into the crowd at square leg. A glance and a place for two each made it into sixteen off the over. Among all this was Kanhai's hundred: dogged, resourceful, finely calibrated.

Dexter bowled his first over of the match, a maiden. Illingworth at the other end beat Alexander with the first ball he'd flighted, and it must have been a hair's breadth.

Kanhai off-drove Dexter to the Coca-Cola board in his next over. The third ball of his third over was a full toss on the leg-stump and Kanhai, hitting it hard but a shade early, saw it curve right to Smith at mid-wicket. He banged his bat in understandable irritation.

This was the crucial wicket. Ramadhin was l.b.w. playing back next ball, so Dexter was suddenly, and fairly inexplicably, on a hat-trick. But he was doing a little off the seam and May could perhaps have found out about this earlier.

Singh, whose name will henceforth have local connotations comparable to the Archduke Ferdinand's at Sarajevo, was considerately treated. For over half an hour May asked him to face nothing fiercer than Dexter, Illingworth and Barrington, all of which he did with some assurance. Allen, the only spinner who might have paid off, was kept inexplicably idle.

As soon as he did come on, at a quarter past three, he took a wicket. Alexander, who had kept watchful vigil for over an hour and a half, pushed forward and the ball lobbed gently, off bat and pad, to Trueman at backward short leg. Trueman took it left-handed in a pose that would not have disgraced Nijinsky.

Singh dejectedly hit Barrington back and was gratefully caught by the bowler. Watson, last man in, played a leaping aboriginal kind of stroke to his first ball and Allen, lying deep at mid-off, took it safely.

Trueman leaped in the air, waving his floppy hat. It was smiles, handshakes all round. May waited for Statham to come in from the deep field and these two, through an avenue of sailors from the Royal Yacht *Britannia*—newly arrived with the Princess Royal—led England off.

There was, in the last resort, an hour and three-quarters in hand. That was the true measure of the victory, rather than the figure of 256 runs, crushing though the latter was.

It had been a great achievement by England's fast bowlers, a very great one, to bowl West Indies out twice on such a pitch. Singh at the very end, and Alexander, could have had no complaints about it. The wickets on this last day had been shared, Allen three, two each to Statham, Dexter and Barrington, one to Trueman, but the real threat had always come from Statham and Trueman.

Who could have envisaged this after the defeat by Barbados?

★ ★ ★

This was a match no one was going to forget in a hurry. The terrific opening barrage by Hall and Watson which brought England to 57 for 3, the perseverance of Barrington despite his clownish mishandling of the bouncer, the stirring driving of Dexter and the flowering assurance of Smith. Statham's and Trueman's beautiful use of seam and swing to sweep the cream of West Indies batting out of the way. The frittering away of time during England's second innings, Ramadhin's accuracy, Hall again, and then Trueman's lumbering onslaught with Illingworth.

Finally, the great questions of time, temperament and technique. In the end it was West Indian technique that ran out. But there remains Kanhai's courageous hundred—correct, poised methods adorned by sudden scarlet spreads of wing—that nearly held England up, the sustained attack of Statham on the last morning and afternoon, the ironic twist that brought the vital wicket to Dexter, and the rolling up of the innings by him and Barrington.

ENGLAND

First Innings			*Second Innings*	
Pullar, c. Alexander, b. Watson ...	17		c. Worrell b. Ramadhin	28
M. C. Cowdrey, b. Hall	18		c. Alexander, b. Watson	5
Barrington, c. Alexander, b. Hall	121		c. Alexander, b. Hall	49
*P. B. H. May, c. Kanhai, b. Watson	0		c. and b. Singh ...	28
E. R. Dexter, c. and b. Singh ...	77		b. Hall	0
M. J. K. Smith, c. Worrell, b. Ramadhin	108		l.b.w., b. Watson ...	12
Illingworth, b. Ramadhin ...	10		not out	41
Swetman, l.b.w., b. Watson ...	1		l.b.w., b. Singh ...	0
Trueman, l.b.w., b. Ramadhin ...	7		c. Alexander, b. Watson	37
Allen, not out	10		c. Alexander, b. Hall	16
Statham, b. Worrell	1			
Extras (l.b.3 w.1 n.b.8) ...	12		Extras (b.6 l.b.2 w.4 n.b.2)	14
Total	382		Total (for 9 wkts. dec.)	230

FALL OF WICKETS—*First Innings*—1–37, 2–42, 3–57, 4–199, 5–276, 6–307, 7–308, 8–343, 9–378, 10–382. *Second Innings*—1–18, 2–79, 3–97, 4–101, 5–122, 6–133, 7–133, 8–201, 9–230.

BOWLING—*First Innings*—Hall, 33–9–92–2; Watson, 31–5–100–3; Worrell, 11.5–3–23–1; Singh, 23–6–59–1; Ramadhin, 35–12–61–3; Sobers, 3–0–16–0; Solomon, 7–0–19–0. *Second Innings*—Hall, 23.4–4–50–3; Watson, 19–6–57–3 Worrell, 12–5–27–0; Ramadhin, 28–8–54–1; Singh, 8–3–28–2.

WEST INDIES

First Innings		Second Innings	
C. C. Hunte, c. Trueman, b. Statham	8	c. Swetman, b. Allen	47
J. Solomon, run out	23	c. Swetman, b. Allen	9
R. Kanhai, l.b.w., b. Trueman ...	5	c. Smith, b. Dexter ...	110
G. Sobers, c. Barrington, b. Trueman	0	l.b.w., b. Trueman ...	31
F. Worrell, c. Swetman, b. Trueman	9	l.b.w., b. Statham ...	0
B. Butcher, l.b.w., b. Statham ...	9	l.b.w., b. Statham ...	9
*F. C. M. Alexander, l.b.w., b. Trueman	28	c. Trueman, b. Allen	7
K. T. Ramadhin, b. Trueman ...	23	l.b.w., b. Dexter ...	0
C. Singh, run out	0	c. and b. Barrington ...	11
W. Hall, b. Statham	4	not out	0
C. Watson, not out	0	c. Allen, b. Barrington	0
Extras (l.b.2 w.1)	3	Extras (b.11 l.b.6 w.2 n.b.1)	20
Total	112	Total	244

FALL OF WICKETS—*First Innings*—1–22, 2–31, 3–31, 4–45, 5–45, 6–73, 7–94, 8–98, 9–108, 10–112. *Second Innings*—1–29, 2–107, 3–158, 4–159, 5–188, 6–222, 7–222, 8–244, 9–244, 10–244.
BOWLING—*First Innings*—Trueman, 21–11–35–5; Statham, 19.3–8–42–3; Allen, 5–0–9–0; Barrington, 16–10–15–0; Illingworth, 7–3–8–0.
Second Innings—Statham, 25–12–44–2; Trueman, 19–9–44–1; Allen, 31–13–57–3; Illingworth, 28–14–38–0; Barrington, 25.5–13–34–2; Dexter, 6–3–7–2.

6

DOWN THE ISLANDS AND MAYARO BAY

BETWEEN whiles I drove around Port-of-Spain, or out to
Maracas, and once across to the Atlantic coast, through Arima
and Sangre Grande, where the swerving surf uncurls below
the deserted coconut beaches of Cocos Bay and Mayaro. Or
else, in my air-conditioned cell at the Queen's Park Hotel,
I would try and write, to the ceaseless questionings of the
yellow-breasted, badger-crested *Qu'est ce qui dit* birds that
flashed through the flamboyants and monkey-pots beneath
my window. Raising my head from my desk I could look
down on the pretty neck of a laundress ironing hard, except
when she turned round to giggle, from what seemed dawn to
dusk, or across at the funnels of steamers just visible through
the tall coconuts.

One Sunday four of us—Freddie Trueman, Tommy
Greenhough, David Allen and I—went on a party 'down
the islands' to lunch with Botha Tench, secretary of the
Queen's Park Club, at his villa on Gasparee.

To go 'down the islands' is the favourite weekend pleasure of the Port Spaniards. Between the north-east horn of
Trinidad and Venezuela—a distance of about fifteen miles
—lies the island-strewn channel of the Boca del Drago, the
Dragon's mouth, so called by the Spanish mariners on account of the dangerous churning waters at the ebb tide. Half
a dozen fair-sized islands, Chacachacare, a leper settlement,
Monos, Huevos, and Gasparee, among them, form a group to
the north of the U.S. Naval Base at Chaguaramas Bay. Off
Coco, nearer to Port-of-Spain, cluster the tiny Five Islands.

Tench's house, half an hour by motor-boat (or ten minutes
in his own speed-boat), stands on the water's edge among

hibiscus and frangipani at the centre of a deep inlet facing out into the Gulf of Paria. The sea is a disappointing muddy green, for the silt of the Orinoco spreads out like a collar round the whole of Trinidad. But a more beautiful, or more isolated, situation it would be hard to find. Dark, wooded headlands; brilliant tropical trees; a boat bobbing off the jetty; a few chickens and pigs as companions.

Some of the chickens we ate during a memorable lunch. Otherwise we drank beer on the terrace, and swam, and slept and swam. At one point the following dialogue—I make the minimum necessary changes—took place between Green-hough and Trueman.

GREENHOUGH (contemplating entry into the sea): 'Can you stand there, Fred?'

TRUEMAN (only his head visible above the glassy surface some ten yards out): 'No, I'm walking on water, you silly clot.'

GREENHOUGH: 'And you could be too, with your bloody luck.'

At dusk we sailed back over a choppy bruised sea, the sun streaking the sky behind the Venezuelan coast and the islands blackening into hard outline before merging with the darkness.

Another Sunday I drove over with Brian Chapman to Maracas, that most vaunted of Trinidadian beaches. The road there, through the steep cedar woods and mahogany forests, rivals any part of the southern French *corniches*. The thick tangle of coffee, cocoa and nutmeg hedges the winding road in, and as you climb into the cool sweet air you can look back on the rust-pink patches of the immortelles—heralds of the dry season—shading the green hillsides of cocoa, and the sudden glitter of sea below.

Maracas—a racing expanse of sand between thickly forested headlands—is a surf beach, with fawn-coloured rollers running up to where the long pirogues of the fishermen lie under a continuous overhang of coconut. At one end the shacks of the fishermen cluster among bamboos and tropical scrub. At the other, far out of earshot, steel bands throb among the parked cars and picknicking bathers.

White skins are greatly outnumbered by black, chocolate, coffee, yellow. The Indians predominate, the young ones a marvellous *corps de ballet* in turquoise and pink costumes, their corpulent elders immersing themselves in dhoti-like shifts as if undergoing rites of purification. Negroes with bulging thighs and negligible waists race in on surf-boards or form a fielding frieze at the games of cricket along the sea's margin. The white sand glistens; the orange sellers slump in the shade of the coconuts, the sun dips, and then the lines of traffic wind back into Port-of-Spain, or seek the longer evening drive over the Saddle with the orchards of the Santa Cruz Valley, where the Spaniards built their first settlements four hundred years earlier, neat as parading soldiers stretching away to the far hills.

★   ★   ★

Trinidad—'land of the humming-bird'—is an oblong with horns at all but the south-eastern corner. Three mountain ranges—the northern, central and southern—run from west to east, more or less parallel to and equidistant from one another, but descending sharply in steepness like tiers as you move south. Cerro Aripo, the highest peak in the northern range, reaches 3,085 feet; Mount Tamana in the central range just passes the 1,000-foot mark; while the Trinity Hills, the Three Sisters, first sighted by Columbus who named them La Trinidad, swell gently up to 718 feet, some hundred feet less than the South Downs.

Driving from Port-of-Spain to Mayaro, returning by Rio Claro, Mitan and Sangre Grande, you encompass in an afternoon most of Trinidad. The bits left out are the strip of northern shore that dips down from the forests of Morne Bleu to Maracas, Blanchisseuse and Toco; and the flat south-west, below the Montserrat Hills, where rice fields alternate with the oil wells of Fyzabad and the sugar refineries of Usine Ste. Madeline.

Much of the country is both Indian-inhabited and Indian in appearance. Miniature white temples gleam among the breadfruit trees; the dome of a mosque catches the sun on the edge of a banana plantation; rows of white flags flap outside thatched huts that are raised on stilts above the swamps. In villages like Mitan and Rio Claro the open street bars give out a nasal whine of Indian music as you stop for a hot roti, a string of oranges, or a mauby, which is a kind of root beer.

The towns have a faintly mysterious air, as if they were surprised to find themselves there. Arima, a nicely-planned little town, with a more decent veneer of age and architectural unity than most, is dominated now by its vast racecourse, to which the rest of the town, originally an Indian mission, seems a mere appendage. Eastward towards the seaward edge of the same plain, Sangre Grande—home of Mr. Benwood Dick—throbs with taxis, lorries, markets, vans, to which the thrumming of steel band music from the rum-shops is a continuous background.

Beyond Sangre Grande all signs of urban life die out. The cocoa and banana plantations give way to thick forests of coconut which, for ten miles down the coast, from Manzanilla Point to Galeota, curve back from the sand into the Nariva Swamp. You drive in cloistered shade—at low tide on the beach itself, if you wish—with ripples of sun on the trunks of the palms, at intervals crossing an oily green river, on whose banks alligators lie shamming after the rains, or passing the bungalow estates of the plantation workers. The Atlantic froths and roars up the beaches of Bande L'Est, where a few pirogues drawn up on the sand or drying seines slung between palms announce the villages of St. Joseph and Plaisance.

Near Rio Claro a group of red, blue and yellow striped chairs, the far side of a bridged gully, blister among ferns and cassia. On the front of an adjacent small shack the words *Fly-Over Barber* present themselves to the eye of the passing motorist or, more practically, to the bored, wicker-hatted gaze of the cart driver urging his bullocks through the heat. Only some twenty miles divides this ancient, rumbling region of blue seas and coconut, of still rivers and bending labourers, from the gleaming, swelling suburban and ugly world of oil and bauxite. Trinidad, no doubt, will shoulder its way to the forefront of Caribbean commerce, but if the thick liana-strangled forests and bamboo tunnels of the northern range and the empty palm-embedded bays of sandy Mayaro and Cocos should ever feel the burden of this prosperity, then not all the native phenomena in the world—neither the Pitch Lake, nor the calypso—will turn the great white winter liners off their blue pleasure grounds and bring them through the Bocas into the calm waters of the Gulf of Paria.

★   ★   ★

After three weeks it began to seem as if one had been in Trinidad all one's life. The diet of oysters and fried French snapper, of chopsuey and ly-chee, had long since palled. The over-iced whiskies no longer rattled promisingly. Reading at night, I could spin out no further those elegant and wonderfully evocative accounts of earlier travellers to the West Indies—Raleigh, Trollope and Froude; Dudley, Waller and Henry Coleridge—which James Pope-Hennessy strung together in *West Indian Summer*.

Then, suddenly, the Test Match was over, the rioting and the bouncers all but forgotten, the great English victory—against all expectations, and on the easiest and most endurable of pitches—safely in the bag.

One dark morning, long before the *Qu'est ce qui dit* were on their perches or the laundress at her post, we drove off to Piarco airport. By the time we had sleepily satisfied immigration and customs, and drunk some disgusting coffee, the sun was stalking up behind the palms of Manzanilla.

An hour late, in a shining Viscount, we took off on the long, dreary flight to Jamaica. Following that northward ducks-and-drakes skid of islands—Tobago, Barbados, St. Lucia, Martinique, Guadeloupe and sundry others—we landed nearly three hours later in Antigua for refuelling. Grey clouds hung like parachutes over the wooden shack where we drank tinned grapefruit through straws. Pools of rainwater ruffled on the tarmac.

Then due west, over St. Kitts and Puerto Rico, on the three-hour lap to Jamaica. In front of me Brian Statham and Freddie Trueman, like exhausted warriors, slept the sleep of the just. At Antigua I murmured words of approval to Trueman, whom I had rarely seen bowl better without help from the elements. He nodded in acknowledgement. 'I was trying a bit, you know,' he said, 'I was trying a bit.'

At long last we swooped down low over the finger of land that once sheltered Bloody Morgan's pirate ships in the harbour of Port Royal. We bumped along Palisadoes' landing strip, wedged between sea and mountain, before emerging, moments later, into the sweltering oven of Kingston's heat.

A glass of free rum—'by courtesy of the Tourist Board'— a flashing smile and 'Welcome to Jamaica' from one of its female minions, and out through passports and customs into a battery of cameras and news-reel men. Ernest Burbridge, British Council Representative in Jamaica, was mercifully there to meet me and soon we were bowling along the inner sweep of Kingston Bay to our hotel, an American-style affair, with chalets built round a swimming pool, under the peaks of the Blue Mountains.

7

JAMAICA: NORTH SHORE AND
THE THIRD TEST

THERE was the best part of a week to spare before the colony match against Jamaica. Ian Fleming, who had been out here as a Commander in Naval Intelligence during the war, had, when we last met in London before Christmas, invited me to stay at Goldeneye, his house near the banana port of Oracabessa. For ten years now Ian, who until recently was Foreign Manager of Kemsley Newspapers, had been coming to Goldeneye in January and February, and the last six of these visits had produced an annual instalment of the adventures of James Bond, secret service agent. *Casino Royale, Live and Let Die, Diamonds are Forever, From Russia With Love, For Your Eyes Only*—these had injected into the staid British thriller pace and sophistication, the offshoots of a stern and idiosyncratic masculine taste. There are those who flinch from the torture and the carnal physical cruelty, but on each of these books something of the rare, genuine poetry of gambling, sport and espionage has rubbed off. The exotic or underworld backgrounds are flicked open like glossy travel folders and never held open too long. The details, whether of diamond smuggling or Russian counter-espionage, are assembled with knowing mastery. Sex is not emasculated. Most of all, these are gay, buccaneering books, written out of an evident and equal love for the intricacies of unarmed combat and the making of a flawless vodka martini, of the correct playing of a difficult hand of bridge and the perfect driving of a Thunderbird. You either warm to these things or you don't. Either way, it is impossible not to admire their expertise.

I accepted the invitation with alacrity. Ian had warned me that he would be involved every morning with the ticklish manœuvrings of a stolen atom-bomb-carrying aircraft and with Bond's hasty counter-manœuvrings to keep the world safe for Uncle Sam or Big Brother.

This suited me fine. And my days there resolved themselves into a delicious pattern of early morning bathe and breakfast of paw-paw and eggs, of work sessions and pre-lunch swim over the reef with Pirelli-mask and spear, of pink gins and shrimps, grilled silk-fish and strawberries, of siesta and swimming and work and dinner and early bed. While Ian slave-drove Bond on the typewriter, Ann painted fish in the great windowless room that looks out over the blue reef as over the rails of a liner.

Sometimes she and Ian would search the coral for conchs to make soup, and I would row Caspar, when he had finished his lessons, over the sea-grass, studded with black-spiked sea-eggs, or roamed by darting sea-snake, and moray eels. Then we would swim off the shelving white beach in a sea netted with sunlight beneath its milky blue.

All afternoon the fussy, emerald-breasted humming-birds, both Doctors and Vervains, would flutter, often in reverse, among the almond trees and bougainvillaea. The black-suited Kling-Klings, with their strident tones of an old-fashioned telephone bell, would stalk pompously along the cliff-edge railings, opening and shutting their long, split-quill tails. Floppy tortoiseshell and cinnamon butterflies of un-natural wing-span cruised the flower-beds.

The waves creamed over the reef below us, and at night, to the raucous croak of tree-frogs and the sparkler-dart of fire-flies, I would try and remind myself that Kingston, that steaming, hideous, shanty suburb of a capital, was five days, four days, three days, two days, one day off.

Once, after dinner, I heard the siren of the banana-boat and strolling down to the sleazy, brilliantly lit wharves, watched the piled green fruit await the long red boats that took them out to the marker buoy beyond the reef. Women lay asleep among the dried leaves. There was a smell of rum, a tinny whine of music. That old never-failing port thrill, a

compound of bustle and activity, of the nostalgias of arrival
and departure, of lights on water, of shouting and engine
noises, sent its familiar shivers down my spine. At intervals
the siren boomed through the night but by morning she was
loaded and away.

The drive back through Port Maria, Castleton and down the
Wag Water River, is like a journey through the coloured plates
of Hakewill's and Kidds' engravings done nearly a century
and a half ago. Erase a villa here, an advertisement boarding
there, and these steep gorges with their Spanish stone bridges
and overhanging foliage are stereoscopic duplicates of those
in the tattered, leather-bound books of prints in the Institute
library at Kingston. Tall coconuts, shiny splays of broad-
leaved banana and plaintain, mango trees and macaw, breadfruit, fern trees roped round with liana and convolvulus, wild
cocoa and cinnamon, these are wedged over the sharp hills in
every conceivable declension of green. Green drips, reflects
and flows, starts up and backs away.

At the roadside, cow's-foot, with its dusty hoof-shaped
leaves, thickens among the trumpet trees and ackee. The
walled road twists over ochre river beds, with women pounding out their washing on the polished stones and sugar
workers padding back from the canefields swinging their
machetes. A mongoose scuffs into the undergrowth, the sun
trains through hollows of feathery bamboo, the long pods of
woman's tongue clack in a light breeze. High up the valley,
above where the banana leaves gleam metallically, the
flowers of a cedar spatter the green with scarlet.

Sir Hans Sloane, in the painstaking colour engravings he
had made for his *Natural History of Jamaica*, records them
all in loving detail, as well as the exquisite birds of the island,
from such rarities as the Solitaire to the ubiquitously flapping John Crow vulture, its fish and solitary yellow snake, a
non-poisonous creature almost polished off by the imported
mongoose. With few snakes left to eat, the mongoose has now
turned its attentions to chickens, and constitutes as much of
a nuisance today as snakes a hundred years ago.

The road from Kingston north-west towards Montego Bay is scarcely less arresting scenically, and much more interesting historically. It is a life-and-death road, for on each of the several journeys which I made along it we came across the scenes of brutal accidents: a car hanging over a bridge, another in a river, a lorry upturned among the banana leaves, its wheels still spinning, a head-on crash at a bend. It was not really surprising, for the Jamaicans cling to the crown of these narrow corniche roads and think nothing, in their huge Cadillacs and Chevrolets, of overtaking, with violent, expostulating honkings, on blind corners.

Not far from Kingston, past Tom Cringle's ancient split, and duppy-haunted cotton tree, stand the forsaken remnants of Spanish Town—Santiago de la Vega, the Spanish capital after the mysterious abandonment of Seville Nueva, the original site on the north coast as well as for over two hundred years, under the name of St. Jago de la Vega (St. James of the Plain), the residence of the British Governors.

The growing dockside facilities of Kingston, its development through the nineteenth century as a commercial port, meant that Spanish Town's days as a capital were numbered.

You can drive through the old part of the town now and scarcely see a soul. The steep verge up which prisoners used to walk to their execution is grassed over and under the penitentiary walls desultory games of cricket stretch over the late afternoon.

But if modern history has by-passed the town, leaving cracked shanty suburbs and peeling advertisements, with negroes asleep outside the fruit-stalls and rum-shops, it has not quite obliterated the splendour of the past. Saint Catherine's cathedral, for example, the oldest church in the British Caribbean, has survived earthquake and restoration, and catches the sun now with the fortitude of an ancient, make-up-encrusted dowager, wearing bits and pieces from every known style of adornment. Aware only too well that its imperial grandeur is past, it faces the future with uncompromised confidence and undiminished zest.

Spanish Town can still boast the most beautiful square in the Caribbean, almost as perfect an architectural unit as the Place de Stanislas in Nancy. The façades of the King's House, the Governor's residence, the Court House and House of Assembly, which form the sides of the square, are in the Georgian-Colonial style, perfectly proportioned, an adroit balance of brick and wood. On the north side, flanked by two eighteenth-century houses and in the shade of a heptagonal rotunda with Corinthian pillars, Bacon's statue in Roman guise of Admiral Lord Rodney, flamboyant, pleasure-loving conqueror of the French fleet at the Battle of the Saints, stands in the centre of a balustraded Ionian colonnade. At his feet, a cannon, taken from the Count de Grasse's flagship, points at the dusty palms in the square garden. The sun flattens along the peach-warm walls and columns, and only the diving dolphins sculptured around Britannia's pedestal as she sails among the wrecked French brigantines seem to have any further taste for action.

Beyond Spanish Town the road twists north, following the thick green waters of the Rio Cobre. Tiny white egrets perch on the rafts being poled down towards Bog Walk and the clustering banana leaves and coconuts hem in the sheer hills over the river. Before the Cobre thins out, lost in the forested ravines of Mount Diabolo, it trails through the citrus orchards of Linstead and Ewarton. Strings of oranges, tangerines, pineapples, limes and grapefruit hang under thatched wayside stalls and eager piccanine vendors race after the car until the dust envelops them. The far side of the mountains, on the long descent into Ocho Rios, the hills are scarred and stained with the deep red aluminum bauxite that reaches the waiting ships in Ocho Rios bay five miles off by overhead buckets, each carrying a ton. For three miles approaching Ocho Rios you drive under a cool canopy of arching ferns and fern trees, the road barely penetrated by thin, rippling filaments of sun. Lianas strangle the encroaching tree trunks and quick-flowing streams silver brief gaps in the vivid green.

Ocho Rios, an upstart rival to Montego Bay, is a glittering

strip of luxury hotels—Jamaica Inn, Tower Isle, Shaw Park, Sans Souci—each with its umbrella-studded beach, its glass-bottomed boats and Bermuda-short bottomed clientele, its yachts and bongo-drummers. They vie with one another in the exoticism of their décor (the Arawak beyond Dunn's River Falls possesses a circular bar ceilinged over with up-turned Mexican straw hats that give the effect of a marine grotto) and the expensiveness of their drinks. A martini will cost you 7s. 6d., a large Scotch 9s., and a continent week in any of their glass-and-bamboo chalets will set you back the best part of £100 (or 300 dollars, since the dollar, with 50,000 American tourists as against 5,000 Canadian, and 5,000 from the rest of the world put together, is the quoted currency).

They are not gay places, though, despite the bongo-drummers and the anxious-to-please calypsoes, for their inhabitants, almost without exception, have long since left their fifties behind them and there is something authentically sad about these unshapely last-fling Darby-and-Joan nuptials. One even begins to long for St. Tropez existentialists, no matter how phony, for the sheer pleasure of seeing a beautiful body again.

All along this Trade-swept north shore vast development areas are being steam-rollered between coral beach and wooded hills, and the Aztec-style skeletons of super-hotels stalk the rocky headlands. Perhaps it will work out all right without too much natural despoliation, but many are those who think that the goose that lays the golden eggs has already been cooked by these absurd prices. Certainly, up to 1959, the tourist trade graph was impressively steep—rising from eight million dollars' worth in 1948 to thirty-two million dollars' worth in 1959—but the peak winter season of 1960, with its bad weather and threats of recession, showed a sharp decline.

Between Ocho Rios and Montego Bay the road follows the coast, swooping round a series of historic coral bays—St. Ann's (site of Seville Nueva), Runaway (where the Arawaks are supposed to have fled the occupying Spanish), Discovery (where Columbus, on his second voyage of discovery, landed on May 4, 1494)—to Falmouth, an elegant little town of early nineteenth-century buildings in the classical style with columns and pilasters, in both stone and wood. The shallow surf races over the reefs beneath the palms, and inland the canefields curve gently up the slopes of low hills. After Falmouth it grows bleaker, the salt marshes littered with the bleached branches of dead mangroves, and the wind scurry-in over the empty country behind Flamingo beach.

Some ten miles out from Montego Bay, halfway up a hill, stand the pink limestone ruins of Rose Hall, most lovely and most notorious of Jamaica's Great Houses. Few of these lavish eighteenth-century plantation houses, built in the heyday of sugar, before the emancipation of the slaves, have survived: mostly the stone crumbles up on the hills, the mahogany woods encroaching more thickly, the long winding drives through the tall canefields scarcely navigable. One or two of the counting houses in Trelawney remain as rivals to such Barbadian plantation houses as Canefield and Drax Hall, but if few have reached such a pitiable state of disrepair as Rose Hall they have not, after all, quite the same excuse.

For at Rose Hall, in January 1832, was enacted one of the great tragic dramas of the old plantation life of Jamaica. Rose Hall belonged at that time to Mrs. Annie Palmer, a young widow of extravagant sensuousness and imperious beauty. Of Irish ancestry, she had spent her girlhood in Haiti, coming to Jamaica as the second wife of a rich plantation owner. She herself, by the age of thirty, had seen three husbands into the grave, each one of whom had died in circumstances of extreme violence. She managed her estates of Rose Hall and Palmyra through the usual hierarchy of overseer, bookkeepers and slaves of both sexes.

In December 1831, a young Englishman called Rutherford, who had inherited an estate in one of the other islands, came out to Rose Hall to learn the business. His post was junior bookkeeper, a status little above the slaves.

Mrs. Palmer took an immediate fancy to him, for he was unusually good-looking. Within twenty-four hours they had become lovers, to the great jealousy and hatred of the overseer, who had hitherto enjoyed his employer's favours. The situation was further complicated by the fact that the coloured mistress-cum-housekeeper who had been assigned to Rutherford to look after his bodily comforts, was not only a beauty in her own right, but grand-daughter of a powerful Obeahman called Takoo. This girl, Millicent, hurt at Rutherford's seduction, wasted no time in telling him the rumours that had long been current: how Annie Palmer had employed Takoo to kill her first husband and that she had herself killed the other two; that during her childhood in Haiti she had been instructed in voodoo and now possessed supernatural powers; that she took a sadistic delight in attending the floggings of her slaves.

Rutherford at first laughed at these stories. But gradually he learned the truth of at least some of them. Then one night the overseer, hoping to break Rutherford's hold on Annie Palmer, reported the presence of Millicent in Rutherford's quarters. Annie Palmer rode down in the small hours and surprised them. She ordered Millicent away, uttering dire threats. A few days later Millicent, believing herself attacked by spirits, sickened and died. Mrs. Palmer had been seen in the area and Takoo, knowing her powers, determined she was responsible. Accordingly, he made plans for his revenge. In the middle of the night he, in company with a group of slaves, entered Rose Hall House through an underground passage. Annie Palmer was pulled from her bed and before the eyes of Rutherford, who had been roused by her screams, Takoo slowly strangled her.

That at any rate is how the story goes. Herbert deLisser has recounted it in detail in *The White Witch of Rosehall*, a book that, whatever its literary merits, gives a vivid description of the workings of a great sugar estate during the last days of slavery.

Whether or not the house is still haunted, as Jamaicans

like to believe, the fact remains that it has never been occupied since the night on which Annie Palmer was strangled.

Walking now among the mouldering rafters and gutted stone, with the sea breaking up on the reefs far below, it is possible to imagine the beauty and elegance, as well as some of the debauchery and violence, of its great days. The canefields rustle around it, ten feet tall, the arrows bend in the north wind. At the foot of the bluff from which Rose Hall, roofless and windowless, but with its handsome outer shell, its sweeping stone steps and columned portico still intact, looks out over the Caribbean towards Cuba, the chimneys of the Rose Hall Sugar Co. fly their pennons of smoke. No other buildings can be seen: the grey exposed landscape, the encircling woods that reach behind the pink house to the dark ridges behind, are exactly as they were when the slaves toiled among the canes and Annie Palmer made merry in her canopied bed.

★   ★   ★

During the three days I spent in Montego Bay, the sun never emerged—or to be quite accurate, it broke through as I was on my way to the airport to fly back to Kingston. Resorts are gloomy places in bad weather and Montego Bay, with its mooning, tanless, fifty-bucks-a-day Americans, was no exception. It is the prettiest of Caribbean urban resorts, a string of minuscule looping bays round a deep V-shaped wooded inlet. The actual town, at the apex, sprawls into slums behind the banana wharves, but thins on the north-east headland into an unbroken, flagged line of French-named shops, clubs, guest houses, hotels and luxury palaces. In full sun, with blue sea lapping up white beaches small and precious as jewels, the atmosphere must be a tolerable approximation to the ritzier portions of the Côte d'Azur. Ritzier in price anyway, for in natural resources Montego Bay come a fairly poor fourth or fifth in the Caribbean alone. Barbados has a dozen better, prettier coral beaches, Antigua, Tobago, St. Lucia all leave Montego trailing.

Yet what Montego has, particularly at Round Hill, the most exclusive and elegant establishment of the lot, is that certain air which the really rich trail around them like a scent. The Mexican straw hats with turquoise ribbons, the bleached hair, the peacock shorts and outhanging shirts, the all-year-round tan and disguising sunglasses, the international faces and vogue clichés carry unmistakable overtones.

Half a dozen of the hotels—Sunset Lodge, Bay Roc, Half Moon, Casa Montego—are elegant by any standards. The vast buffet lunches, the beach parties by firelight, the raft expeditions, the John Canoe fire-dancers, the lolling about at Doctors' Cave beach, would pass the time agreeably enough for all but the most supercilious—for a week or two anyway.

Sometimes I would drive out to the airport and sit on the veranda while the Britannias skimmed in over the swamps from Idlewild, the Avianca Super Constellations from Bogota, the Pan-American Stratocruisers from Miami and Nassau; or one would watch the Viscounts climb into the sunset, Kingston and Caracas bound, the brownskins embarking, the palefaces arriving.

Back at the hotel the dolled-up negress whores would be stationary under the bread-fruit trees.

'My name Earl, wanna sport-girl, Mister?' said a sprawling figure on the white wall beside the night-club called Phebes' Whim-Wham.

'No, I don't think so.'

'Quite right, Mister, sport-girls ain't no damn good. See, here's a sport-girl coming along now.'

The sport-girl, a slinking negress in check toreador pants, wiggled past and put her tongue out at Earl.

'See what I said, Mister?'

Crossing the road one evening to go up to Sunset Lodge for a drink, a taxi-driver ran across.

'I'm going ter show yuh the Limbo, sah, the most sensational dance youse ever did see.'

'No, you're not,' I replied wearily, 'I've seen the Limbo enough times to last me the rest of my life.'

'Ah,' he looked crestfallen, but recovered quickly, 'but yuh ain't never seen the Limbo nude, and when ah says nude, ah means nude.'

I hadn't, but somehow I never managed to get there all the same.

★　　★　　★

One of the major pleasures of my three weeks in Jamaica was the company of Henderson, the British Council driver, whom Ernest Burbridge, the Representative, generously put at my disposal. We not only made various trips around the island, but before play began each day during the Test, Henderson would drive me about the suburbs of Kingston.

On almost every subject—Jamaican history, the arts of colonization, the Maroons, pocomania, the Rastafari—Henderson was gaily erudite. 'In the dark days,' he would begin, his eyes lighting up behind his glasses as he leaned over to whisper confidentially some gloomy incident out of Kingston's blood-spilled past.

The Maroons, the 'Rasta men', the pocomaniacs—these are the three most interesting of the many self-contained groups that are unique to Jamaica. The Maroons, who occupy an area known as the Cockpit country, or the Land of Look Behind, south-east of Montego Bay, have carried on a running battle with the occupiers of the island from the Spaniards onwards. So successful have they been at it, that for over two hundred years they have enjoyed their own form of self-rule and independence within the colony.

The Maroons, generally believed to be of Koromantee descent—the word derives from Cammarones, hill-dwellers —were once the slaves of the Spaniards. When the English, under Penn and Venables, captured Jamaica, the Spaniards, as a departing act, set these slaves free, having previously armed them. They made at once for the hill redoubts near Accompong and, augmented over the years by sundry fleeing criminals, carried out lightning raids on neighbouring properties. Their own hideouts were so difficult of access that nothing short of a full-scale expedition against them had the faintest chance.

Their raids had grown so violent and so damaging that in 1734 the Government determined to put a stop to it. They set up fortifications, brought over Mosquito Indians by sloop from Nicaragua, and these, together with Blackshots and Redcoats, made forays into the mountains against their invisible enemy. They never found them; instead they themselves were ambushed in the wooded defiles and picked off like flies. On the principle that you must treat with those you cannot defeat, the Government decided on a truce. Terms were discussed, and eventually, in 1738, a treaty signed. This laid down that the Maroons were to be granted 2,500 acres, which their descendants would inherit, and within this area they were free to administer themselves. They were to be responsible for returning any future criminals that sought sanctuary, they would owe allegiance to the King in case of rebellion or invasion, and they would accept a British Representative with only advisory powers, in their three main centres—Maroon Town, Trelawney, Accompong. The election of a chief was their own affair.

It could scarcely have worked out better for all concerned. Until 1795—a period of 61 years—there was neither friction nor discontent. Then a series of unconnected events—the arrival of an unbending and unpopular British Representative, the public flogging of two Maroons who committed minor crimes in Montego Bay—led to a fresh outburst of vandalism by the Maroons. Several of their leaders were arrested and a second punitive expedition marched against them. After many initial setbacks and heavy losses, the Redcoats, largely through the importation of Cuban chasseurs and man-hunting mastiffs, succeeded in getting the Maroons to surrender.

The ringleaders and 500 men were deported first to Nova Scotia, then to Sierra Leone; the remainder were allowed to stay.

Now, a hundred and fifty years later, they still inhabit their sweet-scented peaks. A Maroon Commander-in-Chief administers justice and they enjoy their former dispensation from most Colony regulations.

Ken Jones, a young English journalist on the Tourist Board, who had worked previously in South America, told me in Montego Bay of his visit the weekend before to the Maroon country. He had been deputed to accompany a well-known *Life* magazine photo-journalist who was anxious to record the old surviving ways of the Maroons.

To their disappointment, most of the ancient Maroon traditions seemed to have gone the way of all other traditions during these last dollar-clinking years. Maroon society was, visually at any rate, indistinguishable from any other rural Jamaican society.

As a final request they asked the Chief, a Colonel Roberts, whether he would mind dressing up in his uniform—bush shirt, piped khaki trousers, policeman's helmet—for them to photograph. Alas, his only uniform was at the cleaners'.

Could he then arrange some dancing for them? After some delay, Colonel Roberts said this might be possible. They were led into a bar, the juke-box was put on and a young Maroon girl in tight jeans, emerging from the inside room, began to perform a frenzied jive with an equally frenzied partner.

No, this was not quite what they had meant. Did they no longer dance the quadrille, or any of the older traditional Spanish dances?

Colonel Roberts looked thoughtful. He would have to see what could be done. Later that evening, he announced that a number of his friends had volunteered to attempt the quadrille.

The visitors settled themselves, a record was put on, and half a dozen couples of venerable age shuffled into the room.

It was soon apparent that if most of them had ever learned the quadrille, they had long since forgotten it. In next to no time they were turning the wrong way, bumping and boring each other in the most hazardous fashion. The experiment came to a violent halt when one of the ladies, accusing another of deliberately ramming her, landed a fierce openhanded smack on her rival's countenance. Uproar ensued and the subtle, graceful steps of the quadrille were replaced by violent brawling.

I should like to see that copy of *Life*.

★   ★   ★

The Rastafari are another matter. They can be seen individually about Kingston, with matted hair and beards, a hostile depraved look in their eyes, wearing their uniforms of rags and sacking, but they belong essentially to those western, waste areas that lie between the Spanish Town road and the refuse-littered swamps of Hunts Bay.

Henderson took me on extended tours of these infernal regions, with their rusty car chassis and miles of rubbish lying under the mangrove trees along the water's edge. We turned in and out of narrow alleyways, wove round the labyrinths of Back'oo Wall, where escaping criminals immediately make for and the police have to use tear gas to get them out, inched along Darling Street and across the packed markets of Spanish Town Road, ending up, via the dumps of the Dungle (dunghill), the shanties of Boys Town and Trench Town, in the comparative safety of Mayfair cemetery.

The Rastafari, of whom some 20,000 live in this particular area—'the Rasta-men are intent on capturing fresh land elsewhere,' Henderson would lean conspiringly towards me as if this were a military secret—stem from the time of the Abyssinian war. With no logic, since they are none of them Ethiopians, they acknowledge Haile Selassie, the Lion of Judah, as the rightful Emperor of the world. The red, green and orange flag flies above their cardboard huts, many of which consist of old newspapers pasted round strips of wood, or disused cars or bits of packing cases. They are bitterly anti-white. Ninety per cent are probably simple layabouts, nine per cent criminal, one per cent romantic crackpot or renegade middle-class. There are chalked-up signs about

the place urging support of the P.N.P.—Mr. Manley's party
—but generally they are anarchist and anti-Government.

The Rastafari are not politicians, they have no manifesto,
no leaders. They are rather a kind of union of 'anti-men':
anti-life, anti-order, anti-cleanliness, anti-work, anti-civiliza-
tion, anti-almost everything, in fact, except themselves and
Haile Selassie.

Yet, with quaint illogicality, they profess a brotherly fel-
lowship towards all mankind. If, when they hiss at you their
curseword 'Fire', you answer with the code-word 'Peace and
Love', they have to reply, however reluctantly, 'Love again',
for you have called their bluff. They will not molest you—so
it is said, at any rate.

Basically, of course, these rickety, demoralized Rastafari
slums are the resorts of the poorest, therefore most criminal
element, and the affectation of an identifiable group-appear-
ance is merely collective bravado. Many of them grow ganga,
the 'wisdom weed', and from time to time, half-crazed by
marijuana and rum, they start fights or commit crimes of
violence. Thus, few of them expect to spend much uninter-
rupted time outside prison or hospital. It is a vicious circle.
The Government are doing what they can to clear these
areas, but it is bound to be a long business. In the meantime,
the Rasta-men are on the increase and scarcely a day passes
when one or other of their various activities—usually being
found in possession of ganga—is not reported in the criminal
columns of the *Daily Gleaner*.

The Pocomaniacs, a smaller, roving community of nominal Protestants, are less easily located; they hold services,
usually at the weekend, at varying halls, and unless you happen to know one of the congregation or, better still, one of
the shepherds, access to a performance demands some initial
sleuthing. In their own way, the adherents to Pocomania
are as anarchic as the Rastafari. The shepherds, most of
whom are self-appointed, act as father-confessors to their
flocks, and they take to themselves such feudal rights as the
personal defloration—for therapeutic reasons—of any virgin

who happens to take their fancy. Though they practise none of the spells nor indulge in any of the magical practices commonly found among Obeahmen, they have developed the arts of exorcism and possession to an extraordinary degree. Their services reach orgiastic heights and encompass trance-like writhings such as Holy Rollers and Shakers have never even envisaged. Perhaps, like so many of the extreme and eccentric practices of Kingston life, Pocomania too acts as a necessary safety valve.

Driving back into Kingston past the thronged Coronation Market—often called Duppy market because it stands on the site of a hangman's burial ground—we would make detours through quieter areas of little tattoo huts, of schools in leafy lanes and hospitals. Sometimes we would hear the frenzied chants and tambourines of the Holy Rollers coming through an open doorway, a fan revolving above the cavorting matrons in starched blue. Or we would be halted outside Thelma's Beauty Shoppe, where subtle tinting, dyeing and straightening processes are effected, or near the sign that announced, 'Welcome to Mr. Berry's Drinking Saloon'. The Undertakers in Trench Town is the most imposing building of all. Its owner, so Henderson informed me, used formerly to sell bread and sprats, but he suddenly cottoned on to the fact that with a mortality rate such as Kingston once enjoyed, there were better pickings elsewhere. The new premises are a monument to his industry.

Back in Kingston, with the pale blue arcades of King Street scarcely visible for the Cadillacs and Buicks, one sat and stewed in honking lines of traffic. Juke-boxes ground deafeningly out from Indian shops and Free Port shops, and at the seaward end of the street the huge hulls of freighters rose above the domes of the straw market. Near the Myrtle Bank Hotel the pavements grow splotchy with pale American tourists, and in the adjacent gardens calypsonians serenade flattered but nervous schoolmarms on vacation. Donkey-drawn water-coconut carts, each with their tail of green bough pluming up to shade the coconuts, rumble to a halt at corners.

It is an unlovely, hot, frustrating town to move about in, but as with most towns of the Caribbean, initially so gim-crack and formless, it grows on one. In the end one develops a curious kind of affection for it, perhaps because one knows one is merely a bird of passage, with the shipping office and the airline at telephone reach.

★ ★ ★

While we were in Jamaica, the following front-page article by the *Star* Special Investigator, appeared under the black headline KINGSTON WORST PORT IN WORLD.

'MUCH CONCERN IS BEING FELT in shipping circles about the molestation of sailors on Kingston waterfront. An officer of the Seamen's Club, who is in daily contact with sailors and has a lifetime of service on the sea behind him, states categorically that Kingston is the worst port in the world for this sort of thing.

'He says he gets hundreds of complaints a year about the way sailors are ill-treated on Kingston waterfront. He states that many sailors refuse to come ashore here for fear of being misused.

'By permission of the Chief Officer, the entire crew of a British ship recently in port was interviewed by our reporter and asked for their experience in the matter.

' "Kingston is about the worst port we have put in at," was the unanimous opinion loudly expressed by all the men. "No sailor dares go ashore alone in Kingston for fear of being beaten or robbed," they said.

'Touts pestered them, beggars plagued them in the most persistent manner. One older sailor remarked that Calcutta (India) has more beggars than Kingston, but they were not abusive when refused as they were in Kingston. Another, an officer, stated that sailors were not troubled in Barbados as they were here.

' "When they decline the services of a guide," they said, "they are met with a torrent of abuse and remarks such as, 'yu' doan' wan' me because me black' ". Once a group of them were stoned because they refused the services of a "guide".

'Other complaints were that the seamen were grossly over-charged ... 27s. for a bottle of Appleton; 2s. for a pint of Red Stripe Beer: 1s. 9d. for a coke, were a few of the examples they gave.

'Several said they had been threatened with knives when they declined the invitation of male touts to visit houses of ill repute. All without exception complained of the way they were importuned by male pimps and touts seeking to introduce them to women.

'The officers of the ship, when interviewed, agreed that Kingston had an evil reputation among ships' crews, though they personally had no complaints. The Chief Officer said it was easy to avoid the nuisance by taking a taxi to a decent hotel.

'All the men interviewed asked in a puzzled manner why the police did not act to abait the nuisance. "Is there a law against it?" they asked.

'Several of the men said that many ships' crews did not bother to go ashore at Kingston because of the nuisance. One studious-looking sailor asked seriously, "Are the people of Jamaica not civilized?"

'The waterpolice state that they have received no complaints whatever, and they suggest that any sailor who encounters any such thing should report to them immediately.'

Having long had an addiction to ports, and with some experience of such waterfronts as Hamburg, Copenhagen, Murmansk, Barcelona, Bizerta, Marseilles, Genoa, Naples, Port Said, Aden, Batavia, Durban and Sydney, this sent me on immediate investigation. Perhaps it was that I am no longer a sailor, and that the smell of ships and easy money is no more about me. Perhaps simply I struck two bad nights. But I found Kingston deplorably tame. Walking through the sleazy brothel alleys of Rum, Hanover and Paradise streets, people courteously made way. The Madames were warm and welcoming. I don't doubt the girls, some of whom, in yellow jerseys and tiny red pants, looked like footballers, were equally agreeable and accommodating, though they struck my casual eye as being on the prim side. I went, with knowledgeable and agreeable companions, more or less through the social scale of these places, and they seemed, in their different ways, dull though functional. People may be robbed every night in Kingston docks, for all I know, but by serious standards of comparison, it is pure wishful thinking on the part of the authorities to give it such an enticingly black name. Port Royal, the post-earthquake remains of which still cling to the wasted arm of land that holds Palisadoes airport, was once christened 'The Babylon of the West', and 'A Gilded Hades'. Henry Morgan's buccaneers would have thought little of present-day Kingston.

★   ★   ★

THE THIRD TEST MATCH

The colony match against Jamaica, played at Melbourne Park, a few hundred yards away from the Test ground of Sabina Park, was of exploratory, rather than intrinsic interest. Nevertheless, though the match was finally drawn, there were by-products of moment. Most of these concerned West Indies. McMorris, discarded at Bridgetown after having been run out off a no-ball for nought, batted solidly to score 104 out of Jamaica's 374. Scarlett, the other Bridgetown discard, after only summary evidence, made 72 not out before bowling Cowdrey with a prodigious off-break. In view of the failure of West Indies batting at Port-of-Spain, both these performances were significant. Worrell scored a relaxed 75. For M.C.C., Trueman, a fit streamlined version of his Barbados self, bowled beautifully to take 4 for 54. Greenhough was the best of the others with 3 for 58.

M.C.C., having lost Cowdrey early on, batted with the kind of abandon one should expect them to show in a match of this sort. Barrington, who scorns big scores except in the

Tests, was out for 30, but Subba Row played his best innings of the tour in making 92.

The happiest event, however, was May's return to form. He spent an hour over his first 12 runs, but after that, it was like the slow spreading of a peacock's tail. One by one all the old strokes—the force wide of mid-on, the straight drive, the slash past cover—were brought out of storage, oiled and exhibited. He reached his hundred with a towering straight six, a symbolic gesture we all hoped, and an omen of great fertility.

Dexter suffered nothing in comparison with May during an innings of 75, and on the final morning of the match, Smith, with 111, and Illingworth, 60 not out, took M.C.C. up to 525 for 6 declared, their highest score ever against Jamaica.

Jamaica, 151 behind, were thus left to hang on for four and a half hours. Trueman soon had them on edge. He knocked back Holt's middle stump with one yorker, had Lumsden l.b.w. with a second, and bowled Griffith with a third. But once again McMorris, with 74, and Scarlett, with 59, came to the rescue and the match was drawn.

The West Indies selectors had some problems on their hands. Their task was simplified by the fact that Worrell sprained an ankle over the weekend and announced himself as unfit.

Butcher was bound to go after his performance at Port-of-Spain. The question resolved itself into Charran Singh or Scarlett. Had Worrell been all right, Solomon would likely have gone too. In the circumstances it became possible to drop Solomon into Butcher's place, replace Worrell by Nurse and install McMorris at No. 2. This is what the selectors in fact did, and they sensibly preferred Scarlett, before his home crowd, to Singh. Yet Singh was unlucky, for he had acquitted himself honourably enough in his first Test match.

England had no surprise nor problems, though Cowdrey, moping unduly about his comparative failure as an opener,

offered his co-selectors the chance of standing down in favour
of Subba Row.

Nice as it was for May to have Subba Row in such good
form up his sleeve, this could only have been a gesture on
Cowdrey's part. If Subba Row were to have replaced him at
No. 2, then someone else would have had to make way for
Cowdrey lower down.

The only shock arose from the decision to send for Lee
Kow to stand, rather than take on a second Jamaican umpire
to accompany Perry Burke. When this was announced in the
Press Box, there was as much outcry among the Jamaican
correspondents as if their Beauty Queen had been publicly
insulted. But sense eventually prevailed and it was admitted
that Lee Kow, with Burke and Cortez Jordan of Barbados,
was the most suitable and satisfactory.

So to Sabina Park, a steeply enclosed cockpit of a ground
under the hazy peaks of the Blue Mountains.

FIRST DAY

May, without so much as a blush, called right again. A
few clouds were piling up over the Blue Mountains, otherwise it was a humid, fairly limp sort of day. The trees, particularly the smoky-blue lignum vitae, harboured a dozen or
more in their sturdy ship-building branches. The teams were
presented to the Governor, Sir Kenneth Blackburne, a performance now as familiar to them as to guardsmen.

Hall bowled, and you could clearly see Pullar's reflection
on the gleaming tortoise-shell wicket, which looked as if
someone had gone over it with polish. John Goddard had
said, as we were examining the pitch before play, that it
promised to be as quick as ever it had been. Gerry Gomez
contented himself with plucking the loose ends of a few tufts
flattened down just short of a length at the mountain end.

The opening overs did not live up to Goddard's surmise.
Pullar snicked Hall's second ball for four through Sobers at

third slip, then tucked him safely off his legs twice in the over. Off Watson he did the same before leaning him away past cover. Hall tried two bouncers, then two wides. Cowdrey, in a quarter of an hour, faced only two balls. The galvanized roof of one of the stands was now carrying almost as many passengers as the trees under it. A broadcast announcement tried to remedy this, but apart from a general shifting from one buttock to the other, there was no response. Cowdrey now took some quiet runs past the bowler, but a suddenly lifting one from Hall found him gloving it in a gentle arc just short of square leg.

Drinks were taken. Immediately after, Pullar played a careless stroke at a half-volley from Hall on the off-stump and the ball skewed off the edge, waist high, to Sobers at second slip. Alexander, the ball before, had waved Sobers wider into just that spot. Twelve overs only had been bowled in this first hour, sixteen bumpers among them.

At 39 Ramadhin bowled, opening with a maiden to Cowdrey, who let most of them go by with an expression of mild curiosity. Watson changed ends and soon Barrington, ducking into one that lifted little over stump high, took a nasty one below the elbow. England at lunch were 45, the hour before lunch having produced only 19. It had been a plodding business, with Ramadhin hiding it two feet outside the off-stump and Cowdrey pushing half-volleys back like a man on a diet.

Barrington swept Ramadhin to long leg, then, in Watson's next over, he tried to get his bat out of the way of a bouncer. It flicked his glove and Alexander took an easy catch.

Watson immediately hit May on the shoulder with a bouncer, following this with one that would have cleared May's head if he'd been on stilts. May, nonetheless, looked more at ease than in any earlier Test innings and at last one heard the ball hit without the feeling one had cotton-wool in both ears.

But it wasn't for long. Twice in succession Hall pitched vehemently short at May's body; the first time he fended it safely between square and forward short leg, the second it lobbed up off the handle and Hunte, flinging himself forward, cupped his hands under it. So it was 68 for 3, and England scarcely better off than at Port-of-Spain. Hall continued to aim at some mesmerizing spot little over half-way down the pitch, and with not one natural hooker in the England side, he was able to do so without fear of retaliation. But with Ramadhin bowling wide at the other end, it made a dreary spectacle.

Suddenly the tedium was relieved by a noise like a thunder clap. A strip of the galvanized roof had given way. Within seconds the roof was clear, with panicky figures swinging from the rafters like men jumping off a sinking ship. A dozen or more of the several hundred up there had landed upside down on those in the back rows of the concrete stand. Soon the more adroit, having first sought the safety of the field, re-installed themselves between the rails of the upper storey, their legs swinging over the edge. These roof-squatters were in fact pirates: they had entered from the garden of an adjoining house, mounted some privately erected scaffolding, and wormed their way through the barbed-wire netting.

The cost was one broken leg and numerous minor injuries.

At a quarter-past three, spinners bowled at both ends for the first time: Scarlett from the mountain end, Sobers at the other end. Dexter crashed Sobers' first ball off the back foot to deep extra cover, Cowdrey chopped his last for four past slip. That, at last, was 100 in round figures, which Dexter increased by driving Sobers off the front foot. Sobers' two overs cost 14 runs. Ramadhin, who had bowled 14 overs in succession, had therefore to change ends and re-load again before tea.

Rested and refreshed, Hall came back and Dexter, flashing at his second ball, was snatched up by Alexander in front of first slip's very nose. Smith arrived and before the crowd could settle, he was on his way back, well and truly yorked. The trees shook with delight, the piccaninnies cart-wheeled. England, at 113 for 5, had thrown the toss to the winds.

Illingworth survived the hat-trick and Alexander at once

produced Ramadhin for him. But Illingworth this time squashed Ramadhin down into the ground like a beetle. Cowdrey, four hours at the crease, played Ramadhin off his legs to reach fifty, following this with a lovely, flowing off-drive that found the gap. Alexander immediately filled it, giving Ramadhin an arc of five on the off-side.

Hall, rather wearily, bounced one at Cowdrey, and for the only time in the day, he was hooked. Illingworth cut Watson, on in Ramadhin's place, brutally hard to gully where Sobers, shielding his face, got his hands to it, but dropped it. He felt his head as if thankful it was still there.

Solomon had a brief spell with his hurrying little leg-spinners, but twice he dropped short, and each time Cowdrey forced him gratefully away under the blue trees at mid-wicket.

Hall, his looming figure still moving in reflection over the pitch as if it was linoleum, whipped three ferocious bouncers in a row over Cowdrey. Illingworth, who earlier had ducked into a short one from Watson that almost squatted, was rapped by Hall on his bad finger. Batting had suddenly become even more perilous than early on. At this rate, M.C.C. would be faced with demands for danger money.

But these two stuck it admirably, pushing up their partnership to 50, earning the reprieve of night. Then, with only two balls to go, Hall swung one late from Illingworth's off-stump and Alexander scooped up the merest touch. Cowdrey, with almost ostentatious self-restraint, had batted all day for 75. It was a dogged, determined knock, scarcely embellished, never in bloom. But with the new ball due first thing it was worth its weight in gold. Oddly enough, it turned out to be the only time that he had ever played through a whole day.

Hall's figures for the day were 20·4–7–35–5; an unflagging, aggressive performance, marred only by the persistent shortness of his length.

But the talk at dinner that night was not so much of England's disappointing performance, as of how wretched a spectacle such bowling makes of a complex, graceful art.

ENGLAND

First Innings

Pullar, c. Sobers, b. Hall	...	...	...	...	...	...	19
M. C. Cowdrey, not out	...	...	...	...	...	...	75
Barrington, c. Alexander, b. Watson		...	...	...	...		16
*P. B. H. May, c. Hunte, b. Hall	...	...	...	...	...		9
E. R. Dexter, c. Alexander, b. Hall		...	...	...	...		25
M. J. K. Smith, b. Hall	...	...	...	...	...	...	0
Illingworth, c. Alexander, b. Hall		...	...	...	...		17
Extras (w.3 n.b.1)	...	...	...	...	...	...	4
Total (for 6 wkts.)		...	...	...	...	...	165

Swetman, Trueman, Allen and Statham to go in.

FALL OF WICKETS — 1–28, 2–54, 3–68, 4–113, 5–113, 6–165.

BOWLING — (to date) — Hall, 20.4–7–35–5; Watson, 18–5–42–1; Ramadhin, 21–3–45–0; Scarlett, 10–4–13–0; Sobers, 2–0–14–0; Solomon, 4–1–12–0.

WEST INDIES — *F. C. M. Alexander, E. McMorris, C. C. Hunte, R. Kanhai, G. Sobers, S. Nurse, J. Solomon, R. Scarlett, K. T. Ramadhin, W. Hall, C. Watson.

SECOND DAY

Cowdrey again took a guard of middle and off. Both he and May had decided on this as a means of ensuring that they got properly across to the quick bowlers. Watson's line is particularly hard to pick, for every now and again he flashes one through with cocked elbow.

The new ball was soon taken. With it Hall first knocked down Swetman's off-stump with a no-ball, then his middle stump with a more acceptable one. He had played at ten balls without seeming to see any of them.

Watson produced three wides to Cowdrey, as if determined not to let him get near the ball. Hall, with diplomatic tact, bowled at gentle pace to Trueman, and Trueman hit him twice to the square leg boundary.

Next he guided Watson through the slips for four, and he at least looked content. Hall bounced one at Cowdrey and Cowdrey crashed him to long leg; the next ball was similar, as were the stroke and the runs; the third was almost identical, but this time Cowdrey settled for three. These were fine retaliatory strokes and Hall stalked off to fine leg with no show of pleasure. Cowdrey produced a leisurely, rippling off-drive off Watson and England were past 200.

Hall changed ends, Ramadhin bowled, and Cowdrey, turning him to square leg, reached his hundred. This innings of six hours was a unique triumph of technique and determination over disposition; it was also Cowdrey's first hundred for England in fifteen innings as opening batsman.

Trueman, perfectly at ease for almost an hour, swatted suddenly at Ramadhin and Solomon at mid-on caught him at the second attempt. Still, he had helped to add forty-five with Cowdrey.

During the first hour West Indies got through only nine overs, a new low in this respect.

Allen glanced Hall through Watson's legs at long leg, then Watson past Ramadhin at long leg. He pushed Watson through the covers, and that brought him thirteen out of fourteen runs scored. Cowdrey was becoming the sleeping partner.

In the last over before lunch Hall twice in succession hit Cowdrey in the kidneys. Burke, the square-leg umpire, gestured to Lee Kow that the ball should be pitched up, but no one was regarding. England was 299 for 8, Cowdrey 101, Allen 13. Cowdrey took Ramadhin on after lunch, turning his wrist as he flicked him twice wide of mid-on. Ramadhin flighted the next one and Cowdrey, caught between placing and driving, merely reached Scarlett at deep mid-on. This was a pity, for Allen looked to have ample runs in him.

The first ball to Statham was a long hop and Statham hit it hard, at scalp height, through Hall's ringed fingers at long-on. Allen swung Ramadhin from outside the off-stump to the lignum vitae at mid-wicket, then off-drove Watson to the same spot.

Statham drove Ramadhin into the scaffolding of the Radio Jamaica box behind the bowler, and the crowd began to shout for the return of Hall.

So Hall, shirt tails flapping, returned and at once sent Statham's off-stump whirling. His figures, 6 for 38, when he bowled Swetman this morning, ended at 7 for 69 in 31 overs. England's last three wickets added 45, 30 and 32; and the final score of 277, for all its inadequacy, was more than any-one had a right to expect overnight.

England, under a heavy overcast sky, were quickly on the attack. Statham bowled a magnificent opening over, twice beating Hunte with outswingers that Swetman failed to hold. In his third over Hunte tried to drive a half-volley on the leg-stump and the ball flew off the inside edge to Illingworth, the squarest of three backward short legs.

Truemen, two overs later, got one to lift and the ball lobbed off McMorris' buttoned-down wrist to Smith, central of the short legs. There was general appeal, but the umpire, Lee Kow, reckoned it too high. Trueman looked dis-appointed. He flipped a short one past Kanhai's ear, nearly yorked him, then was nicely on-driven.

McMorris, with virtually no back lift, got well into the line and the ball came off the bat with the discouraging plop of a discharged cockroach. After an hour, with West Indies 26, May brought on Dexter for Statham.

He bowled one over before tea, after which Statham re-turned, with Dexter taking Trueman's end. This was the beginning of a long, strokeless siege. Dexter, with mid-on, mid-wicket and short square leg, aimed at middle and leg, and neither batsman could get him away. Statham, attack-ing the off-stump, ran the ball away. Every now and then he found the edge, and as often the gaps between the slips. More often he beat the bat.

At a quarter to five, with Statham near the end of a long, cruelly fruitless spell, help came from a quarter least ex-pected. McMorris edged yet again; Cowdrey, at second slip, turned and chased it. Kanhai, facing the throw, called and raced for a third. McMorris however turned his back on him. Kanhai was virtually home at the wrong end when Cow-drey's throw arrived. Swetman threw the ball up to Statham, by which time Kanhai was smouldering on his way back to the pavilion.

May kept Statham at it, curiously long it seemed, for with Dexter bowling with pinpoint accuracy, it might have been wiser to have used Statham and Trueman in short bursts at the other end.

Statham, in his fourteenth over, bowled his first bouncer of the afternoon. Sobers hooked at it and Allen, at mid-wicket, reached up, got his hands to it, but couldn't hold it.

Trueman, who had earlier dealt McMorris several body blows, came back and Sobers flashed two full tosses to the boundary. The north-east stand that had collapsed the day before was again laden, and now the roof reverberated to the dancing of its exulting incumbents.

But that was about it for the day. McMorris, patient to the end, pushed forward at three overs from Allen; Sobers merely cruised. West Indies, 81 for 2 after nearly two and three-quarter hours' batting, were 196 behind. It was anybody's game.

ENGLAND

First Innings

Pullar, c. Sobers, b. Hall		19
M. C. Cowdrey, c. Scarlett, b. Ramadhin		114
Barrington, c. Alexander, b. Watson		16
*P. B. H. May, c. Hunte, b. Hall		9
E. R. Dexter, c. Alexander, b. Hall		25
M. J. K. Smith, b. Hall		0
Illingworth, c. Alexander, b. Hall		17
Swetman, b. Hall		0
Trueman, c. Solomon, b. Ramadhin		17
Allen, not out		30
Statham, b. Hall		13
Extras (l.b.4 w.10 n.b.3)		17
Total		277

FALL OF WICKETS—1–28, 2–54, 3–68, 4–113, 5–113, 6–165, 7–170, 8–215, 9–245, 10–277.

BOWLING—Hall, 31.2–8–69–7; Watson, 29–7–74–1; Ramadhin, 28–3–78–2; Scarlett, 10–4–13–0; Sobers, 2–0–14–0; Solomon, 4–1–12–0.

WEST INDIES

First Innings

C. C. Hunte, c. Illingworth, b. Statham	...		...	...	...	...	7
E. McMorris, not out	...	...	...	...	...	...	31
R. Kanhai, run out	...	...	...	...	...	...	18
G. Sobers, not out	...	...	...	...	...	...	17
Extras	...	...	...	...	...	...	8
Total (for 2 wkts.)		...	...	...	...	...	81

*F. C. M. Alexander, S. Nurse, J. Solomon, R. Scarlett, K. T. Ramadhin, W. Hall, C. Watson to go in.

FALL OF WICKETS — 1–12, 2–56.

BOWLING (to date) — Statham, 14–4–33–1; Trueman, 12–6–21–0; Dexter, 6–3–9–0; Allen, 3–0–10–0.

THIRD DAY

The clouds higher over the mountains, another tree-hung, roof-draped crowd. Sobers was off with a burst of fours off Trueman: a firm push to mid-wicket, a cut through May's right hand at third slip. Next he cut Statham over May, again at third slip, for a third boundary. But generally Statham preferred to attack Sobers' leg-stump, than his more profligate but vulnerable off.

Trueman worked up a formidable pace: mostly he was just short of a length and he got several to fly. McMorris took raps on thigh, rib and forearm with a phlegm that suggested either Fakir-like imperviousness or invisible mattressing. Sobers quickly revenged him with three fierce boundaries in one over: an on-drive, a force through the covers, a turn off his legs.

Allen replaced Statham and Sobers twice cut savagely through the covers. These twenty runs, scored in two overs, took him to a fifty of thrilling virtuosity. Allen must, and should, have been cursing himself for his unusual miss the evening before.

McMorris, immobile as a statue, should have been run out

Third Test, Kingston. M. C. Cowdrey, who made 114 and 97, in action against Hall. Above, he gets up on his toes to flick a half-volley to the boundary, and below, he hooks a bouncer. From this stroke on, Cowdrey was the master: whenever Hall bounced, Cowdrey hooked. Usually it meant four runs.

Garfield Sobers. In eight innings he made three hundreds and one fifty. Altogether he scored 709 runs, averaging 101·28.

Watson bowling to Illingworth. The more harmless
kind of bouncers passed yards overhead.

The roof of a stand, grossly overloaded, collapses
during play. Casualties included a broken leg.

Watson bowled by Statham for 3. The ball came to rest on the hole that the middle stump had vacated. West Indies, after being 329 for 3, were all out 353.

McMorris hit over the heart by Statham, ironically the only one of the four fast bowlers who scarcely ever threatened the batsman's physical safety. Hall and Watson bowled persistently short, Trueman used the occasional bouncer.

lay bowled by
all for 45. A
eautiful ball,
f great pace,
hat split the
iddle stump
nd sent the off
one spinning.

Iunte's fine
ffort to bring
Vest Indies vic-
ory, was ended
y Trueman,
vho hit the
tumps four times
n the last after-
noon.

FOURTH TEST, GEORGETOWN. Cowdrey st. Alexander b. Singh 27. Pullar is at the other end, Walcott, seduced from retirement, at slip.

Sobers st. Swetman b. Allen 145. Allen, who took the wickets of Worrell and Sobers in three overs after they had added 121, finished with 3 for 75.

FIFTH TEST, PORT OF SPAIN. Sobers, during his innings of 92. Square third man on the boundary kept his offside slashes down to singles. Parks, brought in to replace Swetman, keeps wicket in a Test for the first time.

Clyde Walcott, in almost certainly his last Test, made 53 and 22.

FIFTH TEST. J. M. Parks, who made 43 and 101 not out, batting against Ramadhin. For the only time in the series Alexander was obliged to put two men out when Ramadhin was bowling. Parks either went right back and pulled him, as above, or made ground to him and drove.

soon after this. He pushed to square leg, hesitated as Sobers called, then ran on: had Pullar's throw to the bowler's end been hard and straight, he would surely have been out.

But while McMorris plodded on, adding a mere nine runs before lunch, Sobers played Barrington, Illingworth and again Statham with perhaps greater sobriety, but no less certainty. West Indies, by lunch, were 144 for 2, McMorris 40, Sobers 70. Dexter, whom one had expected May to use to seal up one end while Statham and Trueman fired in short bursts at the other, had not bowled at all.

With fifteen overs before the new ball, May set Barrington and Illingworth against Sobers. The curly-headed McMorris was still there, to be sure, but one had to continually remind oneself of the fact during the lullaby of his innings. The fielding was ragged, the bowling accommodating, if not inaccurate. Barrington, bowling round the wicket, aimed at the rough outside Sobers' off-stump and occasionally hit it.

The heat in this packed bowl was drugging. Fans fluttered listlessly in the stands, the flags above the pavilion hung limp, the coconut palms seemed made of tin. The hundred for the partnership was feebly applauded, McMorris' fifty—the result of four and three-quarter hours' labour—rather more vigorously. Sobers had exchanged his earlier aggression for an armchair quiet. It was an afternoon of siesta all right. At 178, after an hour of the spinners, May took the new ball, for what it was worth.

Trueman soon hit McMorris on the pads, but an insistent appeal was rejected. This was just what Trueman needed. His next four balls, two bouncers, two beautiful outswingers, to one of which McMorris got a profitable edge, were twice as quick.

Statham, bowling one of his rare short balls, hit McMorris under the heart. He was obviously hurt, but played another ball before dropping his bat and spitting—as it turned out—blood. A medical conference lasting a good ten minutes took place on the pitch: doctor, captain, colleagues, drink-waiters, each had a hand in it, and at the end McMorris, who is as tough as they come, was reluctantly led off for X-ray. West Indies were 189, McMorris 65.

Nurse, making an appropriate, if unfortunate, entry to his first Test innings, began by hitting Statham effortlessly through the covers off the back foot.

Dexter now had his first bowl of the afternoon. Sobers at once swung him to long leg to reach his second century of the series. It was the innings one had feared from him. The second 50, as a matter of curiosity, took twice as long as the first.

The evening belonged entirely to the West Indies. Nurse took three fours in a row off Statham and virtually disposed of him for the day. Sobers drove, hooked, and cut anything the veriest inch short. Barrington made one or two run away outside the off-stump, and an odd one squatted. But these, one felt, were merely to cheer up the fielders, if not those of them that were batsmen. At ten past five West Indies passed England's score. By the close they were 291 for 2, Sobers 142, Nurse 46. It looked ominous indeed, for this was batting of smoothness, power and total certainty.

ENGLAND

First Innings

Pullar, c. Sobers, b. Hall	...	...	...	...	...	19
M. C. Cowdrey, c. Scarlett, b. Ramadhin		...	...	...	114
Barrington, c. Alexander, b. Watson	...	...	...	...	16
*P. B. H. May, c. Hunte, b. Hall	...	...	...	...	...	9
E. R. Dexter, c. Alexander, b. Hall	...	...	...	...	25
M. J. K. Smith, b. Hall	...	...	...	...	...	0
Illingworth, c. Alexander, b. Hall	...	...	...	...	17
Swetman, b. Hall	...	...	...	...	...	0
Trueman, c. Solomon, b. Ramadhin	...	...	...	...	17
Allen, not out	...	...	...	...	...	30
Statham, b. Hall	...	...	...	...	...	13
Extras (l.b.4 w.10 n.b.3)	...	...	...	...	...	17
Total	...	...	...	...	...	...	277

FALL OF WICKETS—1–28, 2–54, 3–68, 4–113, 5–113, 6–165, 7–170, 8–215, 9–245, 10–277.

BOWLING—Hall, 31.2–8–69–7; Watson, 29–7–74–1; Ramadhin, 28–3–78–2; Scarlett, 10–4–13–0; Sobers, 2–0–14–0; Solomon, 4–1–12–0.

WEST INDIES

First Innings

C. C. Hunte, c. Illingworth, b. Statham	...		...	...	...	...	7
E. McMorris, retired hurt		...	...	...	...	...	65
R. Kanhai, run out	...	...	...	...	...	...	18
G. Sobers, not out	...	...	...	...	...	...	142
S. Nurse, not out	...	...	...	...	...	...	46
Extras	...	...	...	...	...	...	13
Total (for 2 wkts.)	...	...	...	...	...	...	291

*F. C. M. Alexander, J. Solomon, R. Scarlett, K. T. Ramadhin, W. Hall and C. Watson to go in.

Fall of Wickets—1–12, 2–56.

Bowling (to date)—Statham, 26–6–69–1; Trueman, 25–8–61–0; Dexter, 12–3–38–0; Allen, 17–3–50–0; Barrington, 17–6–31–0; Illingworth, 13–2–29–0.

FOURTH DAY

The vital wicket came unexpectedly early this morning. Sobers had cut Trueman square under the laden branches of the lignum vitae tree, and the firecrackers were exploding in preparation for his one hundred and fifty and for Nurse's fifty. But Trueman, having attacked Sobers from round the wicket, changed back to over: he got one to move in off the pitch, and Sobers, deceived by the difference in angle, pushed outside it and was l.b.w. Trueman had taken Sobers' wicket each of the four times so far. Yet, if 145 of Sobers' runs were, in fact, gratuitous, his cutting and delicious timing placed his innings technically high up the list of those played by such overseas left-handers as Donnelly, Morris, Harvey and Sutcliffe.

The spinners were soon on, Illingworth and Allen, both bowling to a slip and ring of five on the off-side. May could only hope to contain West Indies as much as possible; in so far as they were restricted to 28 in the first hour he could be said to have got off to a good start. The fielding, with Barrington and Illingworth making brilliant stops, was certainly better. Unfortunately, just when both Nurse and Solomon had got thoroughly bogged down, Swetman dropped Nurse off Illingworth, a sharp catch off the bottom edge.

In the half hour before lunch Nurse and Solomon were reduced to ten runs: one would have thought they were trying to save the game. Illingworth bowled nine overs for seven runs, Allen seven overs for five. It was, though they should never have been allowed to do it, a finely sustained performance. Words would pass over lunch, one surmised, between Alexander and his batsmen, and if wickets fell hastily as the result of them, then this pawky morning's batting would be responsible.

During lunch the crowd shifted over the boundaries and swarmed up the tall floodlight pylons. The branches of the lignum vitae sagged ominously, like rigging in a gale.

Allen's first ball of the afternoon was short and widish; Solomon flashed, got a top edge and Swetman took the catch. Nurse tried to drive Illingworth back over his head in the next over and sent it steepling up to deep mid-on. Smith circled under it, flung off his cap, and held the ball safely. England were suddenly right back in the match. Trueman came back and in his first over flattened Alexander's off-stump. Three wickets had gone for no runs.

McMorris now returned and Trueman, having got his wicket, gave way to Allen. With eleven overs to go before the new ball, May evidently meant to keep back the two quick bowlers.

Twenty-seven minutes went by before West Indies advanced their by now thoroughly constipated total; then Scarlett twice snicked Illingworth wide of slip. For some reason May replaced Allen, who had been doing exactly what was wanted of him, by Barrington. The first ball was a half-volley, and McMorris crashed it through the covers. May, however, soon had cause for self-congratulation, for Barrington suddenly bowled McMorris with a googly.

The stands were again bulging like distended frogs, and a fierce piece of infighting broke out in one of them. While this was going on, Scarlett lunged out at a half-volley from Illing-worth, and Statham took a nice running catch at long-off.

With the score 329, 76 overs having been bowled, Statham took the new ball. A run later, he knocked Watson's middle stump out of the ground, the ball coming to rest ex-actly between the remaining two. Ramadhin survived a couple of overs, then precisely the same thing happened to him. The last seven wickets had fallen for 24 runs.

The later batting had been psychologically confused and rickety against bowlers who can scarcely have believed their eyes. As a matter of interest, one bouncer, by Trueman, was all that was bowled by England during the day.

So England batted again in mid-afternoon, a mere 76 be-hind. This was about four hours ahead of schedule and about 200 runs to the good.

Hall began at a great pace: he used two forward short legs, three backward, two slips and a gully. Pullar on-drove him for four, then received three bouncers in six balls. Next he cut Hall to the scoreboard and received another pair of bouncers for his pains. Watson pitched violently short to Cowdrey and soon hit him. Alexander at once brought up an extra leg slip. There was no word from the umpires, who might well have paid attention to Watson's cocked elbow too. Pullar steered Hall for a third four past gully, but he was playing dangerously far from his body. Cowdrey hooked a bouncer from Hall and then drove Watson to the mid-off boundary. He then produced another hook, one of the mem-orable shots of the tour, that thudded the ball off the mid-wicket palings. England at tea were 29 for no wicket.

Hall and Watson looked oddly deflated in their second spell. Hall bowled several wides and neither of them recaptured much pace. At 36 Alexander brought on both his spinners, Scarlett from the mountain end, Ramadhin from the cathe-dral. They spun the ball enough to beat each batsman in turn, and Ramadhin got several to squat nastily. Solomon had a short spell at the end, and Sobers might have snapped up Cowdrey at leg-slip. But, in the last over of the day, Pullar put away a full toss and a long-hop to set England only eleven runs behind.

Seldom, if ever, can an afternoon's play so dramatically have transformed a Test match. At lunch, West Indies, 329 for 3, were racing towards victory. Eighty minutes later, on a pitch that developed no sudden malice, they were all out for 353 and tumbling towards possible defeat. It was a justifiably disappointed and despondent crowd—at 20,000, easily the largest to cram into sweltering Sabina Park—that streamed away into the melting, flamingo sunset. How could it have happened? And, indeed, one asked oneself over the first magical scotch and soda of the evening, how did it? It was simply that, having lost Sobers early on, the West Indians allowed themselves to get dammed up completely by the spinners bowling to a defensive field. They got rattled going for the runs after lunch, and suddenly, before they knew where they were, the bowlers were through and on top of them.

It has happened before and would—sooner than we knew —happen again.

ENGLAND

First Innings		*Second Innings*		
M. C. Cowdrey, c. Scarlett, b. Ramadhin	114	not out		17
Pullar, c. Sobers, b. Hall	19	not out		40
Barrington, c. Alexander, b. Watson	16			
*P. B. H. May, c. Hunte, b. Hall	9			
E. R. Dexter, c. Alexander, b. Hall	25			
M. J. K. Smith, b. Hall ...	0			
Illingworth, c. Alexander, b. Hall	17			
Swetman, b. Hall	0			
Trueman, c. Solomon, b. Ramadhin	17			
Allen, not out	30			
Statham, b. Hall	13			
Extras (l.b.4 w.10 n.b.3) ...	17	Extras (l.b.4 w.3 n.b.1)		8
Total	277	Total (for 0 wkt.) ...		65

FALL OF WICKETS—*First Innings*—1–28, 2–54, 3–68, 4–113; 5–113, 6–165, 7–170, 8–215, 9–245, 10–277.

BOWLING—*First Innings*—Hall, 31.2–8–69–7; Watson, 29–7–74–1; Ramadhin, 28–3–78–2; Scarlett, 10–4–13–0; Sobers, 2–0–14–0; Solomon, 4–1–12–0. *Second Innings* (to date)—Hall, 7–2–19–0; Watson, 7–5–8–0; Ramadhin, 5–3–7–0; Scarlett, 7–3–10–0; Solomon, 3–0–13–0.

WEST INDIES

First Innings

C. C. Hunte, c. Illingworth, b. Statham	7
E. McMorris, b. Barrington	73
R. Kanhai, run out	18
G. Sobers, l.b.w., b. Trueman	147
S. Nurse, c. Smith, b. Illingworth	70
J. Solomon, c. Swetman, b. Allen	8
R. Scarlett, c. Statham, b. Illingworth	6
*F. C. M. Alexander, b. Trueman	0
K. T. Ramadhin, b. Statham	5
C. Watson, b. Statham	3
W. Hall, not out	0
Extras (b.6 l.b.7 w.1 n.b.2)	16
Total	353

FALL OF WICKETS—1–12, 2–56, 3–299, 4–329, 5–329, 6–329, 7–341, 8–347, 9–350, 10–353.

BOWLING—Statham, 32.1–8–76–3; Trueman, 33–10–82–2; Dexter, 12–3–38–0; Allen, 28–10–57–1; Barrington, 21–7–38–1; Illingworth, 30–13–46–2.

FIFTH DAY

Hall quickly beat Cowdrey with a good one that left him. There followed one of those purple patches of great batsmanship that send a fast bowler shaking his head vainly down to long-leg. Hall bowled a yorker on the leg-stump and Cowdrey, with an instinctual turn of the wrists, sent it skimming into the fence at square-leg. Next came a lethal-looking bouncer and Cowdrey hooked it to the identical place. Hall followed this with a high full toss which Cowdrey swung just out of long-leg's reach. He drove the next for four through the covers and then took a run off one that dropped a few yards from his glove. Pullar took a single off Watson's first ball and Cowdrey flicked the next off his toes first bounce into the stand at square-leg.

So, within half an hour, Ramadhin and Sobers were on, and Cowdrey, who had begun with 17 to Pullar's 40, had overhauled him. He swatted a half-volley from Ramadhin, all right-handed, back so hard that Ramadhin tactfully withdrew his hand. A four through the covers off Sobers took Cowdrey past 50, the partnership past 100. Kanhai, in the same over of Ramadhin's, failed to hold a sharp, low chance at mid-wicket from Cowdrey.

Drinks were taken by patently rattled West Indian fielders, then Cowdrey lay back to Sobers and bisected the central gap between the five off-side fielders. He tried now to ginger Pullar along into some sharp but safe singles which Pullar rejected with the stern air of a verger who was being urged to put his hand in the vestry box.

Pullar, however, ran a nippy one for his own fifty. There was time now to recollect that this was England's first century opening partnership on tour since Richardson and Bailey scored a hundred before lunch at Durban early in 1957. More extensive research revealed that in thirty-five Test matches this was only the sixth century opening partnership, and that Cowdrey, in his mere eight Tests as an opener, had shared in three of them.

Scarlett replaced Ramadhin, and Cowdrey, with effortless and complete certainty of timing, stroked him through the deep-set, defensive field for three fours in an over. Hall returned, and Cowdrey leaned him away past mid-off to the paling. He hit the next ball majestically to the mid-on boundary for his twelfth four of the morning. He took a third four past mid-on in the same over, which took him, in the last two overs before lunch, from 68 to 93. It was batting of an opulence that one is lucky to see once in a series. At lunch England, having added 99 in the 90 minutes before lunch, were 164: Pullar 61, Cowdrey 93.

Pullar, rendered totally broody against Ramadhin and Scarlett for half an hour afterwards, at length mistimed Ramadhin's low-slung, quicker one, and was l.b.w. Two balls later Cowdrey went to square-cut Scarlett; it lifted, and Alexander did the rest. Cowdrey was three runs off joining Compton as the only other English batsman to score two centuries in a Test since the war. Compton did this at Adelaide in the 1946/1947 series, and four other Englishmen—Sutcliffe, Russell, Hammond, Paynter—have done it altogether.

These two wickets, both falling at 177, were the sad result of the total misappropriation of time since lunch. Alexander now brought up two forward short legs for Ramadhin and England, in the persons of Barrington and May, were suddenly struggling ludicrously. Ramadhin pitched one on Barrington's leg-stump and it turned a couple of feet. Scarlett, in the next over, got one to shoot along the ground to May. In the hour since lunch England scored 23 for two wickets. It should have been for three because Barrington, as if beset by a gnat, swished at Ramadhin, the ball soaring straight to Kanhai at long-on. Kanhai took it in front of his face with both hands, but the ball bounced out and over his head. Alexander brought Solomon on and Barrington, pushing forward to the googly, was l.b.w. in his second over. It was like watching money pouring out of a hole in a wealthy man's pocket.

Dexter and May had time to take a four at each end and then, at 202 for 3, Alexander brought on Hall to take the new ball. Dexter cut Watson late for two successive fours, but in the same over he was literally torpedoed by the second of two that whipped in low, to take the leg-stump. At 211 for 4, England were 135 on.

The cracks in the pitch that had been evident before play started, began to make themselves felt with some viciousness. Hall and Watson were skidding one an over all along the ground. May kept out a squatter, then turned Watson off his legs to the square-leg boundary.

Alexander had a word with the incoming bowler before each over, and this slowed down the tempo at a crucial stage.

Hall bounced one over May's head; the next ball was a high full toss which May pushed back just wide of the bowler for four. Another bouncer shot past May's head, then he jabbed a shooter for two. Both May and Smith sported the cottonwool-padded vests designed by Harold Dalton; it looked as if they would come in handy. What they needed on this crabby pitch were ankle-guards as well. A bouncer from Watson flipped May's collar two balls before tea. England, having scored 64 for the loss of four wickets during the two afternoon hours, were 288 for 4 — 152 runs ahead.

Alexander, after only 8 overs with the new ball, began the day's final session with Scarlett from the cathedral end, Hall from the mountain.

Scarlett bowled only one over, for Watson to change ends; then Smith, having glanced Watson for four, seemed to get his bat caught in his pad and was l.b.w. to a lowish break-back. Illingworth flicked Watson off his legs for four and looked purposeful enough for Alexander to summon up Ramadhin. It was the obvious move and Ramadhin, without a smile, bowled Illingworth round his legs. Three short legs were there to greet Swetman, who could almost have touched Hall's floppy cap with his bat. Instead, he swished Ramadhin to square leg, in one stroke making his highest Test score since Bridgetown. May produced a lovely off-drive to Scarlett and then Hall was back on again. His fourth ball, of ferocious pace, hit and split May's middle stump. May had batted pleasantly, if not decisively, for two and a half hours.

Swetman was l.b.w. in Watson's next over and England were 269 for 8. Trueman edged Watson through the slips and England at long last were 200 on. Allen, who, one felt, should have come in two places earlier, hit a full toss from Hall back to the sight-screen. Watson beat Trueman four times in a row and Trueman, having taken buffoonish sights from all angles, affected to face up to him left-handed. It might have done as well, for he was l.b.w. to a full pitch in the next over, the last but one of the day.

Nine wickets had fallen since lunch for 116 runs. The wicket had contributed rather more to this than to the West Indian collapse the day before. But the truth was that England batted quite as badly during this period. Dexter alone was out to a ball that no one could have stopped. At the same time, if West Indies had bowled straighter than they did, they would have had England out long before the end.

The general pattern, however, was much the same as on the Saturday; a confining, accurate spell by the spinners— Ramadhin bowled twenty overs for 34, Scarlett ten overs for 12 at one point—a couple of consequent wickets, and then the bowlers on top for the rest of the day.

ENGLAND

	First Innings		*Second Innings*	
M. C. Cowdrey, c. Scarlett, b. Ramadhin	114	c. Alexander, b. Scarlett	97
Pullar, c. Sobers, b. Hall ...	19	l.b.w., b. Ramadhin ...	66
Barrington, c. Alexander, b. Watson	16	l.b.w., b. Solomon ...	4
*P. B. H. May, c. Hunte, b. Hall	9	c. Alexander, b. Hall	45
E. R. Dexter, c. Alexander, b. Hall	25	b. Watson	16
M. J. K. Smith, b. Hall ...	0	l.b.w., b. Watson ...	10
Illingworth, c. Alexander, b. Hall	17	b. Ramadhin ...	6
Swetman, b. Hall	0	l.b.w., b. Watson ...	5
Trueman, c. Solomon, b. Ramadhin	17	l.b.w., b. Watson ...	4
Allen, not out	30	not out	7
Statham, b. Hall	13	not out	0
Extras (l.b.4 w.10 n.b.3) ...	17	Extras	20
Total	277	Total (for 9 wkts.) ...	280

FALL OF WICKETS—*First Innings*—1–28, 2–54, 3–68, 4–113, 5–113, 6–165, 7–170, 8–215, 9–245, 10–277. *Second Innings*—1–177, 2–177, 3–190, 4–211, 5–239, 6–258, 7–269, 8–269, 9–280.

BOWLING—*First Innings*—Hall, 31.2–8–69–7; Watson, 29–7–74–1; Ramadhin, 28–3–78–2; Scarlett, 10–4–13–0; Sobers, 2–0–14–0; Solomon, 4–1–12–0.

WEST INDIES

First Innings

C. C. Hunte, c. Illingworth, b. Statham ...	...	...	...	...	7
E. McMorris, b. Barrington	...	...	...	...	73
R. Kanhai, run out	...	...	...	...	18
G. Sobers, l.b.w., b. Trueman	...	...	...	...	147
S. Nurse, c. Smith, b. Illingworth ...	...	...	...	...	70
J. Solomon, c. Swetman, b. Allen	...	...	...	...	8
R. Scarlett, c. Statham, b. Illingworth ...	...	...	...	...	6
*F. C. M. Alexander, b. Trueman	...	...	...	...	0
K. T. Ramadhin, b. Statham	...	...	...	...	5
C. Watson, b. Statham ...	...	...	...	...	3
W. Hall, not out	...	...	...	...	0
Extras (b.6 l.b.7 w.1 n.b.2) ...	...	...	...	...	16
Total	...	...	...	...	353

Fall of Wickets—1–12, 2–56, 3–299, 4–329, 5–329, 6–329, 7–341, 8–347, 9–350, 10–353.

Bowling—Statham, 32.1–8–76–3; Trueman, 33–10–82–2; Dexter, 12–3–38–0; Allen, 28–10–57–1; Barrington, 21–7–38–1; Illingworth, 30–13–46–2.

SIXTH DAY

The debates having gone on most of the evening were going strong first thing. There were those who roundly declared West Indies would be lucky to raise 150: others who felt West Indies had a better than even chance if they got rid of the last England pair straight away.

Trueman put his finger down the cracks on the pitch before play began and was pleased to be photographed doing so. They were certainly an astonishing sight, though the Assistant Secretary reported that one of the umpires had said he had never known a wicket which would play so well on the sixth day. We were, wrongly as it proved, sceptical about that.

Be that as it may, both Allen and Statham had to stab down on at least one shooter an over early on. But they got their heads down and they positioned themselves behind the line of the ball in a way that was a model to more than one of their predecessors.

In the fourth over Allen glanced Hall a foot short of Nurse at backward short leg. Nurse threw the ball up as if he'd made the catch and it looked as though the fielders were about to depart. This was inexcusable cricket on Nurse's part, and took away much of the pleasure from his first innings. Hall, however, had fallen over after his delivery, and Lee Kow sensibly took no notice of Nurse.

All in all, Statham and Allen saw out the fast bowlers for forty minutes. Drinks were taken and the unexpected prospect of a declaration began to open up. But Ramadhin came on and Statham was l.b.w. to a creeper in his first over. He and Allen had taken England from 280 to 305, and they had played admirably.

West Indies therefore needed 230 to win in just over four hours. It was a tall order under any circumstances.

Statham, who had been suffering all weekend with bad blisters, bowled two balls, then had to finish his over from a two-pace run. He retired for attention, but returned in time for his next over. Hunte took an immediate rap from Statham, then gloriously hooked Trueman for four. Mc-Morris, wearing a chest protector like an inflated Mae West, glanced Statham down to long leg. May was allowing his fast bowlers only one slip and a gully, one backward short leg. Each had third man and long leg on the boundary edge, cover, extra and mid-wicket.

Hunte drove Statham to the square-leg boundary and generally looked to be after the bowlers. But Trueman got the third ball of his third over to whip back, and over went McMorris' stump.

Hunte again drove Statham off his legs to the boundary, a lovely stroke made with quick turn-over of the wrist. Two balls later he repeated the shot for four more. Then he cut Statham to beat third man.

Kanhai took three to mid-wicket off Trueman's first ball, which meant that fifteen runs had come in three minutes.

Next Hunte hooked Trueman from outside the off-stump over mid-wicket's head, a combative stroke if there ever was one. By lunch West Indies, after thirty-five minutes, were 30 for 1. Statham had consistently over-pitched on the leg-stump, not a wise tactic against Hunte.

Hunte drove him to the mid-off boundary in the first over of the afternoon and the rise and fall of noise between each ball became as regular as the waves on a surf beach.

Trueman bowled and Hunte drove him skimming past a worried-looking May at mid-off. Statham went off for further repairs, so at 45 Allen went on in his place. His first ball beat Kanhai and Swetman had the bails off in a trice. It was a near thing.

Trueman produced a beauty in his next over, a replica of the one that beat McMorris, and this time Hunte's off-stump went cartwheeling.

This was not before time, for Hunte was in hot pursuit, with increasing certainty, as well as daring, of stroke.

Sobers flicked Trueman between slip, standing fine, and gully, a gap that should never have been left at this stage. He crashed Allen marvellously through the covers, swung at Trueman and survived a confident appeal for l.b.w.

Dexter looked to be the right pace for this pitch, but May preferred Illingworth, using him at Allen's end.

He pitched one in the rough and it zipped past Sobers' nose for four byes. Kanhai, during his next two overs, cut and missed at him half a dozen times.

Trueman, having bowled with great heart for ten overs, gave way to Statham. This opened the way to customary West Indian tragedy.

Kanhai pushed a ball out to Dexter in the covers, Sobers raced down the pitch and now, suddenly, Kanhai saw him. With a look of horror he shouted him back, but Sobers was too far gone. Dexter threw in underhand to Statham and Sobers was out by a yard.

Sobers walked back in shocked silence. Kanhai rested on his bat and turned his eyes to the hills. Nurse, though, was soon forcing Statham through the covers: Statham, whether because of his foot or not, was without sting.

The hundred went up in four minutes under two hours. West Indies wanted 130 at exactly a run a minute. It depended largely on these two. Nurse, despite an initially, rather crouching stance, straightens up to an easier position as the bowler delivers and his timing was melodiously rhythmic.

Illingworth bowled ten overs, just short of a length, for 19 runs: not spectacular bowling, but it pushed the batsmen behind the clock—which suddenly and mysteriously stopped —for the first time, and it was excellently directed.

Ten minutes before tea Trueman returned and his third ball sent Nurse's off-stump spinning. He played back and again the ball moved sharply in off the seam. 115 for 4 at tea; half-way in runs, 90 minutes left to play.

Kanhai took six runs off Illingworth's first over, five off Trueman's next, and again the West Indies were on the attack. Scarlett snicked, then cut, Illingworth for fours, so that in ten minutes the score raced up by twenty-one. West Indies had their noses in front once more. Kanhai seemed to have several spasms of cramp and once, playing at Trueman, the bat flew out of his hand and landed near Swetman.

Statham replaced Illingworth, and Scarlett, playing across one right up to him, was plainly l.b.w. second ball. 140 for 5; 90 needed in 75 minutes. The balance was shifting every over. Kanhai reached his fifty, a dogged performance taking him two and a half hours.

In the last hour of the match West Indies wanted 85 to win. Kanhai suddenly went down with cramp but, after a minute or two of massage, he carried on in great discomfort. He could scarcely run at all now. Alexander called for a runner, which May appeared to refuse. Alexander went over to the square-leg umpire, Burke, who conferred with Lee Kow. Hunte, who came out to run, was waved away.

The game went on to a storm of booing and catcalls. Trueman quieted it temporarily by removing two of Kanhai's stumps with a yorker.

May, with four wickets to get in half an hour, switched to his spinners: Barrington and Allen. Both tended to pitch outside the off-stump and precious minutes were wasted.

Statham was brought back and Barrington at slip, unsighted by Swetman, dropped a low catch from Alexander. Allen bowled to three short-legs but Alexander and Solomon dropped safely down on anything they needed to play.

The booing dwindled away; instead, each defensive stroke was greeted with a great roar. Ten minutes before the end, the crowd began to stream slowly away. A soft, golden light spilled across the ground. Cowdrey bowled the final, genial over, and as the umpires took off the bails, firecrackers exploded all round the boundary. West Indies were 55 runs, England four wickets, short.

Scarcely a ball had shot or turned all day. That was another oddity, just as was May's reluctance to use Dexter. Trueman had bowled magnificently, but Statham was far below his best. In the circumstances, he was probably brave to have bowled at all.

Each side had looked, at certain moments, to have been on the verge of winning. For West Indies the removal of Hunte, the running-out of Sobers, the loss of Scarlett, and, finally, Kanhai's cramp, had been successive blows to four surges towards victory.

Bailey, Tyson at half pace, Alec Bedser, would probably have bowled England safely home. Without a medium-pace bowler able to cut the ball, and with Statham so reduced in venom, there were not quite the guns there.

★   ★   ★

There was, not surprisingly, both dismay and ill-feeling about May's refusal of a runner to Kanhai. The Laws of Cricket (Law 2) state quite clearly that he was in no position to do so. He made not only a misjudgement, but a mistake, for which, half an hour after the match, he rightly apologized to both Kanhai and Alexander.

The umpires were at fault also. Lee Kow correctly maintained that Kanhai, with only courtesy reference to May, was entitled to a runner, as a matter of course; Perry Burke disagreed.

It was an unfortunate business, which left a nasty taste in the mouths of some; but with the match petering out as it did, no great harm was done. On May's behalf it must be said that he had justifiable reason to be irked when McMorris, having not fielded throughout the previous innings at all, came out to bat with Hunte. May perhaps thought that with quinine or salt tablets, Kanhai's cramp would pass. It had been a nerve-racking, harassing day, with the match in danger of being lost one minute, and with victory in his grasp the next, so that a detached view of what was, and what was not, legitimate cannot have been as easy as all that.

Yet nothing can take away from this match its extraordinary quality. No one watching it could remember any Test to have ebbed and surged so repeatedly or so extremely.

It contained, too, remarkable performances: Cowdrey's two innings, during the second of which he experienced that almost dream-like certainty about where the ball would pitch that every great player knows a few times in his career. Later, he described to me how he would almost instinctively position himself for a certain stroke before the ball was bowled and, sure enough, the right ball for it came along. In the course of this innings he learned something about hooking too: that, judiciously played, the hook or swing was a defensive weapon as well as an offensive one, and that, if you were in the right frame of mind for it, that is to say in anticipatory mood, it was not necessarily as impossible or as unbusinesslike as some had thought.

No other batsman played particularly well for England. Dexter twice showed true class for short periods, May's second innings was more like it, Allen, with 30 not out and 17 not out, must even have impressed on his captain that he was wasted at No 10. But both Barrington and Smith had poor matches, and Pullar's running lost many runs. That England emerged with a creditable draw was due almost entirely to the batting of the last pair, Statham and Allen, who added 32 in the first innings, 25 in the second, and gave West Indies rather over an hour and a half less batting.

The two fast bowlers again did all that could have been expected of them. Statham's unfitness on the last day perhaps cost England the match, but Trueman, knocking out the off-stump four times on the last day, was a fine sight to the end.

Allen bowled rather indifferently in the second innings, but Illingworth, having settled on an offside attack, bowled most tidily to his field in each innings.

For West Indies, Hall's 7 for 69 was a devastating piece of bowling over the first two days, but both he and Watson were wildly inaccurate with the new ball. Sobers came properly into his own in West Indies' first innings and Nurse showed that he has come to stay. McMorris proved that he was the right choice to partner the smiling Hunte, whose own second innings of 40 was a joyous achievement.

The two run-outs in which Kanhai figured—making five in all so far—allowed England to get back into control when the tide was running firmly for West Indies. These, from West Indies' point of view, were the saddest and most costly things of all.

ENGLAND

	First Innings		*Second Innings*	
M. C. Cowdrey, c. Scarlett, b. Ramadhin	... ...	114	c. Alexander, b. Scarlett	97
Pullar, c. Sobers, b. Hall	...	19	l.b.w., b. Ramadhin ...	66
Barrington, c. Alexander, b. Watson	... ...	16	l.b.w., b. Solomon ...	4
*P. B. H. May, c. Hunte, b. Hall		9	c. Alexander, b. Hall	45
E. R. Dexter, c. Alexander, b. Hall		25	b. Watson	16
M. J. K. Smith, b. Hall	...	0	l.b.w., b. Watson ...	10
Illingworth, c. Alexander, b. Hall		17	b. Ramadhin ...	6
Swetman, b. Hall	... ...	0	l.b.w., b. Watson ...	5
Trueman, c. Solomon, b. Ramadhin	... ...	17	l.b.w., b. Watson ...	4
Allen, not out	... ...	30	not out	17
Statham, b. Hall	... ...	13	not out	12
Extras (l.b.4 w.10 n.b.3)	...	17	Extras	23
Total	... ...	277	Total (for 9 wkts.) ...	305

FALL OF WICKETS—*First Innings*—1–28, 2–54, 3–68, 4–113; 5–113, 6–165, 7–170, 8–215, 9–245, 10–277. *Second Innings*—1–177, 2–177, 3–190, 4–211, 5–239, 6–258, 7–269, 8–268, 9–280, 10–305.

BOWLING—*First Innings*—Hall, 31.2–8–69–7; Watson, 29–7–74–1; Ramadhin, 28–3–78–2; Scarlett, 10–4–13–0; Sobers, 2–0–14–0; Solomon, 4–1–12–0. *Second Innings*—Hall, 26–5–93–1; Watson, 27–8–62–4; Ramadhin, 28.3–14–38–2; Scarlett, 28–12–51–1; Solomon, 6–1–20–1; Sobers, 8–2–18–0.

WEST INDIES

	First Innings		*Second Innings*	
C. C. Hunte, c. Illingworth, b. Statham	... ...	7	b. Trueman	40
E. McMorris, b. Barrington	...	73	b. Trueman	1
R. Kanhai, run out	... ...	18	b. Trueman	57
G. Sobers, l.b.w., b. Trueman	...	147	run out	19
S. Nurse, c. Smith, b. Illingworth		70	b. Trueman	11
J. Solomon, c. Swetman, b. Allen		8	not out	10
R. Scarlett, c. Statham, b. Illingworth	... ...	6	l.b.w., b. Statham ...	12
*F. C. M. Alexander, b. Trueman		0	not out	7
K. T. Ramadhin, b. Statham	...	5		
C. Watson, b. Statham	... ...	3		
W. Hall, not out ...	... ...	0		
Extras (b.6 l.b.7 w.1 n.b.2)	...	16	Extras	18
Total	... ...	353	Total (for 6 wkts.) ...	175

FALL OF WICKETS—*First Innings*—1–12, 2–56, 3–299, 4–329, 5–329, 6–329, 7–341, 8–347, 9–350, 10–353. *Second Innings*—1–11, 2–48, 3–86, 4–111, 5–140, 6–152.

BOWLING—*First Innings*—Statham, 32.1–8–76–3; Trueman, 33–10–82–2; Dexter, 12–3–38–0; Allen, 28–10–57–1; Barrington, 21–7–38–1; Illingworth, 30–13–46–2. *Second Innings*—Statham, 18–6–45–1; Trueman, 18–4–54–4; Allen, 9–4–19–0; Illingworth, 13–4–35–0; Barrington, 4–4–0–0; Cowdrey, 1–0–4–0.

★   ★   ★

The Press Box at Sabina Park must rank high among the most uncomfortable on Test match grounds. With perhaps eight present it might be bearable; we mustered around twenty. The chairs were hard and each time anyone of the seven in each row wished to remove himself for any purpose, the remaining six needed to tilt or cower and hold their breath. For the more bulky among us it would have been little more difficult to go through the eye of a needle. Similarly, the passing of a cable from inscriber to messenger required a relay operation that the most experienced chain-gang worker would have found taxing. Very often one would have to pass a cable for someone in mid-sentence, only to find, on return to composition, that the idea had flown. Doubtless, some very complex and weighty images foundered.

It was also a box so hot and airless that a pressure-cooker could scarcely have been less inviting. Lunch had to be fetched from the pavilion a long way off, and the ordering of this presented problems of its own. For instance, after several failures in giving verbal orders to the waitress, we composed a daily list. The first time we were two cokes short and two cakes to the good; the thirst-maddened coke-less ones could neither be persuaded to eat nor pay for the cakes. 'I thought it was a hay not a hoe,' said the understandably disgruntled waitress. By the time the match was ending we had a fine service of ham sandwiches, hot rotis and beers in operation. I don't know if the cakes were ever eaten.

There was danger in the box too. Glasses crashed to the ground, beer bottles got crunched underfoot, and once Brian Chapman, bumping his head for the fifth time on the overhanging wooden shutter just above it, sent a thermos cascading onto my forehead and cutting it open. Many American Purple Hearts were less valiantly won.

There were compensations, however. We were directly behind and above the bowler's arm, and so near that Trueman could wink or scowl at us on his walk back. Wesley Hall almost disappeared from sight under us as he turned at the end of his run. Ahead were the hazy slopes of the Blue Mountains, with the military hill-station of Newcastle glittering 2,000 feet up under its customary cottonwool cloud packing.

There were few incident-free days within the box, though I am happy to say that the British and West Indian camps warred within rather than against each other. On one occasion, the *Barbadian Advocate*, incensed at Kanhai's running out by a Jamaican, wrathfully flung down a pocketful of dollars in front of the *Daily Gleaner*'s sports editor and called upon the neutral British to support his own allocation of responsibility for the misfortune. 'Only a Jamaican could have done a thing like that,' he fumed.

It was a sartorially colourful box; from the dapper Mr.

O. Seymour Coppin of the *Barbados Advocate*, zoot-suited and tie-pinned, to Mr. L. D. (Strebor) Roberts of the *Gleaner*, whose cynical, amused and cigarette-holdered profile was offset by shirts of daily more dazzling hues. There were blue shirts, canary shirts, even a long, unidentified youth in crimson shirt with gold-braided collar. There were cigars, cheroots, cigarette-holders, and, I don't doubt, marijuana going. The aromas of rum and scotch vied with those of beer and curried goat. Sometimes the girls' school in the garden behind burst into piping song, preparing, it seemed, for next year's carols.

At times it was like an overcrowded raft, with tempers frayed, sailing through equatorial waters out of all touch with the outside world. Barry Osborne, in charge of cables, would come in and announce unavoidable delays (which were usually quickly cleared), but which—with Jamaica five hours behind London time—created anxieties and problems. Agreement could not be reached between us then on whether the ordinary or urgent rate should be used by all, and this caused the most heated controversy of all.

No, there was never a dull moment, but I sometimes think we were lucky to get out of it in one piece.

When the time came to leave I became increasingly conscious of the things I hadn't done in Jamaica. Though I spent a lovely Sunday on the white sands of University Beach, beyond Morant Bay, I never reached Port Antonio, described by Ella Wheeler Wilcox as 'the most beautiful harbour in the world'. I failed to get to the south-west tip, Negril Beach and Savannah La Mar, where Ian Fleming had told me the most marvellous birds were to be seen. I did not even get to the much-vaunted Botanical Gardens or into the Blue Mountains. They must wait another day.

But such of the evening as was left after getting de-pressurized from the Press Box at Sabina Park I passed agreeably with Jamaican friends. Dining at Blue Mountain Inn, with the floodlit waterfall pouring through steep woods, dancing in the open-air Colosseum atmosphere of the Havana Club, with its fabulous band, or in the smoochy darkness of Club Michel, where one recognized people by contour, rather than feature. Edna Manley, the talented sculptress wife of Jamaica's distinguished Premier, Norman Manley, gave a party for me to meet Jamaican writers, as did Ernest Burbridge, most helpful of British Council Representatives, and his wife, and that Johnsonian, extravagantly-bearded figure, John Figueroa, poet, professor, educationist. These were warm, friendly gatherings which I shall remember.

Unfortunately, our hotel, for all its chromium glitter, its peacock-blue swimming-pool, and gardens, was twenty minutes out of Kingston. One was suspended there nocturnally in a kind of limbo of absurdly-priced drinks and indifferent service. Once, maddened beyond endurance at having sat for half an hour at the dinner table without attention, we sent ragingly for the Manager. But, alas, it was Mr. R. W. V. Robins who innocently arrived.

The day of our departure for Antigua, Henderson drove me to Palisadoes. As we were saying goodbye, he slipped into my hands a paper-bound copy of the *Folk Songs of Jamaica*. These, on that long, wearying flight, gave me endless pleasure. Basically British in tune, African in rhythm, the best of them are the digging songs like *Missa Ramgoat*, about a randy overseer, *Judy Drownded*, and *De Ribber Ben Come Dung*:

> Me tek piece-a deal bud
> Me tek piece-a deal bud
> Me tek piece-a deal bud
> Me chuck it pon de water
> Whai yah, whai yah, whai yah,
> An' a how you come ovah?

There are fine chorus songs like *Linstead Market* about the woman who carried her ackees to market early, but failed to sell a 'quattie wat'.

> Ef ah married to a Nayga man,
> An' ah lef him for a Chiney man,

> Nobody's business but me own.
> Ef me even old old like Taggoram
> An' me wan' fe pose as twenty-one,
> Nobody's business but me own.

Some of the other songs, like *House an' Lan'*, are Maroon in origin; others, like *Docta Bud* and *Monkey Draw Bow*, describe animals or birds. There are love lyrics such as *Dallas Gawn* and masochistic school songs like *Teacher Lick de Gal*:

> One shif me got,
> Ratta cut i', same place i' cut,
> Mama patch i', same place i' patch,
> Fy-ah bun i', Teacher lick de gal,
> I' tun right o-vah.

8

EAST TO ANTIGUA

THE Viscount to Antigua was an hour, or several Rum Collins, late. When at last it did arrive, it was discovered to be over-booked and had to be off-loaded. We stifled, assuaged our thirsts, and hoped for the best.

We took off from Palisadoes finally at one o'clock. Four hours later, having flown over the southern tips of Haiti and the Dominican Republic, we landed at the shining lily-pool-and-glass airport of San Juan, capital of Puerto Rico.

I passed some of the flight by reading the next instalment of C. L. R. James' dramatic serial, 'M.C.C. Without Malice', in *The Nation*. The issue of February 5 contained a sensible leader on the bottle-throwing. 'What took place on Saturday, January 30, at the Oval, was disgraceful, inexcusable.... The dominating motive in *The Nation*'s condemnation is that if the Trinidad public, any section of it, takes it upon itself to decide when a man is out, or not out, then big cricket in Trinidad is finished. ... Two things must be said at once. The first is that if you merely boo an umpire, you are interfering with the game. It is not so disgraceful as throwing bottles, but you are making that most difficult of all jobs, more difficult still. Not only must the umpires be left alone. When they step on to the field to start the next Test in Port-of-Spain, *The Nation* hopes that the whole crowd will stand and cheer them all the way to the wickets.'

A forlorn hope this proved to be. However, it was a mere sideline. The main front-page headline was ALEXANDER MUST GO. Page two carried the box insert: What to Do. (1) Make Worrell Captain, (2) Wire Gilchrist to Come at Once. Frank will control him and we shall beat England in four days. (See next week's *Nation*.)

Beneath this was another heading. THE CHOICE—Lose with Alexander or Win with Worrell.

Having agreed that the better side won the Second Test, the writer returns jocularly to the bottle-throwing. 'A bottle-thrower hurled his bottle of whisky into the air. Then it suddenly struck him that in his ballistical enthusiasm, he had forgotten that there was still some whisky in the bottle. He rushed to it, picked it up, drank off what remained with great speed, and then hurled the bottle again. For the life of me, disgusted as I am of the whole business, I cannot help laughing at that fellow and his mercurial temperament.'

Next, he discusses the fast bowling. 'All this talk about bumpers should be dismissed. Hall and Watson bowled no excessive amount of bumpers. Cowdrey was hit in the stomach, on the side, on the finger and the toe. What kind of bumpers were those? Barrington was so eager to duck that he was putting himself in danger. . . . What is happening is this: both Hall and Watson can get a ball very little short of a length to rise. This demands that the batsmen get most resolutely behind the ball, particularly if it is on the wicket. And, if a fast, short ball makes him disinclined to get right behind, so much the better. Test cricket is not for children.'

Agreed, but what Mr. James does not seem to face is that a law exists forbidding the persistent bowling of the short-pitched ball. A very sensible law, which should have been invoked more often than it was. For no one cares tuppence about bouncers: they are a bore and a waste of time. But what takes much of the beauty and nearly all the arts out of batsmanship is precisely that endlessly repeated banging of the ball down that never allows the batsman on to the front foot. He has one stroke, the fend, left to him, and that is an ungainly stroke to have to play, and to watch, throughout a sweltering day. The issue then resolves itself not into the bowler's crafts against the batsman's, but simply into the stamina of one against the physical endurance and patience of the other.

Mr. James goes on: 'Man for man, the West Indies team

is as good as or even better than the M.C.C. It is bad captaincy that is causing us to be scrambling as we are doing.
Everybody is whispering and shrugging shoulders.'

Alexander is blamed for bowling Hall and Watson into
the ground, for lack of strategy, for poor field placing, for the
indifferent batting of his side.

Mr. James winds up: 'I hereby give notice I shall not let
this question rest until it is corrected. Even if Alexander is
appointed captain for Australia, that will not stop me. When
we were last in Australia, Goddard had to stand down for
the last Test. If he is selected, I shall do my damndest to see
that Alexander is stood down as captain for the first Test. . . .
This fooling with West Indies' captaincy has gone on too
long. Hour after hour, in 1957, I had to sit and suffer the
consequence of Goddard as captain. The cricket world be-
lieves that in 1951–52, in Australia, we lost through bad
captaincy. It has to stop, and the time to stop is now.'

A man of uncompromising views, this editor of *The
Nation*, and I could not help wondering, as the pale, green
shapes of St. Croix, St. Kitts and Nevis swung like camouflaged aircraft-carriers at their moorings, whether there were
many who thought like this, and how much Frank Worrell
valued such advocacy.

★　　★　　★

The furnishings of our first few days in Antigua were half-
a-dozen coconut palms, a white beach, and a peacock-blue
sea breaking up on a coral reef. The sun poured down; a constant Trade wind took the edge off the heat and riffled the
palms and sea-grape. Occasionally, sandpipers skimmed the
dark patches of seaweed or a pelican plummeted down
greedily on an unsuspecting fish.

The royal yacht, *Britannia,* with the Princess Royal on
board, lay in St. John's Bay, and the flags flew in the villages
and streets of the island. Bunting was arched at the entrance
to each settlement, with 'Welcome to Your Royal Highness'
flapping in huge letters above it.

M.C.C. played a three-day match on the pretty little ground here, flying the flag in their own way under Cowdrey's genial captaincy. The Leeward Islands pleased their supporters by scoring 286 and 190 for 3. M.C.C. rattled up 440 for 5, declared, Cowdrey, Subba Row and Dexter scoring hundreds. Dexter six times cleared the ring of mahogany trees planted to celebrate Queen Victoria's Jubilee and his hundred was scored before lunch in only 88 minutes. It was good country-house cricket, which Peter May, cruising with his wife in the *Flandre* to Port-of-Spain, missed out on.

Antigua is often compared to Barbados in its physical and social characteristics. It struck me as being not only appreciably smaller, but altogether more relaxed. The Trades blow day in, day out, cooling temperaments as well as bodies. The men are tall (though not as tall as those of Barbuda, its dependency, which was regarded as the ideal breeding ground for slaves, who often reached six feet seven and eight), slow-moving, and good-humoured. Race relations are generally regarded as ideal. Much of the island, like Barbados, is given over to sugar cane: the rest is pasture-land, or sea island cotton. The north-east, badly scarred by United States missile bases, scarcely seems tropical at all: low, treeless hills, scrub, occasional wood villages, with tin-roofed church and scattering chickens, a cluster of huts.

But from St. John's, the neatly laid-out port, with blue-and-white painted wood houses, on the north-west, down through English Harbour in the south to Long Bay, half-way up the east coast, the island swings along a series of stunning bays, with coconut palms curving round seas of a brilliant green-blue, and empty white beaches, as on Fry's Bay, backing onto dappled coconut estates. Inland, beyond Columbus' Old Road, Fig Tree Hill Drive winds through packed, rain-forested ravines of mango, banana, breadfruit, and fig. Donkeys nibble on the edge of lagoons beyond which the high mauve smudges of Montserrat, thirty miles away, sheer out of the horizon.

Nearer English Harbour, the road, with its arrow-root

verges, curves gently along the shallow, ibis-scored waters of Falmouth Bay, before looping more steeply under the headland overlooking Nelson's Dockyard.

This latter is shaped like a turtle, inside whose flippers, almost land-locked, calm mirroring waters gather blue of sky, green of cliff. There can be few safer natural harbours in the world, few lovelier anchorages. The headlands, save for the biscuit-coloured balustrades of Clarence House, occupied by the Duke of Clarence (later William IV) when in command of H.M.S. *Pegasus*, remain unscarred. Yachts lie tied up to the wharves where Nelson's ships were careened by the hanging of hoisted-out guns to the mast-heads. The splayed stone quays echo to hammering and planing, just as they did 200 years ago, when naval ships, engaged in running fights with the French or Spanish fleets, or with privateers, darted in for urgent attention or for re-fit. The sun dazzles off stone and brick, part ruin, part intact: the pillars of the two-storeyed boat house, its roof torn off in the hurricane of 1871, stride purposefully to the water's edge; lizards race among the ring bolts of the wet dock.

Saw Pit Shed; Joiner's Loft; Copper and Lumber Store; the long rectangle of the Naval Officers' Quarters; the surviving wall of the Capstan House; the Galley; the Cordage, Sail, Canvas and Clothing Store; the Pay Office; in differing states of disrepair and restoration, neat ruins returning to model life, they litter these empty quays and jetties, unmistakably British, unmistakably eighteenth-century, unmistakably naval. The Admiral's House, with newly-painted jalousies and double-tiered wood surround, gleams like a pavilion. Should the bust of Admiral Lord Nelson, shadowed by a solitary coconut palm, turn suddenly into the living, twenty-six-year-old figure of Captain Horatio Nelson, captain of the 28-gun frigate *Boreas*, and Senior Captain of the Base, how much would he find unfamiliar?

The answer is, very little; ten years ago, Nelson's Dockyard, hurricane-hit, termite-attacked, indifference-smitten, was derelict. Now, through the activities of the Society of the Friends of English Harbour, founded in 1951, the original buildings, a good dozen of them, are being put back into use with painstaking thoroughness and attention to detail. Various funds in England, as well as private donations, helped to swell the revenue of the Society, and by 1956 the £40,000 needed to reconstruct the whole site had already been exceeded.

That is half the task; but annual maintenance will need almost £1,500, if the same cycle of decay is not to start again. An alert Committee, however, has sensibly decided that English Harbour should be something more than a museum piece, a mere monument to British Naval power during the eighteenth and early nineteenth centuries. Plans are being made now for the development of English Harbour as a re-fitting station for every kind of ocean-going yacht. A small hotel for yachtsmen and a restaurant are being designed to occupy the old Copper and Lumber Store.

Nelson, were his ghost to walk the wharves in a dozen years from now, might discover that he could find his way about blindfolded. It would be a handsome testament to the devotion of those who, like the former Governor of the Leeward Islands, Sir Kenneth Blackburn (now Governor of Jamaica), and Commander V. E. B. Nicholson, R.N., envisaged the scheme and have given such loving time and attention to it.

Sir Kenneth Blackburne, in his pamphlet *The Romance of English Harbour*, outlines the story of the harbour itself and goes on to describe Nelson's own part in it. It is the story of the hundred years of naval conflict between Britain and France that was to culminate, in a chase that briefly took in these shores, at Trafalgar.

By the 1720's English Harbour was established as a Naval Base, capable of completely re-fitting men of war. The original site, St. Helena, was on the opposite shore, but the growing need for increased facilities demanded an altogether more elaborate project. Accordingly, a new plan was made, and the present site developed

The slowness of the work, the lack of funds (the Government of Antigua, though quick to criticize the Navy for the mounting losses of merchant ships at the hands of French privateers, found itself unable to contribute), the hurricane of 1772, meant that English Harbour only really came into its own during the last twenty years of the eighteenth century. This was the crucial period in the Caribbean when Rodney and Hood sparred among the Leewards with de Grasse, before finally defeating (and capturing) him off Dominica in the Battle of the Saints in 1782.

From this decisive victory onward Britain held complete control of the Caribbean. English Harbour, under the governorship of Sir Thomas Shirley, was extensively fortified. Clarence House was completed. And in 1784 Captain Nelson and H.R.H. Prince William arrived in their respective frigates *Boreas* and *Pegasus*.

If English Harbour was at its most useful and most handsome during Nelson's experience of it, it nevertheless provided—despite its apparently idyllic situation—a hazardous and boring life for the several thousand sailors who often found themselves there for months at a time. The tideless harbour encouraged disease and 'putrid distempers', and Sir Kenneth quotes from an address given by the President of the Leeward Branch of the British Medical Association, in which he says: 'It often happened that a well seasoned Soldier would be seized with furious delirium while standing Sentry, and be carried to his barracks at Monks Hill to expire in all the horrors of Black vomit within three or four hours of his attack.'

By 1803 over a thousand troops were engaged in the defence of the Dockyard. In the autumn of that year thirteen schooners sailed from Guadeloupe to attack the harbour, but Captain James O'Bryan in the *Emerald* intercepted them, capturing three and scattering the remainder.

In 1805 the French and Spanish fleets, with 15,000 men aboard, passed close in shore. Nelson arrived five days later in the *Victory*, anchoring with twelve line of battle ships off

St. John's. Then he was off and away to the spectacular, and for him, final, rendezvous off Cape Trafalgar.

English Harbour lingered on, gradually declining in importance as a naval base until it was abandoned by the Royal Navy in 1899.

For Nelson it held many memories. He spent the three hurricane seasons of 1784, 1785 and 1786 there. He met his future wife, Mrs. Nisbet of Nevis, while stationed there; and in his last year he was appointed to succeed Sir Richard Hughes as Commander of the Station.

A year later Prince William gave away the bride at Nelson's wedding in Nevis. Antigua may not have had quite the same romantic associations for Nelson as did later the haunting ballrooms of Naples and Palermo, during his long, tender and tortured courtship of Emma Hamilton, but he was not then the battered, heroic conqueror of the Nile, simply a young, bored and largely untried captain, probably as anxious for the experience of love as for that of war.

Driving away from English Harbour and turning for a last look at the blue still waters, one felt one was leaving not only a place, but a period. Was it imagination, or did one really at noon hear the distant pipe of 'Up! Spirits!' and smell, among the odours of pitch and sacking, of rope and mortar and shavings, the sharp whiff of rum?

★   ★   ★

The whole coastline of Antigua is a series of linked bays and white sand beaches, the best of them dominated by modern beach-house-style hotels: the Anchorage, Long Bay, Half Moon, Antigua Beach, White Sands and Trade Winds. Rum punches clink under shadowing palms, the reefs are groped by goggled divers, and predatory birds dive out of the sunset. High white clouds sail over the disused sugar mills that dominate every eminence of the interior, the light changes from minute to minute, the sea breeze rattles the shutters day-long, night-long.

For a week it is perfect; then one is ready to move on.

9

CARNIVAL IN TRINIDAD

WE landed at Piarco Airport at ten o'clock, after a three-hour flight through the darkness. The Bel Air Hotel was all muddle and confusion, with six sleeping to a room. The team were off next morning, though, for Georgetown, British Guiana, so it was only for one night. I had determined on three: two for Carnival, one for sleep. It should have been the other way round.

I asked the taxi-man on the way in to Port-of-Spain how it was going. That morning, Monday, February 29, had been Jour Ouvert, the opening of the two-day Bacchanal that is the climax of Carnival. At five o'clock in the morning the steel bands had set out roving the city, their followers, dressed mostly in 'hot' shirts and jeans, shuffling and pirouetting behind in their thousands, arms linked. A whole community on the move. For five hours they had kept going, drenched but revived by three downpours. Up-town, down-town, past Lapeyrouse, up Tragarete road, through Maraval and round by the Savannah. The bands, those 'playing mas'', converge from all parts of Port-of-Spain, weaving in and out, forty thousand people in this great annual act of mass participation.

Though the Carnival itself covers only the two days before Ash Wednesday, the celebrations had started the Friday before with various stage contests and parades: parade of Tamboo-Bamboo band and Old Time Steelband, Best Road March Steelband Contest, parade of Queens and Funnymen. Saturday is the Calypso Fiesta, when the calypsonians from the tents—from the Original Young Brigade and the New Victory, from the Senior Brigade and the Big Bamboo—compete for the title of Calypso King. The ones I had heard the month before—Mighty Sparrow, Lord Melody, Mighty Spoiler, Lord Christo—had variously distinguished themselves, Mighty Sparrow being elected Calypso King after the final on Dimanche Gras.

'What were the best calypsoes of the year?' I asked Jake, my driver. 'Why, *May-May*, man, and *Ice, Ice*—they're the top two, man, they're the top two. But you'll be interested in the *Test Match Riot*, Lord Brynner's *Test Match Riot*, man, ho, ho, you'll be interested in that one, man.'

'And how does that go?'

'Ah'm going to sing you dat, never you worry. Jes' you listen.' And along the Beetham Highway, with the lights twinkling above us on Laventille Hill and the sloops in the port washed in moonlight, he croaked out the song. I got the words (which were composed and first sung by Lord Brynner) later:

> Don't doubt me don't doubt me
> Because I was there and ah see—
> Right after tea interval
> The thing happened in Queen's Park Oval,
> From the time Charan Singh got run out,
> Ah don't know where all these bottle and stone came out.

> Chorus
> It was bottle and stone riot in Queen's Park Oval,
> The whole test match turn to a carnival,
> I had to hide me clean head inside a canal,
> To get away from the big scandal,
> Right in the middle of the Federal Capital.

> It's a shame and was so bad,
> And a disgrace to this place Trinidad,
> After we had such good sporting name,
> One little thing happened to make us shame.
> It will take about fifteen or more years,
> To get back this good name I'm sure,

So M.C.C. take this apology please,
From Trinidad, Brynner and the West Indies.

I was on me heel,
When the Premier and the Governor came out on the
     field,
They started raising their hands up,
Signalling the rioters to stop,
Oh brother but they kept on pelting,
And shouting to bring back Charan Singh,
Then I only hear thing like a bottle fly,
It near lick out the Premier glasses clean from he eye,
What a disgrace to know that Constantine had to be in
     place
To catch a bottle from the Governor's face.

Anyhow I'm sure,
These kind of things won't happen no more,
Because I'm sure everybody understand,
West Indian back-bone of cricket is England,
Because the Charan Singh who didn't get the run,
Might be in Lancashire League a few months to come,
And when he come back to the West Indies,
We have to say Mr. Charan Singh if you please.

Dimanche Gras develops the whole historic theme of Carnival. The winning calypsonians perform, the Limbo Cham-
pionship takes place, and the various characters from the
Old Time Carnivals are presented: Nègres Jardin, the 'bat-
toniers' of the stick-fighting bands, Gros Tete, Pai Banan,
Jolle Range, Pierrot Grenade, Police and T'ief, King Papa
Diable. This year, I learned, the Bacoulou Folk Group of
Haiti had danced the Voodoo rituals. I was sad to miss that.
    It was after eleven when we reached the Savannah. The
wooden bleachers that would hold the huge audience for the
next day's spectacle—the parade of the Bands—were dimly
discernible. The Queen's Park Hotel, as if under siege, was

wire-netted off from the road. The streets were quiet, save for the distant bubbling of a steel band, whose members, as they approached on the last stages of the day's 'jump up', seemed to be dying on their feet. The city, having been up since five a.m., was gathering its strength for the morrow.

★　　★　　★

After breakfast, Margaret Maillard drove me round the town to see the bands forming up. At street corners one would see last-minute alterations being done to the trailing cloak of some Roman Emperor or to the gorgeous costume of a Nile Princess. Groups of Bad Sailors swung along to their rendez-vous. A masked robber held up some protesting citizen, extorting the traditional ransom. We passed Assyrians and Barbarians, English bowmen and Siamese Princesses, Red Indians and African Tribal Chiefs.

The mounting noise of the pans downtown drew us into Marine Square where fabulous papier-mâché bird head-dresses—some of them twice the size of their wearers—bobbed above the crowd. Here Ancient Greeks jostled among Aborigines from New Guinea, Queen Pauha cast her eyes over Ben Hur, Genghis Khan threw lascivious glances at Aphrodite. The pans throbbed their rhythmic rearrangement of barely detectable tunes like *Among My Souvenirs* or *Liebestraum*, or *Loch Lomond* and *Little Brown Jug*. Sweat poured, the masqueraders shuffled, the crowds, jeaned to a woman, craned.

So it went on all morning. We drank our rum punches in the cool of the China Clipper, and then, fortified, set out for the Savannah.

Connoisseurs of Mardi Gras from New Orleans to Rio de Janeiro, of Italian *festas* and French *fêtes*, incline to put Port-of-Spain's Carnival as one of the best two—on a level with Rio's. The parade of the Bands, some of them five hundred strong, lasts from noon until dusk. They mime their way round the Savannah, perform before the judges on a platform, and finally jump-up round the town. As a result, each band may be six or seven hours on the go. When one considers what some of the individual members are wearing—ermine, crinolines, togas, cloaks, Elizabethan costumes—it is an astonishing feat of physical endurance alone.

All afternoon we stood in the sun and watched the slow strut of these heroes out of history and legend. The main bands enact certain themes out of ancient and modern history, sometimes covering a vast period like Siam 1250–1767, sometimes a single episode like the Cuban revolution. Usually it is the former, because of the scope provided for gorgeous contrast within a single band. So we saw Ye Saga of Merrie England, with its negro Richard Coeur de Lion, its Bryan de Boeuf Gilbert, and its battlemented float, escorted by Crusaders, English Kings and Queens, Vikings, Romans, and Sherwood foresters. Saint George, the sun flashing off his armour, bestrode a white charger, his spear impaling a dragon.

Time passed before us. The splendour of Mother Africa, Italia 900 B.C. to A.D. 14, the Eternal City with its sinuous wine-carriers and decadent Emperors, Viva Zapata, the Golden Age of China, the Assyrian Court, Dakota Indians, Realm of the Inca, Sioux Uprising, Black Ebo Snake Charmers (with real snakes), Aztec Gods, Ghost Ship Raiders, Kemalu Ju Ju, Parisian Dandies, Stray Bats, Tiger Worshippers, Satan Kingdom, on and on until the flares of sunset, then dusk, bled the colours from these marvellously imagined and lovingly copied embodiments of the Trinidadian dream. These stately processions are wish-fulfilments or re-enactments of fantasy, rather than satiric comments. As such, they are often incongruous, sometimes anachronistic. But more than anything, taken individually or *en masse*, they are breathtakingly beautiful consummations of vision.

Later on, downtown, it gets rowdier, the satire more ribald. Saga Ting dancers, Sailors Ashore, Fugitives from a Chain Gang, Cute Chicks, mix it with decreasing relevance to theme and increasing jollity. Heat, rum, tiredness, fight a battle with the pan-inspired determination to go on. For the hundredth time the steel band starts up *May-May*, or *Ice*, *Ice*, and the rhythm is re-established, the flagging feet and pistoning elbows returned to action.

There is a lull around seven o'clock. Then, at half-past eight, the thirty or so steel bands—Invaders and Desperadoes, Silver Stars and Cross Fires, Samba Boys and Mexicans —muster at their headquarters for the 'last lap'. As they move off, crowds adhere to them like ants for the final near-exhausted, shuffling jump-up on to midnight.

In the early hours, thighs aching, soaked through, I landed up at my besieged hotel, there sleepless to shuffle mentally through to dawn. Were the bubbling silver notes of *May-May, Rich Man, Poor Man, Ice, Ice*, really coming from Maraval and Laventille Hill, or was it only in my brain? It was impossible to tell, and I really no longer cared.

★   ★   ★

Carnival seems to have begun in its present form in the 1780's, though, until Emancipation, in 1833, the slaves were not permitted to take part and even the free coloureds, though allowed to mask, were subject to stringent regulations. In the second half of the nineteenth century the races increasingly blended, with the higher bourgeois tending to drop out as the proceedings took on a more African character. In 1858, Carlton Schuler records, Governor Keate forbade the wearing of masks because of the rioting, pilfering and house-burning that had developed into part of the ritual.

Each year now there are fights between the steel bands, sometimes serious, sometimes not.

This year, 1960, the papers called it a 'clean carnival'. The fire services were only called out thirty times, arrests were kept down to double figures, there were a mere handful of gun duels and knifings.

All in all, though, most people, whether they'd 'played mas'' or not, seemed relieved when it was over. George Bailey's Saga of Merrie England carried off the first $500 prize, which, considering his production was estimated to have cost $75,000, seemed inadequate recompense. Harold Saldenha's wonderful Siam 1250–1767 was narrowly and, I thought, undeservedly, beaten into second place. Sparrow's *May-May* emerged as Road March 1960.

When I left Port-of-Spain to fly down to British Guiana two days later, it was like leaving a city of the dead.

GEORGETOWN: THE FOURTH TEST

MEANWHILE, in Georgetown, a curious little drama was being enacted. Peter May, who had been due to fly down with his team from Port-of-Spain, had in fact gone on ahead. His wife, Virginia, the object of many unsympathetic attacks during the last M.C.C. tour of Australia, was not, in fact, sailing back to Europe on the *Flandre* as arranged, but spending a few days in Barbados preparatory to coming to Georgetown.

It was not until Walter Robins arrived in Georgetown that May acquainted him with this change of plan. Robins, bearing in mind the adverse criticism that May had received in Australia for spending too much time with his then fiancée and too little time with his team, both expressed surprise at the decision and doubted the wisdom of it. He intimated to May that there was bound to be unfavourable press reaction. Would he not think again?

Relations had at no time been exactly close between captain and manager, and May remained adamant. He wanted, and intended, to have his wife with him. Robins had no express powers to forbid it, and there could be reasons to support the argument that if the captain was happier with his wife at his side, he might also be a better captain. Not everyone took this view. Dexter's wife, Susan, had joined him in Jamaica, but had since left to return to her work as a model. Subba Row's fiancée, Ann Harrison, had also gone. There were those who thought that May should, for the month remaining, devote his time and his energies to his team.

Robins, having done his best to put this to May, without success, left it at that for the time being. Later that evening

May asked Robins to come and see him. He expressed his concern at Robins's attitude, to which Robins replied that his own responsibility was to the interests of the team as a whole, and so on and so forth.

At this May finally came clean and confessed that for several weeks—since the Second Test in fact—he had experienced discomfort and some bleeding from the internal abscess for which he had been operated on back in July. He had kept this largely to himself, confiding only in Colin Cowdrey, his vice-captain, and Brian Statham, his senior professional.

Robins, understandably, was astounded at this information, as well as at the fact that it had been kept from him. Now May's daily and unexplained visits into town before play began became clear. He had been receiving attention from doctors in both Port-of-Spain and Kingston, and when these had not been at hand to dress his wound, he had done it himself. Statham had noticed him one day in the dressing-room so he had had to be told.

Presumably, May's reason for secrecy was that he felt he could carry on in this way until the end of the tour. If he had told Robins, he might—almost certainly would—have been advised to consult a specialist. The consequences of this might have been that he would have had to withdraw.

May's behaviour can be regarded as admirably courageous and determined, or simply misguided, or unfair to his manager, his team and himself. Perhaps it was a mixture of all of these.

With this new, more complicated aspect of the matter in his mind, Robins went over to the Park Hotel to sound the various correspondents about their views. It was obvious that, with Mrs. Peter May due to arrive in a couple of days, some kind of story was going to break: the sooner the whole affair was put in true perspective, the better, and the less painful for everyone concerned.

The matter was fairly fully discussed and the general opinion emerged that the first essential was a detailed doctor's report.

Accordingly, Robins took May along for examination the next morning, which happened to be the last day of the British Guiana match. May had already fielded for the best part of two days.

After lunch Robins came to the Press Box with a written statement which he handed round. This said quite simply that owing to the reopening of his operation wound, May had been advised by his doctor to rest for at least fourteen days. It was hoped that, with luck, he would be fit for the Fifth Test.

So there it was. What May had feared, happened. He was out of the side. Had his wife not been joining him in Georgetown, the odds are that the matter would never have come to light. Whether—purely from a cricket point of view, and leaving every other aspect aside—that was a good or a bad thing remained to be seen.

The day's drama was not over. Trueman ricked his back batting and there were doubts as to the extent of his injury. Barrington, who'd had flu earlier in the week, had a relapse and went to a nursing home with bronchial asthma. Jim Parks was accordingly flown in from Trinidad, where he happened to be coaching, during the early hours of the morning. If Barrington did not immediately respond to treatment, Parks would have to play in the Fourth Test, due to start in four days' time. Our resources had suddenly grown very slender.

★   ★   ★

The colony match was otherwise devoid of incident. British Guiana batted for nearly two of the four days to score 375 for 6, declared, while M.C.C., batting for the remaining two, replied with 494. British Guiana's innings was notable for a grandiloquent performance by Clyde Walcott, whose 83 showed him to be still, at thirty-four, one of the world's great players. England, it seemed, could thank their lucky stars that he had retired so early from Test cricket.

M.C.C., on a pitch of curious deadness, began with a partnership of 281 by Cowdrey and Pullar. Cowdrey, who had made a hundred in Antigua, as well as 114 and 97 in the Kingston Test, thus came near to making four centuries in a row. His timing was now perfect and his off-driving of lordly magnificence. He hooked Stayers' bouncer and the merest flick of his wrists sent the ball scudding to the pickets.

Pullar, whose first century of the tour this was, not unnaturally suffered in comparison. But he, too, helped along—as was Cowdrey—by disastrous catching, played increasingly handsomely through the covers.

The West Indies press had, since Kingston, been loud in its demand for the inclusion of a third fast bowler for the Fourth Test. Stayers, of British Guiana, was the obvious choice. He was conceded generally to have a suspect action, especially with his bouncer, and it became known that one of the Test umpires had been asked to have a look at him in the nets. The opinion had been unfavourable.

However, whatever chance Stayers might have had, dissolved quickly. He was unlucky not to get an early wicket with his bouncer, which flies up quickly off little short of a length, but this apart, he looked little over medium pace. A hundred runs were struck off him before he took a wicket, and he looked more and more deflated as the innings wore on.

Smith made a reassuring 97, getting stuck there for twenty minutes before playing no stroke at a ball from Stayers that bowled him.

★   ★   ★

During the weekend before the teams were announced, it looked as though the West Indies selectors were bent on exercising all their persuasive powers on Walcott. It was a weekend of rumour and of anti-climax, with one player after another reporting temporarily unfit. By Monday—the Test was due to start on Wednesday—Cowdrey was confined to his room with a heavy chill: the same day Barrington, recovering from his congestion of the lungs, rose from his bed and tottered to the nets. Trueman was still uncertain.

Late that afternoon West Indies announced their side.
Nurse (most unfairly), Solomon, Scarlett were out. Walcott,
Worrell, and Charan Singh were in. Lance Gibbs, the British
Guiana off-spinner, was in the twelve named in case Rama-
dhin, who developed a shoulder injury, was unfit.

The West Indies press was jubilant about Walcott, as well
they might be. It only needed Everton Weekes now, and the
famous triumvirate would be complete. Gibbs, with a convul-
sive little run and high action, had bowled well in the Colony
match. Singh was on hand in case the wicket, as it showed
signs of doing on the last day of the M.C.C. match, took spin.

Only Nurse, who had made a brilliant début at Sabina
Park, could count himself unlucky.

England announced her side on the eve of the match. The
invalids, hopefully perhaps, were pronounced fit. So the only
change turned out to be Subba Row for May. Parks, whom
several in their secret hearts might have preferred to Swetman, was chosen as twelfth man.

FIRST DAY

At ten o'clock thick grey clouds came rolling in over the
estuary in the wake of the north-east Trades. Five minutes
later it was raining; not exactly a downpour, but enough to
rattle the corrugated-iron roofs on Main Street.

By the time we reached the ground at 11 o'clock the rain
had stopped, but the covers were on and the outfield muddy
in patches. Early news was that neither Ramadhin nor Gibbs
was fit, and that Scarlett would play after all.

The covers, when they were removed, revealed strips of
damp in the middle of the wicket, and the pitches alongside,
despite a generous coating of dried grass, remained slithery.
Consequently, it was half-past twelve before Alexander and
Cowdrey were able to toss. The usual happened—Cowdrey,
like May, having called 'tails'—and Cowdrey and Pullar
were making their way out behind the West Indies a quarter
of an hour later.

There was time only for three overs before lunch, but it was enough for Hall, despite several bouncers that nearly cleared the wicket-keeper, to demonstrate the suety slowness of the pitch. This was, by a long chalk, the deadest pitch so far. Cowdrey, with contemptuous disinterest, twice off-drove Watson before flicking Hall to the square-leg boundary. England, at lunch, were 11, Cowdrey 9, Pullar 2.

Pullar steered Watson past slip to the boundary, then glanced him for another. Hall pitched short and Cowdrey hooked, safe as houses, to beat long leg. Thirty came up in half an hour, so Alexander replaced Hall with Worrell. Watson, it was noticeable, had looked much the quicker of the two from the northern end.

Worrell, bowling over the wicket to a ring of four men fairly deep on the leg side, opened with three maidens. Hall had a go at Watson's end but, though he looked quicker this time, his most significant achievement was to skim Cowdrey's cap with a bouncer.

The fifty was quietly raised, but scarcely acknowledged, though the gates had been closed on the biggest crowd ever to enter Bourda. England's opening partnerships so far had been 50, 71 unfinished, 37, 18, 28, 177—an average of over 76. West Indies had scored 6, 22, 29, 12, 11—an average of 16.

At 50 the spinners came on, Scarlett at the north end, Singh from the Press Box. Scarlett opened with two maidens, Singh with five gently dropping full-pitches. Cowdrey, perhaps filled with compassion, contented himself with two twos and a single, despite the absence of a deep square leg or midwicket. Singh never found a length, but Cowdrey settled further and further back into somnolence and Pullar never quite managed to time the series of half-volleys and full-pitches that reached him. They were soon to suffer for this, for after a score of runs had gone down the drain Hall, looking more buoyant and refreshed than when he started, came back.

Pullar followed his first ball round to leg and Alexander

was across to take the catch. 73 for 1, or just about par for the wicket.

Subba Row snatched a single off his first ball and now Alexander brought on Watson at the other end for one over before tea. Hall set two short legs forward of Subba Row and went flat out just short of a length. Two balls before tea he got one to kick and Subba Row fended it high just between the two of them. England, at tea, were 82, Cowdrey 44.

Subba Row, who had been given the job of vice-captain, gave off an air of assurance Cowdrey had forfeited some time ago. He sliced Hall past gully for four, pushed him off his legs and genuinely seemed enthusiastic for the imaginative single. Sobers came on to bowl, as usual, in his cap, and his opening overs were worse than Singh. Subba Row, just reaching a wild long hop, swept it for four one-handedly.

Cowdrey swung a full toss to the score-board at mid-wicket, and there was an atmosphere of such self-indulgence and dissolution on both sides that it was hard to believe that any of it counted. Yet in the midst of it all, Subba Row was out. Sobers, bowling from the back of the hand, produced yet another wide long hop, Subba Row followed it round, and Alexander caught him. 121 for 2, Subba Row 27.

Hall and Watson, like darkly spectral figures of fever, returned to welcome Barrington, pale from his days indoors. Hall at once hit him on the elbow with a ball he ducked into. But the lesson was learned, if painfully. Twice more in succession Hall tried to bounce and each time Barrington hooked him hard and true to square leg.

Sobers returned and continued to get away with full-pitches, long hops, half-volleys. Cowdrey had gone on a fast, though he seemed neither to be suffering nor fretting. Barrington clowned away some bouncers from Watson. The sun had slunk away behind the stands, the palms scarcely moved.

England, with 75 minutes lost, couldn't complain at the score of 152 for 2. Cowdrey, in this period of plenty, had done a good job all day. He was never in the faintest trouble, but in mid-afternoon, the dynamo had unaccountably run down. The result was a slow march into dusk, not a gallop.

For West Indies, it had been disappointing. The fast bowlers had found little life in themselves and none in the wicket. The spinners, though Scarlett was tidy, were otherwise lamentable. Only Worrell, in his limited way, had looked anything of a bowler at all.

Ramadhin, inscrutable and wary, had been sorely missed. He is the necessary link to the fast bowlers. Had he been playing, 152 for 2 would have been a reasonable score. As it was, it ought to have been 200.

ENGLAND

First Innings

Pullar, c. Alexander, b. Hall	...	...	...	...	...	33
*M. C. Cowdrey, not out	...	...	...	...	...	65
R. Subba Row, c. Alexander, b. Sobers	...	...	...	...	27
Barrington, not out	...	...	...	...	...	22
Extras	...	...	...	...	...	...	5
Total (for 2 wkts.)	...	...	...	...	...	...	152

E. R. Dexter, M. J. K. Smith, Illingworth, Swetman, Allen, Trueman and Statham to go in.

FALL OF WICKETS—1–73, 2–121.

BOWLING (to date)—Hall, 13–1–49–1; Watson, 12–1–35–0; Worrell, 8–4–7–0; Scarlett, 11–5–12–0; Singh, 6–1–17–0; Sobers, 9–0–27–1.

WEST INDIES—*F. C. M. Alexander, C. C. Hunte, E. McMorris, G. Sobers, F. M. Worrell, R. Kanhai, C. L. Walcott, W. Hall, C. Watson, C. Singh, R. Scarlett.

SECOND DAY

A sweltering morning, another crammed ground, and the prospect of a large score. Hardly had one settled, though, when Cowdrey, pushing forward to the third ball of the day from Hall, was caught at the wicket.

Barrington, still looking pale, played a few overs, but the crack above the elbow he received from Hall the previous evening was obviously paining him. He, therefore, sought attention from a doctor and Smith came out in his stead. He was all but l.b.w. first ball to Hall; the second flicked his off-stump. 161 for 4 and Barrington's return problematic.

Alexander called up Sobers for Illingworth, hoping he might step into Ramadhin's shoes, on this occasion anyway. He pitched his googly half-way down the pitch on the leg stump, it turned and kept a shade low, and Illingworth, heaving as if to clear the trees, was pitiably bowled.

Swetman emerged, and the fast bowlers began pawing the earth. Alexander brought them both back and Swetman, having edged four runs, was totally l.b.w. to Watson. 175 for 6, and the match seemingly thrown away in one terrible hour.

The pity was that Dexter looked in as fine fettle as one had seen him. He pulled Watson, turned Hall off his legs and drove each bowler straight in turn. Scarlett, fielding at cover, practically had his leg amputated by a square cut. Sobers returned, and now Dexter crashed him to the sight-screen. The first hour had produced only 17, a score not exactly aided by Alexander's fiddling slowness and advices at the start of each over. The half-hour before lunch, in contrast, took England from 167 to 206. All the same it had been, in perfect conditions, a disastrous morning for England. Alexander had handled his bowling with the utmost skill, and it was impossible to avoid the feeling that he had got pretty well every batsman's weakness finally weighed up.

Hall's first delivery with the new ball after lunch went for four widish byes. England could be grateful for anything they got now. Dexter lashed Watson hard and often into the covers, but only once managed to steer his way past the bruised and battered Hunte.

Things were looking up generally when Dexter, still admirably belligerent, went to hook a near bouncer from Hall. He got it high up the bat and Hunte, diving forward at square leg, held a fine catch.

Barrington, heavily bandaged, came back now to try to

hold the fort with Allen who, once again, looked blandly unruffled.

With Alexander not disposed to risk Charan Singh again, Worrell returned to give the fast bowlers deserved rest during the full heat of the afternoon. He began with his habitual accuracy, visibly chagrined only when Allen edged successive balls for four on either side of the wicket.

Singh, at length, in response to loud vocal appeals from the Indian sections, replaced Worrell. He soon quieted his admirers with copious full tosses which only Barrington's infirmity prevented him from dispatching. Allen, less handicapped, hit two successive boundaries, then drove Scarlett for a third through the covers. Sobers tried again, this time from a different end, and Allen placed an opening full toss to the score-board. The bowling, in its airy vagueness, was scarcely credible.

England had thus, in easy stages, struggled past 250 before Barrington, almost immobile, prodded Sobers's googly into Walcott's stomach at slip. He had done nobly to continue his innings at all, but the 70 extra minutes he had struggled were worth that number of runs in another contest. Hall soon knocked back Trueman's middle stump, but this time Statham proved himself of sterner stuff. He drove, he snicked, he placed; and the bowlers found it increasingly hard to look civil about it. Allen, meanwhile, had reached an altogether becoming fifty—his first in Test cricket—so that, once again, West Indies had failed to wrap up the tail.

Scarlett, Sobers, finally Worrell had all to be pressed into action. Mostly they were played with deliberation and care, though once Statham slashed Worrell savagely to the palings.

Alexander dropped Allen off Worrell, which, though hard on Worrell, served Alexander right for several fairly disgraceful appeals. Tea, put back half an hour, had eventually to be taken with these two still together, and England 295 for 9.

Hall's second ball of the evening had Allen taken at the wicket: Alexander's fourth catch of the innings, Hall's sixth

wicket. After 175 for 6, with Barrington virtually out of commission, 295 wasn't unreasonable. West Indies had only their
spinners to blame for it. Hall, scarcely pitching short at all,
had bowled with fine concentration before lunch, but once
he had tired, there was no one to fill the gap. Singh would
have nightmares about his performance, while Sobers,
though he picked up three wickets through the sheer novelty
of it, was little less erratic.

West Indies batted for three-quarters of an hour and it was
not without incident. Each batsman took a brace of boundaries through the short legs, then, within the space of an
over from Statham, Hunte might have been caught and run
out. The catch flew shin-high to Trueman's right at leg slip,
but though he got both hands there, he couldn't hold it. Two
balls later Pullar, making a fine stop at short square leg,
found the batsmen changing their minds in mid-wicket. Unfortunately, he dropped the ball as he turned and Hunte
scuffled back.

Neither Statham nor Trueman threatened much after this.
Hunte on-drove Trueman between the legs of a mounted
policeman stationed alongside the sight-screen, then turned
him through the short legs. McMorris, sleeves buttoned, ex-
pressionless, managed to look like something in Madame
Tussaud's.

ENGLAND

First Innings

Pullar, c. Alexander, b. Hall	...	...	...	...	...	33
*M. C. Cowdrey, c. Alexander, b. Hall	...	...	...	...	...	65
R. Subba Row, c. Alexander, b. Sobers	...	...	...	...	...	27
Barrington, c. Walcott, b. Sobers	...	...	...	...	...	27
E. R. Dexter, c. Hunte, b. Hall	...	...	...	...	...	39
M. J. K. Smith, b. Hall	...	...	...	...	...	0
Illingworth, b. Sobers	...	...	...	...	...	4
Swetman, l.b.w., b. Watson	...	...	...	...	...	4
Allen, c. Alexander, b. Hall	...	...	...	...	...	55
Trueman, b. Hall	...	...	...	...	...	6
Statham, not out	...	...	...	...	...	20
Extras (b.5 l.b.2 w.2 n.b.6)	...	...	...	...	...	15
Total	...	...	...	...	...	295

FALL OF WICKETS—1–73, 2–121, 3–152, 4–161, 5–169, 6–175, 7–219, 8–258, 9–268, 10–295.

BOWLING—Hall, 30.2–8–90–6; Watson, 20–2–56–1; Worrell, 16–9–22–0; Scarlett, 22–11–24–0; Singh, 12–4–29–0; Sobers, 19–1–59–3.

WEST INDIES

First Innings

C. C. Hunte, not out	...	...	...	...	...	22
E. McMorris, not out	...	...	...	...	...	10
Total (for 0 wkt.)	...	...	...	...	...	32

*F. C. Alexander, G. Sobers, F. M. Worrell, R. Kanhai, C. L. Walcott, W. Hall, C. Watson, C. Singh, and R. Scarlett to go in.

BOWLING—Trueman, 6–1–21–0; Statham, 5–1–11–0.

THIRD DAY

A morning of growing cloud, with queues curving outside the gates for several hundred yards. Cowdrey now was depressingly faced with the same task as May at this stage at Kingston. It was as much in his interest to keep runs down as to take wickets.

Statham and Trueman had the briefest of opening spells

together, Cowdrey soon bringing on Illingworth to bowl to a packed off-side field. Hunte, having added only three in half an hour, got an edge to one from Illingworth that went with the arm, but Swetman dropped it. Statham came on at Trueman's end and three times in a dozen balls he had McMorris pushing forward vainly. Illingworth meanwhile pitched with the monotony of a dripping tap on the line of the off-stump and neither Hunte nor McMorris could do other than prod into the covers. Once only McMorris got through them in an hour.

Shortly before lunch Barrington had a trundle in place of Statham and Hunte immediately scooped him just out of Smith's grasp at mid-wicket. Otherwise he, too, commanded the push and the prod. The result was that a bare 31 runs came in the 90 minutes before lunch; and this, despite the 24 overs England had bowled compared with 16 by West Indies the day before. Round one, then, both tactically and morally, to Cowdrey.

Hunte determined to get moving after this, and time after time he lay back to carve unsuccessfully at Allen, who, with Trueman, began the afternoon's bowling. At length he connected, and Trueman, at short slip, took a low, swift catch. 67–1–39.

Trueman bowled four fast and splendidly accurate overs for six runs. Then Statham, in heavy drizzle, came back to bowl at McMorris. The first ball flew between wicket-keeper and slip for four, the third found the edge of the bat for Swetman to take an easy catch.

The drizzle continued for twenty minutes, with both fast bowlers going now against the new batsmen. Not until Trueman had skidded did Cowdrey approach the umpires for a halt to be called. At half-past two, with West Indies 79–2, Kanhai 5, Sobers 0, they went off.

Twelve minutes later they were back. Trueman at once hit Kanhai, shuffling back on his stumps, hard on the right pad, but Lee Kow, peering from his butler-at-the-keyhole stance, refused a confident appeal. A leg-bye resulted, then

Sobers, hooking at the next ball, skied it between mid-off and mid-on. The rain was soon banging down again on the corrugated iron of the stands and, after enduring this for a couple more overs, sanctuary was again sought, by some more eagerly than by others.

The tree-dwellers, inside and outside the ground, who had hoisted up their lunch on baskets attached to ropes, scampered down now, leaving only a top layer of the most determined. The level of the dykes round the ground was soon rising. From their dressing-room the England players could sniff the freshness of the air with wry pleasure.

Suddenly it cleared, and with tea being taken meanwhile, only twenty minutes of the afternoon was actually lost.

Cowdrey, in steamy conditions, began with his fast bowlers, but there were no signs that the wicket had livened up. Sobers drove Statham beautifully past mid-off and flicked him to the fine-leg boundary. But he was hustled by Trueman who twice had him stabbing down in the nick of time. Yet he drove Trueman to the sight-screen when Trueman, keeping a very full length, tried to blast a way through.

For the last hour Allen and Illingworth bowled in gloomy light. Once Kanhai, with his customary overbalancing sweep, sent Illingworth to the square-leg boundary. Once he pulled Allen to mid-wicket. Otherwise there wasn't a stroke of note. Both bowlers, in the manner that Ramadhin had taught them, pitched a foot outside the off-stump, with extra-cover on the boundary and four other off-side fielders half-way. Only the short, snatched single could have broken this up. But these two, after the ruinous run-outs of the previous Tests, were taking no chances this time. So West Indies, after four and a quarter hours' play, were a mere 107 runs on their way.

ENGLAND

First Innings

Pullar, c. Alexander, b. Hall	...	...	...	...	...	33
*M. C. Cowdrey, c. Alexander, b. Hall	...	...	...	...	65
R. Subba Row, c. Alexander, b. Sobers	...	...	...	...	27
Barrington, c. Walcott, b. Sobers	...	...	...	...	27
E. R. Dexter, c. Hunte, b. Hall	...	...	...	...	...	39
M. J. K. Smith, b. Hall	...	...	...	...	...	...	0
Illingworth, b. Sobers	...	...	...	...	...	...	4
Swetman, l.b.w., b. Watson	...	...	...	...	...	4
Allen, c. Alexander, b. Hall	...	...	...	...	...	55
Trueman, b. Hall	...	...	...	...	...	...	6
Statham, not out	...	...	...	...	...	...	20
Extras (b.5 l.b.2 w.2 n.b.6)	...	...	...	...	...	15
Total	...	...	...	...	...	...	295

FALL OF WICKETS—1–73, 2–121, 3–152, 4–161, 5–169, 6–175, 7–219, 8–258, 9–268, 10–295.

BOWLING—Hall, 30.2–8–90–6; Watson, 20–2–56–1; Worrell, 16–9–22–0; Scarlett, 22–11–24–0; Singh, 12–4–29–0; Sobers, 19–1–59–3.

WEST INDIES

First Innings

C. C. Hunte, c. Trueman, b. Allen	...	...	...	...	39
E. McMorris, c. Swetman, b. Statham	...	...	...	...	35
R. Kanhai, not out	...	...	...	...	...	...	31
G. Sobers, not out	...	...	...	...	...	...	33
Extras	...	...	...	...	...	...	1
Total (for 2 wkts.)	...	...	...	...	...	139

*F. C. M. Alexander, F. M. Worrell. C. L. Walcott, W. Hall, C. Watson, C. Singh and R. Scarlett to go in.

FALL OF WICKETS—1–67, 2–77.

BOWLING—(to date)—Trueman, 20–5–44–0; Statham, 16–3–42–1; Illingworth, 20–7–23–0; Barrington, 3–2–4–0; Allen, 16–3–25–1.

FOURTH DAY

Cowdrey took the new ball straight away this morning. With rain spattering into the canals all round this city of weather-boarded, stilt-raised houses, and the atmosphere at Bourda steamy, but rainless, he could expect some swing out of the fast bowlers, but though he gave them five overs each, Statham alone beat the bat during that time. Kanhai was uncomfortable against anything short from Trueman, and once he fended him just out of short leg's reach. Trueman wisely kept the ball right up to Sobers, but this time the consequence was three lovely strokes through the covers. Yet, only 11 runs came in half an hour, only 25 in the hour. Illingworth, with extra cover deep on the boundary and the usual off-side ring, was the first change.

There were few pickings here, though Dexter, when he came on for Statham, allowed Kanhai liberal exercise at the square cut. However, magnificent fielding generally kept both him and Sobers down to singles, whatever the fierceness of the stroke. Sobers, increasingly solid, reached fifty. The hundred for the partnership followed and then, in a matter of minutes, Kanhai's fifty. Like Sobers it had taken him well over three hours. The bowling had been a shade less accurate than on Friday.

It was Yorkshire at both ends to begin the afternoon. Sobers took two singles, then Kanhai, when Trueman immediately fed him with a short one, hooked it first bounce into the pavilion. The next ball was slower and a full pitch. Kanhai, startled, miscued it and Dexter, at short mid-wicket, received a ludicrously easy catch. This was a wicket out of the blue, but it brought in Walcott, that noble Othello among contemporary batsmen. His opening strokes, including a crash through the covers off Illingworth, made Kanhai's innings suddenly shrink in quality and range. Sobers, put on his mettle, produced lazily handsome off-drives against each bowler, and now at last West Indies were really moving. But Trueman, refusing to be browbeaten, continued to

pitch at Walcott's toes and suddenly, with about the fourth
yorker in half a dozen balls, he sent the leg stump wheeling.

Trueman, at great pace, bowled a tremendous over to
Worrell, who, three times during it, stabbed the ball out at
the last second. Worrell, however, had habitually been
Statham's rabbit and Cowdrey soon brought him on. Worrell
was not to be gobbled up though, nor did Statham manage
much more than three-quarters of Trueman's speed. Illingworth contented himself with cooping Sobers up and for the
most part he succeeded pretty well. At intervals Sobers
chopped him past slip, very occasionally he drove him hard
enough to beat mid-off. After 90 minutes of Illingworth,
Allen took over and Sobers hit a full toss to the mid-wicket
boundary. Barrington, too, had a bowl, aiming to pitch into
the rough outside Sobers's off-stump.

Sobers was past bothering much about such natural
hazards and twice in an over he sent leg breaks skimming into
the palings. The second of these took him to his third hundred of the series and a faultless, if often muted, effort it was.
Worrell had settled in now, the spinners far more to his liking.
West Indies at tea were 227 for 4, or 18 behind.

Refreshed, Sobers drove Allen in his first over with a third
onto the tin roof of the press box. From there the ball rolled
into the narrow canal behind, where it lay until a small boy,
shinning down an overhanging tree, darted in, salvaged it
and made off like a Macdonald Bailey. It took five minutes
to select a suitable replacement. With it, Trueman whistled
one past Worrell's ear and himself rolled half-way down the
pitch after it. Soon after half-past four West Indies sailed past
the England total. Worrell was now scoring run for run with
Sobers and, for the first time in the series, the West Indian
running between the wickets was sharp and imaginative.

But, all in all, Cowdrey could be thankful that only 193
runs had come in the day. After lunch Trueman had
threatened to wreck the innings and perhaps Cowdrey took
him off a couple of overs too soon. But once Worrell was freed
of him, he batted with his usual relaxed elegance.

It was Sobers's day, though. A hundred is an insignificant landmark to him. He merely shifts the gum from one side of his mouth to the other, and on he goes. And West Indies, with the weekend ahead of them and two days left, were 37 ahead. Cowdrey, who kept a stately tempo in great heat, was faced with a left-hander at one end all day. He was rather unjustly criticized for delaying tactics, but compared with Alexander, he seemed a hare. Sobers is not easy to set a field for, and Cowdrey, one way and another, had little cause for regret.

ENGLAND

First Innings

Pullar, c. Alexander, b. Hall	33
*M C. Cowdrey, c. Alexander, b. Hall	65
R. Subba Row, c. Alexander, b. Sobers	27
Barrington, c. Walcott, b. Sobers	27
E. R. Dexter, c. Hunte, b. Hall	39
M. J. K. Smith, b. Hall	0
Illingworth, b. Sobers	4
Swetman, l.b.w., b. Watson	4
Allen, c. Alexander, b. Hall	55
Trueman, b. Hall	6
Statham, not out	20
Extras (b.5 l.b.2 w.2 n.b.6)	15
Total	295

FALL OF WICKETS—1–73, 2–121, 3–152, 4–161, 5–169, 6–175, 7–219, 8–258, 9–268, 10–295.

BOWLING—Hall, 30.2–8–90–6; Watson, 20–2–56–1; Worrell, 16–9–22–0; Scarlett, 22–11–24–0; Singh, 12–4–29–0; Sobers, 19–1–59–3.

WEST INDIES

First Innings

C. C. Hunte, c. Trueman, b. Allen	...	...	...	...	39
E. McMorris, c. Swetman, b. Statham	...	...	...	...	35
R. Kanhai, c. Dexter, b. Trueman	...	...	...	...	55
G. Sobers, not out ...	...	...	...	...	142
C. L. Walcott, b. Trueman	...	...	...	...	9
F. M. Worrell, not out	...	...	...	...	38
Extras (b.4 l.b.8 n.b.2)	...	...	...	...	14
Total (for 4 wkts.) ...	...	...	...	...	332

*F. C. M. Alexander, W. Hall, C. Watson, C. Singh, R. Scarlett to go in.

FALL OF WICKETS—1–67, 2–77, 3–192, 4–212.

BOWLING (to date)—Trueman, 34–6–92–2; Statham, 30–7–67–1; Illingworth, 35–10–56–0; Barrington, 6–2–22–0; Allen, 33–7–61–1; Dexter, 5–0–20–0.

FIFTH DAY

This was, in the equation of runs and time, a crucial morning for West Indies. It was the sultriest day so far, the mosques behind the stands glinting and the palms ruffled by only thin spasms of breeze. Cowdrey, with the new ball due in five overs, began with his spinners, Allen and Illingworth. West Indies, at 332 for 4, were 37 ahead.

Sobers took a single off Allen's first ball of the morning. Worrell pushed forward to the third, he was outside it and it came in to take the top of the off stump. Allen in his next over drew Sobers out, again the ball turned, and Swetman whipped the bails off. This was an admirable piece of bowling, a slick bit of stumping. So both overnight batsmen were gone for six runs. Alexander, at the other end, wore the expression of one whose house is falling about his ears.

Cowdrey declined the new ball and Alexander, joined by Scarlett, raced now for singles off practically every ball. Once Alexander looked to be clearly run out, but Illingworth had broken the wicket in taking the throw. Twenty-five had been added before Cowdrey finally called his fast bowlers up.

Scarlett picked Trueman's first ball to him hard off his toes and Illingworth at short leg knocked it up and then, diving for it, all but brought off a stupendous catch.

But Alexander and Scarlett, having had forty minutes' gratuitous look at the bowling, were not to be so easily shifted now. Trueman, into what had suddenly become a fair breeze, was less on a length than usual, and Statham, with all manner of worries on his mind (his small son had been seriously ill the past week), troubled neither greatly. Alexander played some handsome strokes, as well as several profitable pushes; Scarlett, in his ungainly fashion, cracked anything short, and he steamed up the pitch when called like a branch-line train suddenly put onto express service. By lunch, West Indies were 392, Alexander 33, Scarlett 22. The tide was flowing again for West Indies.

But in the first over of the afternoon Alexander pushed Trueman to Smith at deepish mid-on and called. Perhaps Scarlett's great bulk hid the fielder. Anyway, Smith raced in, lobbed at the stumps from five yards and Alexander ran on into the pavilion.

Trueman quickly bowled Singh. But it was forty minutes and only ten runs later that Alexander, at 402 for 8, declared. West Indies were 107 ahead; just over eight hours remained for the match.

Hall, with three backward short-legs and one forward, two slips and a gully, attacked Pullar's leg stump from the start. Watson, who had damaged an ankle earlier in the match, did not field, so Worrell, with his medium-paced, left-arm seamers, had to do duty at the other end.

Hall was soon bouncing them at Cowdrey and the first one that came within reach Cowdrey hooked hard to the square-leg boundary. Two more cleared his head, then he hooked him for four to fine leg. He hooked the next two to mid-wicket and long leg for two and four. That meant five bouncers in eight balls and fourteen runs to Cowdrey. So Alexander, a good deal earlier than he can have anticipated, had recourse to Scarlett.

He opened with a full toss which Cowdrey drove through the covers. Worrell, in contrast, put the ball exactly where he wished and there was monastic silence at his end. He used three short legs for Cowdrey, with Hall banished to the trees at long leg, and aimed in Trevor Goddard-like fashion at the pads, with one an over going the other way. Scarlett, with a ring of five on the off, settled to a length and Pullar, hitting firmly off the back foot, could find no way through.

Worrell, shirt soaked as if he'd been caught in a heavy shower, came off with figures of 8–5–5–0. Singh at once spun one between Pullar's bat and pad and nearly bowled him. He followed this up with several thoughtful and accurate overs that even Cowdrey found testing. Ten minutes before tea he beat Cowdrey with one that spun sharply, Alexander deftly took the bails off, and Cowdrey was given out. 40–1–27.

Sobers had a friendly bowl, on an assortment of lengths, before and after tea. Pullar, managing to hit about one full toss in three, thankfully got off 7, which score he had stuck on for thirteen overs. Scarlett was soon back, with Singh hurrying Dexter with an occasional quicker one at the other end. Dexter, having had half a dozen scorching off-drives cut off by Sobers at short extra, at last got one through. He then drove Scarlett hard at the mounted policeman on the extra-cover boundary, a stroke of violence and breeding.

So, at 76, with fifty minutes of the day left, Hall wound himself up for a final fling. Dexter, looking very upright and straight, played him with time in hand and Alexander again allowed him only three overs. Walcott replaced him and Dexter pulled two long hops to the pavilion. Worrell was called up in the last ten minutes and he too began with a long hop which Pullar hooked first bounce towards the scoreboard.

Worrell bowled the last over of the day. The first ball shot cruelly and Pullar, playing across the line, was l.b.w. It was a sad end to a solid and dogged innings. Yet England, 110 for 2—four runs on—were virtually out of the wood. Dexter, 30 not out, had looked more the part of a classical No. 3 than anyone on view for a long time.

ENGLAND

First Innings			*Second Innings*	
Pullar, c. Alexander, b. Hall ...	33		l.b.w., b. Worrell ...	47
*M. C. Cowdrey, c. Alexander, b. Hall	65		st. Alexander, b. Singh	27
R. Subba Row, c. Alexander, b. Sobers	27		not out	0
Barrington, c. Walcott, b. Sobers	27			
E. R. Dexter, c. Hunte, b. Hall ...	39		not out	30
M. J. K. Smith, b. Hall	0			
Illingworth, b. Sobers	4			
Swetman, l.b.w., b. Watson ...	4			
Allen, c. Alexander, b. Hall ...	55			
Trueman, b. Hall	6			
Statham, not out	20			
Extras (b.5 l.b.2 w.2 n.b.6) ...	15		Extras (b.6)	6
Total	295		Total (for 2 wkts.) ...	110

FALL OF WICKETS—*First Innings*—1–73, 2–121, 3–152, 4–161, 5–169, 6–175, 7–219, 8–258, 9–268, 10–295. *Second innings*—1–40, 2–110.

BOWLING—*First Innings*—Hall, 30.2–8–90–6; Watson, 20–2–56–1; Worrell, 16–9–22–0; Scarlett, 22–11–24–0; Singh, 12–4–29–0; Sobers, 19–1–59–3.

WEST INDIES

First Innings

C. C. Hunte, c. Trueman, b. Allen	39
E. McMorris, c. Swetman, b. Statham	35
R. Kanhai, c. Dexter, b. Trueman	55
G. Sobers, st. Swetman, b. Allen	145
C. L. Walcott, b. Trueman	9
F. M. Worrell, b. Allen	38
*F. C. M. Alexander, run out	33
R. Scarlett, not out	29
C. Singh, b. Trueman	0
W. Hall, not out	1
Extras (b.4 l.b.12 n.b.2)	18
Total (8 wkts. dec.)	402

C. Watson did not bat

FALL OF WICKETS—1–67, 2–77, 3–192, 4–212, 5–333, 6–338, 7–393, 8–398.

BOWLING—Trueman, 40–6–116–3; Statham, 36–8–79–1; Illingworth, 43–11–72–0; Barrington, 6–2–22–0, Allen, 42–11–75–3; Dexter, 5–0–20–0.

SIXTH DAY

'Dead as Marley's ghost,' roared a young negro in striped shirt as the first ball was bowled. Not everyone in the English camp shared this view, though only early disaster could prove it false. The ground, after five record-breaking days, was barely a third full. The pitch bore great scooped-out hollows in the bowler's footmarks and it was surprising it had not done more. Most were clear of the stumps, but by no means all.

Hall this morning bowled with bandaged wrists, for trying to bounce one at Dexter the night before he had cartwheeled down the pitch. Alexander, saving him for the new ball twelve overs hence, gave him only a couple first thing, then he brought up Scarlett, with Worrell going at the South end. Subba Row several times tickled Scarlett down to long leg, Dexter sliced Worrell to the third-man boundary. Singh came on and Dexter, after a fallow period, skied him inches over McMorris at deep mid-on.

For a long time now it was dour, laborious batting, with Singh much on the spot and runs coming mainly in deflections. After an hour, Sobers replaced Singh, occasionally hitting the rough, sometimes firing in a slinger, and rather more accurate than in the first innings. The 150 went up and Scarlett, changing his tactics, bowled round the wicket to three short legs. He pitched one short and Dexter, pulling it to the pavilion, reached fifty. He had not so far looked the commanding player he had done at the start of his innings. Sobers, in his Comptonish manner, now bowled a long hop too and Dexter, crashing it flat-batted to the sight-screen, was off the leash. In the next over he picked Scarlett off his toes first bounce into the wire-netting at mid-wicket. As a result, Alexander brought Hall back for one over before lunch. Dexter weathered it and England went in at 163 for 2, Dexter 60, Subba Row 22.

Hall took the new ball, which had been available twelve overs back, in his first over after lunch. Subba Row, moving well inside the line, nudged him safely off his hip and once Dexter had flashed an express half-volley to square leg, Hall's straight-backed equine head went down and he was the gloomy shambling figure he becomes when wickets elude him. Worrell, who can scarcely have bargained for these long bowling stints, gave nothing away for forty minutes. Then Dexter drove him most beautifully through the covers.

In some curious way this shot seemed to seal West Indies' fate. The batting at both ends grew even more ample. Subba Row cut Scarlett for four and England were 200 for 2. In Worrell's next over Subba Row cut him through Alexander's gloves and England were a hundred on. Another square-cut off Scarlett took Subba Row to a fifty of gathering momentum, his first in Test cricket.

At ten to three Walcott bowled and Dexter pierced the ring of five offside fielders. He sliced past slip, he square cut. Singh returned and Dexter struck him to the mid-wicket trees. Then he drove him straight, a scorching stroke that took him to his hundred. In terms of pure technique, this was as admirable a partnership as England had produced yet. Subba Row was finding the gaps whenever he lay back to cut and the score bounded up quicker than at any time in the match. Suddenly Dexter let fly at a half-volley from Walcott, and Worrell, deceptively idling at deep mid-off, took a startling catch, without change of expression, head-high to his right. 258–3–110; a partnership of 148, that had hauled England from a struggling position into a comfortably cruising one.

Smith was next and Walcott, one thought, would have been gentle enough in pace for him. But he peered out at the first ball, as if suspicious of its shape, got an outside edge, and Alexander dropped it. Twice in his last three innings Smith had been bowled first or second ball, his bat caught in his pads. So close does he play to the ball that when he misjudges the line he is late and impeded.

England at tea were 278 for 3, Subba Row 80. Smith was caught one-handed off a full toss by Scarlett after this, a quixotic end to a lamentable innings. Subba Row, in increasing danger of seizing up altogether, finally reached his hundred, then got out.

Barrington was out to Worrell in the same over, so there were now more wickets around than runs, which, considering that before tea only 18 had fallen in six days, did more than was decent to restore the balance.

It had been a better match than the scores suggest. England, it is true, came out of it perfectly honourably, but there were more anxious moments than may seem likely. Had Ramadhin been fit, and Watson not crocked for the second innings, it could have been different. But Alexander's spinners failed him, except for Singh's one teasing spell to Cowdrey on the penultimate evening. And more than this, his great players, Sobers and Kanhai, perhaps fearful of what followed them, dared too little during their long partnership. Alexander and Scarlett showed what the short disruptive single could achieve, and it was reasonable to suppose that what they could do, Sobers and Kanhai could do better.

Allen's quick dismissal of Worrell and Sobers on the fifth morning had perhaps been decisive. That, and the constant threat of Trueman, Cowdrey's hooking to demoralize Hall, and finally the handsome batting of Dexter and Subba Row.

Not a dramatic match it is true. But the tension held, and for England there was always something of significance going on.

Walcott's failure was a sadness; one always wants a great player to return in triumph. Yet how good he had looked while he was there: a giant still among numerous pygmies.

It was announced on the last evening that Brian Statham would fly home next day to be with his sick son, seriously ill in Manchester with complications after chicken pox and a tonsil operation. Peter May, too, was returning at the weekend.

West Indies, it seemed, might in the circumstances have an even chance to level the series at Port-of-Spain. Who would have thought that, with May and Statham both out of it, England could still feel fairly happy? Yet, and not without reason, they did.

ENGLAND

First Innings			*Second Innings*	
Pullar, c. Alexander, b. Hall ...	33		l.b.w., b. Worrell ...	47
*M. C. Cowdrey, c. Alexander, b. Hall	65		st. Alexander, b. Singh	27
R. Subba Row, c. Alexander b. Sobers	27		l.b.w., b. Worrell ...	100
Barrington, c. Walcott, b. Sobers	27		c. Walcott, b. Worrell	0
E. R. Dexter, c. Hunte, b. Hall ...	39		c. Worrell, b. Walcott	110
M. J. K. Smith, b. Hall	0		c. Scarlett, b. Sobers ..	23
Illingworth, b. Sobers	4		c. Kanhai, b. Worrell	9
Swetman, l.b.w., b. Watson ...	4		c. Hall, b. Singh ...	3
Allen, c. Alexander, b. Hall ...	55		not out	1
Trueman, b. Hall	6			
Statham, not out	20			
Extras (b.5 l.b.2 w.2 n.b.6) ...	15		Extras (b.6 l.b.4 n.b.4)	14
Total	295		Total (for 8 wkts.) ...	334

FALL OF WICKETS—*First Innings*—1–73, 2–121, 3–152, 4–161, 5–169, 6–175, 7–219, 8–258, 9–268, 10–295. *Second innings*—1–40, 2–110, 3–258, 4–320, 5–322, 6–322, 7–331, 8–334.

BOWLING—*First Innings*—Hall, 30.2–8–90–6; Watson, 20–2–56–1; Worrell, 16–9–22–0; Scarlett, 22–11–24–0; Singh, 12–4–29–0; Sobers, 19–1–59–3. *Second Innings*—Hall, 18–1–79–0; Worrell, 31–12–49–4; Scarlett 38–13–63–0; Singh, 41.2–22–49–2; Sobers, 12–1–37–1; Walcott, 9–0–43–1.

WEST INDIES

First Innings

C. C. Hunte, c. Trueman, b. Allen	...	...	...	...	39
E. McMorris, c. Swetman, b. Statham	...	...	...	...	35
R. Kanhai, c. Dexter, b. Trueman	...	...	...	...	55
G. Sobers, st. Swetman, b. Allen	...	...	...	...	145
C. L. Walcott, b. Trueman	...	...	...	...	9
F. M. Worrell, b. Allen	...	...	...	...	38
*F. C. M. Alexander, run out	...	...	...	...	33
R. Scarlett, not out	...	...	...	...	29
C. Singh, b. Trueman	...	...	...	...	0
W. Hall, not out	...	...	...	...	1
Extras (b.4 l.b.12 n.b.2)	...	...	...	...	18
Total (8 wkts. dec.)	...	...	...	...	402

C. Watson did not bat

Fall of Wickets—1–67, 2–77, 3–192, 4–212, 5–333, 6–338, 7–393, 8–398.

Bowling—Trueman, 40–6–116–3; Statham, 36–8–79–1; Illingworth, 43–11–72–0; Barrington, 6–2–22–0, Allen, 42–11–75–3; Dexter, 5–0–20–0.

* * *

Georgetown I shall remember for the nocturnal baying of its dogs, the hooting of steamer sirens on the Demerara river, the ceaseless, querulous chirping from the mango-trees of the *Qu'est-ce qui dit* birds.

The town itself has the air of Holland transported to the tropics, though in fact the French, during their short tenure between the Dutch occupation and its secession to Britain in 1812, laid it out. The main avenues, with canna lilies, saman-trees and flamboyants in the central walks, are wide and shady. Intersecting streets are lined with white, weather-boarded houses, usually on stilts with a kind of bell-tower. Most of them are clouded in bougainvillaea, stephanotis, zinnias, gladioli and poinsettia, so that, driving by, one flashes past a blur of pink, purple, scarlet, orange, green and white.

The city, wedged between the estuary of the Demerara and the muddy Atlantic waters that are kept out by miles of

sea-wall, generates a feeling of space and of deceptive leisureliness. Many of the roads were once canals, and though the
dykes remain, only a handful of canals, with slow-moving
clouds mirrored between punts and barges, still exist.

Georgetown, unlike Kingston and Port-of-Spain, has not
merely architectural unity, but a style and a flavour. The
British being what they are, it may lack the vibrations and
exoticism, the *douceurs* as well as the squalors, of such
French *départements* as Martinique, such Dutch colonies as
Surinam, which lies adjacent to the south.

But you can walk through the air-terminal-style commercial centre (rebuilt after the fire of 1945) to the docks at the
river mouth in five minutes; or to the sea-wall, where at
sunset, during weekends especially, a *passegiato* takes place
in the Italian manner, with rows of young negresses and
Indians in pink and lemon cotton dresses passing and re-
passing strolling bands of youths; or you can wander through
the exciting smells of Stabroek Market and watch the river
boats, unloading vegetables and spices.

The crescent of the public buildings, with its flaking colonnade and glinting dome, exceeds its counterparts in Jamaica
and Trinidad. The gabled and balustraded Law Courts, the
Town Hall, quasi-Scottish Baronial, quasi-Aztec, the white
Cathedral, the largest all-wood building in the world, both
astonish and please. Shady parks, lily-ponds, and sudden
sheets of canal water, soothe the eye wherever you go.
Georgetown is not a metropolis, still less an interesting shopping centre. The gentleman of pleasure, except at his most
down-at-heel or suburban, is not catered for. Yet, undeniably,
from a visual point of view, it is the most successful of the
British Caribbean capitals.

The sea-wall, completed in the 1850's, curves round the
city like a protecting arm. Seaward of it, mud, to the width
of a football pitch, follows the wall virtually down the seventy
miles to the Berbice river.

On this flat coastal strip of reclaimed silt, where a constant
battle is waged against erosion, ninety per cent of British

Guiana's people live. The original settlements were at the far-thest navigable points of the four main rivers—the Essequibo, the Demerara, the Berbice and the Corentyne—but with the establishment of sugar on the coast, and to a certain extent rice, the centres of population shifted. Now an almost un-broken line of villages, each with its sugar refinery, its com-munity centre, its range of Anglican, Catholic and Methodist churches, its mosque and Hindu temple, its school, extends down the coast past New Amsterdam to the Surinam border.

The pattern of these contiguous villages, some of which bear French names like Le Plaisance and Bon Repos, or the English names, like Buxton, of those who did pioneer work for emancipation, is identical. To the north-east the Trade-ruffled, coffee-coloured sea, a strip of mud beach fenced with brushwood, an area of marsh, the sea-wall and the Berbice road. Inland of the road, parallel dykes, known as side-lines, run for about a mile, marking the village boundaries. Some-times a central canal, the middle-walk, still exists, but this has usually been filled in to form the village street. Behind the villages the canefields spill like a green sea up to the edge of the coconut-estates and the bush. Farther inland still, per-haps fifty miles off, the forested plateaux, veined with rivers and sprayed with roaring waterfalls, rise up in tiers towards Brazil. Down south, near the frontier, the Rupununi tribu-tary of the Essequibo twists through vast cattle-bearing savannahs, a kind of South-American middle-west, where the plains lose themselves in strips of forest, the forest is fringed with orchid and cactus, and finally the sandpaper-trees and pink rivers die away under the mountain barriers that separate Guiana from the Rio Branco grasslands in Brazil. This is the air-passenger's view, as the Dakota swings him in a wide curve over the lake of Amuku, where wiser and more foolish men before and since Raleigh sought the legen-dary gold of El Dorado.

Not that its gold-bearing properties are entirely legen-dary. There has always been gold in Guiana, and generations of bush-negroes, or 'pork-knockers' as they are called, have

devoted their lives, with a gambler's or narcotic-addict's des-
perateness, to finding it. But the finds, though not rare, have
been quick to run dry, and the economics have yet to prove
more than modestly satisfactory. The dream of a Guianese
reef, to compare with Johannesburg's Rand, dies hard all the
same.

The coastal villages have a stagnant sort of charm. During
daylight they give off an air of somnolent abandon, the men
out in the canefields, or in the refineries, or at work on the
dykes. I used to drive out sometimes to Le Plaisance, and
walk along the canals, their punts moored among the water-
lilies, to watch small Indian children of affecting beauty, or
negro urchins with their rolling eyes, chasing each other
under the dark of their stilted, anti-termite huts. The rum
parlour, with the most unlikely advertisements for Ovaltine
or Vin Fou, would be open; and I would hear, if I took long
enough over it, the scandals of the village, its hopes and sor-
rows and sudden impatient acts of violence.

Unfortunately, though Guiana has its East Indian majority, with negro, Chinese, Amerindian and various species of
ex-European minority, the ethnological groups tend to form
pockets. The Europeans as top executives in Bookers and
industry, in banks and administration, in sugar and bauxite;
the Chinese in business; the East Indians in politics, trade
and shopkeeping; the negroes in all of these, as well as in
government and the canefields. These are loose generaliza-
tions, and the professional worlds consist of every group in
varying ratios. But, socially, as in Trinidad, they prefer to
keep to themselves, so that you tend to find a predominantly
Indian village, white-flagged and with miniature temple,
here, a negro village there. And driving back at night to
Georgetown, with the coconut palms leaning against the sunset and the swamps running with colour, you move through
a dusk of alternating noise, of steel band and the nasal,
fluting, repetitive whine of the music of India.

★　　★　　★

The Sunday of the Test match Anthony Tasker, Public Relations Officer of Bookers, who own not only seventy-five per cent of the sugar estates, but seemingly every second general store in Georgetown, lent me his 14-foot speedboat. He himself had to leave for Jamaica, but in the end his wife Elizabeth was able to come and five of us set out with picnic baskets, ice-box and rum bottles for the trip up the Demerara river, to the Amerindian settlement at Santa. Santa is half a dozen miles along the Kamuni Creek, but for an hour we bounced at 20 knots over the choppy cross-currents of the Demerara to reach the enfolded opening of the creek.

The Demerara, for much of its length, is over half a mile wide. Sugar estates, signalled by the glinting tin of refineries and house roofs, dot each bank, and for ten miles up the estuary, wharves and stellings interrupt the low, wooded shoreline.

We slewed past scattered marzipan-looking islands, one of which, Borselen, was the original Dutch capital. Not a stone of it remains. Creeks opened out of the undergrowth, and rafts bearing timber, launches, a bauxite ship nosing its way down from Mackenzie, passed us going the other way and sent us banging over their wakes.

The wind flew in our faces, the rum slopped from our glasses, the roar of the outboard—most anti-social of machines—made all conversation impossible. Not since war-time trips in M.T.B's out of Felixstowe had my liver had such a shaking as on this pink, muddy river.

Around noon we turned into the narrow Kamuni, the choppy, coagulated pink giving way to glass-smooth coffee water, that farther up turns into pure Coca-Cola. Navigation becomes tricky, because endless tacoubas—floating bits of wood, half-submerged logs—litter the surface, and the various transport craft and Amerindian corials, a form of dug-out canoe, ignore the accepted rule of the road.

We tied up for a delicious picnic lunch, then cruised smoothly but noisily up to Santa. Much of the Kamuni runs through tropical forest, a solid wedge of saltbush, mangrove, mocha-mocha, and mango, with grey ropes of liana festooned around the branches and sudden feathery sprays of bamboo arching out over the creek. Mocha-mocha, the Amerindian word for 'plenty', is a long-stalked, waxy plant, with large vivid leaves like a breadfruit's. The twisted, elephant-coloured roots of the mangroves are three-quarters exposed, producing a dead, skeletal effect. Above them, the thick, tropic greens begin, a sequence of overhanging shades that bury themselves in the water, so that it seems one is skimming through the foliage itself. Spurwings and parrots break from cover, and vast emerald and turquoise butterflies flop about as if half-drugged.

Suddenly the forest comes to a stop, we round a bend and seem to have entered upon the flat, civilized sweep off Maidenhead. A little less green perhaps, but the punts the Amerindians affectedly call *bateaux* lie moored among the reeds and the banks curve gently away under peaceful skies. A pleasure launch, with a party of bikini-clad Chinese girls, negresses, Indians and assorted youths, throbs past us. Two Amerindians of vast age, bearded and faintly Mongolian in feature, paddle by, waving a dignified salute.

Santa itself is on a low hill, the reeds cut away to make a narrow beach. A wooden church hall, a schoolroom, a score of thatched rondavel-style huts, are scattered among starapple, sapodilla, pineapple, coconut, and avocado pear, with a cotton-tree of great antiquity, as their natural forum. Magically, too, there is a dusty, bumpy cricket pitch among the coconuts and when we arrived a game was in progress. What a setting for a Walcott or a Weekes to emerge from! For did not the bumpy unpredictable ground of Bowral produce Bradman? We learned later that the annual match against a rival mission up-river had been a fiasco: the Santa team had set off for the day in high spirits, only to be seen returning a few hours later. There had been a failure in communications and of the opposition there were no signs. Perhaps they simply feared the might of Santa and had prudently fled. But it must have been a disappointing business all the same.

The Santa Mission consists of about two hundred Amerindians, chief of whom is Mrs. Patterson, mother, grandmother and great-grandmother of most of the rest. An idiosyncratic woman of unusual character, she told us with some scorn that it was fifteen years since she had set foot in Georgetown. Or was it fifty? None of us could tell. But it was quite plain that she thought it a congested, murderous place with none of the calm delights of Santa.

The school, for the last twenty years, has been presided over by 'Teach' Fraser, a pepper-and-salt-pated negro from Suddie, on the Essequibo. I could not at first make out whose voice Teach's resembled. I knew it was uncannily like some friend's in inflexion, and the facial mannerism and carriage of the head were similar too. I realized suddenly that it was Cecil Beaton's; how on earth could those high, witty, ironic, self-mocking but self-assured tones, with correspondingly amused or distant lift of the head, have carried here?

The only adult bachelor in the settlement, Teach taught the three R's during the day, cooked for himself at night, read or played the piano.

We sat on the steps of his hut and talked. He showed us his schoolroom with its blackboard, maps and royal photographs, took us round the other huts whose inmates were mostly stretched out in their rope hammocks (the hammock is the Amerindian's main legacy to civilization, and to the Royal Navy in particular), only the pale soles of their feet visible, instructed us in the arts of distilling *parivari*, a beer-like liquid made from cassava, and finally excused himself, saying it was time to go and ring the three-o'clock bell for Sunday school.

Santa is an Anglican Mission, and our last view of it was of Teach, in his khaki shorts, white shirt, grey socks and brown shoes, ringing his bell, and of neat children in Sunday best clothes climbing to the church hall.

'Come again on a week-day,' Teach called out, 'you'll see

us at work then.' Did he say 'my dears'? I couldn't be certain. The men are engaged mainly on the cutting and shaping of wallaba-trees for telegraph poles, and even on this Sabbath we encountered great laden barges making their way downriver to Georgetown.

We said goodbye to Mrs. Patterson, who beseeched us to take care in the great city, and sailed with the dipping sun on our wake back through the cool, arched shadows of the Kamuni.

Again in the Demerara, the sky had begun to flood saffron behind the palms. Georgetown, an hour later, rose from the evening waters like a distant prospect of Venice in a painting by Canaletto. A grey smudge of domes and spires, hardening gradually into the marine outlines of Water Street. We swooped past the islands, squadrons of gulls escorting us, ducklas and egrets flurrying out of the mangroves. The transition from eighteenth-century Venetian to twentieth-century South American became brutally distinct and final, the replacement on a magic lantern of one slide by another, two centuries and several thousand miles apart.

It was dark when we tied up. A thin horn-shaped moon hung seaward above the masts of sloops and cargo-boats.

★   ★   ★

Each evening after the day's play we lay out in the high, domed patio of the Park Hotel, our legs up in the Berbice chairs whose wooden arms extend several feet for just this purpose. The posture is inelegant, bad for digestion, and in the last resort uncomfortable.

The local press, which must rank high among the most blatantly chauvinistic in the non-Soviet, non-Afrikaans-speaking world, was daily ruder about the English players, their Captain and the slowness of the play. Yet, though West Indies had led England on first innings three times in four Tests, they had proved imaginatively unequal to the task of outpacing them. Each time, their tempo had been wrong from the start, and on the one occasion, at Kingston, when they had suddenly switched from the shuffle to the gallop they had floundered hopelessly. Even such fine stroke players as Sobers and Kanhai had allowed themselves to be confined to a jog-trot for hour after hour. There was never a moment after the Barbados colony match when the England bowlers were basically discomfited. At Bridgetown, Everton Weekes showed May how fields should be set, and Ramadhin gave a flawless example of how an off-spinner may bowl defensively. The lessons had been learned and soon the pupils exceeded their masters in skill. Throughout the series England had scored the faster of the two, and though they bowled their overs fractionally slower (one less per hour on average) the constant presence of a left-hander in Sobers more than made up for this.

I could not, moreover, agree with those who found the play boring. Slow, yes, but not boring. It's true that, in a five-hour day, with frequent interruptions from the water-cart, 200 runs were rarely exceeded (when it was, it was by England). Alexander, being a wicket-keeper, tended against his own interests to slow West Indies up between overs, especially since he found it necessary to have lengthy consultations with his bowlers before each over. Both May and Cowdrey, on occasion, took their time too, but only once—on the Saturday of this Fourth Test—was it obtrusive.

Yet it was not until the last afternoon that England were finally out of the wood. At Kingston the match was in doubt until the last hour. At Port-of-Spain England won with only two hours to spare. How can play be dull in such circumstances? One has to regard each session of play as crucial parts in a lengthy contest whose balance shifts from hour to hour. I have no patience with those who say that only the cricket matters, not the result. To believe this is to miss the whole point of Test cricket. The importance of the result is what gives atmosphere and tension to the whole thing. Fast, bright, one-sided cricket, as anyone who saw England demolish West Indies, New Zealand and India during our last three home series must agree, is the most boring thing in the world. But these four Tests had been, for all their slowness, tautly contested; there was uncomfortable edge to them. What is more, every run mattered, that was the significant thing.

Of course, even Test cricket must be played by losers and by winners with grace, charm and sportsmanship. One takes that for granted. But what makes the slowest Test of absorbing interest is uncertainty about the result. Many people were encouraged to believe the England–South Africa Tests of 1956/57 were dull. They were nothing of the kind. The series was finally drawn two all, and the drawn match was the most exciting of the five. What is desperately tedious is to watch Test batsmen taking their ease against a demoralized attack.

No side in this series got properly on top; it was a struggle from first to last, in which character, courage and technique were at a premium. No player, except perhaps Sobers, and on occasion Dexter, scored fifty without scars of battle. Hall and Watson on the one hand, Trueman and Statham on the other, saw to it, with no help from the pitch, that there would be proper dignity to a century. A morning's survival against the new ball became an achievement in itself.

Those who find a stern, level contest unendurable, merely because runs trickle rather than flow, have no place in modern Test cricket. They are suited to our southern counties, our clubs and villages. Cowdrey's hooking of Hall, Dexter's tremendous driving, acquired that much more splendour from the austerity of their context.

I always remember Leonard Hutton saying to me that the infallible guide as to whether a player would make the real grade as a Test cricketer was that, deep down, he should respond to it, almost prefer it. He did not mean that batsmen enjoy being hit or that they should never be apprehensive. What he meant was that the true Test player grows in stature under tension, that he raises his game according to the demands of the situation. It is not necessarily a surface pleasure. I don't suppose Hutton actually *liked* facing Lindwall and

Miller, with the new ball. He patently didn't. It is more an affair of the blood, an instinctual appetite, a coolness of temper. He himself was one of the greatest examples of it, Miller another, Evans, Bailey, Fingleton, O'Reilly, Edrich, Benaud in their different ways others. Cowdrey has, to a certain extent, got to be stung into it. One recognizes at once those who, despite the highest natural gifts, don't have it, nor ever will.

★   ★   ★

There is a traditional work-song in Georgetown that goes like this:

> Georgetown got some worthless gals,
> *Mind how* you swing you' tail,
> Swing you' tail in a decent way,
> *Mind how* you swing you' tail.

> Georgetown gals don't fetch no price,
> *Mind how* you swing you' tail,
> Give dem a shillin' an' kiss dem twice,
> *Mind how* you swing you' tail.

Whatever the general truth of these observations, the Georgetown streets at night bear a liberal sprinkling of what Earl in Montego Bay termed 'sport girls'. The city as a whole has a dead, desolate air by early evening, but from the white pavilion of my mosquito-net I could hear far into the morning the blare of music from isolated pockets of resistance—the balustraded London Hotel, near the docks, the Palm Court, the Woodbine.

The disappointing thing about Guiana, Britain's solitary possession in South America, is that, with over a hundred miles of coastline, it lacks a single bathing-beach. The pink detritus twines against the shore at a width of several miles. The Trades blow more or less constantly through the day, though Georgetown, being below sea-level, can get uncomfortably humid at night.

Whatever its defects as a country to visit, British Guiana is a real place. One is out of the false world of tourists and into the hard world of affairs, of strident nationalist politics, of economic struggle. If the myth of El Dorado has died, there are still those who believe there are fortunes to be made. Scratch a Guianese and you will find a pork-knocker. The hydro-electric potential of this 'land of many waters', the country of Kaiteur, one of the most spectacular falls in the world, is enormous. So that, even if today Guiana, the size of the British Isles, but with only a hundredth of its population, appears a sparse and bitterly parochial place, it may yet justify the five-hundred-year-old dreams of Raleigh and his successors.

NOTES IN TOBAGO

M.C.C. are down on the Berbice river, playing a three-day match against the county, who include Kanhai, Solomon and Butcher. Parks keeps wicket for M.C.C. for the first time: on his performance must depend his chance of playing in the last Test. One thing: whatever the result of that Test I shall have kept up my proud record of never having reported a losing series. Since I succeeded R. C. Robertson-Glasgow on the *Observer* in 1953, I have covered three winning series against Australia, a win at home and a draw abroad against South Africa, home victories against West Indies, India, and New Zealand, a rainy, one-sided draw against Pakistan. The only series England have lost during these eight years—in Australia 1958/9—was when I was unable to go.

★ ★ ★

So, after an early morning flight from Georgetown to Port-of-Spain, an afternoon at Piarco airport, and a twenty-minute flight up here, to Robinson Crusoe's island. Defoe's tedious story is known to be based on the life of Alexander Selkirk, who was shipwrecked on Mas-a-Tierra, one of the Juan Fernandez islands in the Pacific. But that Defoe transferred the site to Tobago is evident from one of Crusoe's entries in his journal. 'And the land which I perceived on a bearing west-south-west was the great island of Trinidad.'

My patio at Arnos Vale looks out on a half-moon of white sand, with fishing-boats drawn up under awnings of coconut. Off the headlands on either side the long swell boils and pounds as it hits the reef. The beach, which, after a fortnight's deprivation at Georgetown, one gazes at with thirsty eyes, shelves deeply and the tide marks are strewn with shells.

It is as pretty a bay as I've seen in the Caribbean yet. From bed to sea is a matter of twenty seconds, which is about the same as when I was on Hayman Island, in the Great Barrier Reef. Tobago, on a miniature scale, reminds me of the Great Barrier, though the island itself is five times the size of any of the Queensland cays. But the nylon pool and kaleidoscopic coral gardens at Buccoo, the high-flying, predatory frigate birds, who force the gulls to disgorge by diving on them and then scoop up the falling fish, the dazzle of blue and white on the reefs, keep reminding me of Hayman. Only here it is coconut palms instead of pandanus, she-oak and casuarina.

★   ★   ★

What, I ask myself, shall I remember with most pleasure about these three months? In Barbados, the blue of the water, as clear as the eyes of any Scandinavian beauty; driving back through the Careenage at sunset, with the palmistes black against the syrupy sky; the surf at Crane and Bathsheba; the coral-stone plantation houses, cool and elegant, rising out of the canefields.

In Trinidad, the Saddle Road to Maracas Bay, with the immortelles open like parasols over the cocoa-trees and nutmeg; the hibiscus hedges and the islands of the Bocas, the white, creaming Atlantic through the coconut plantations at Manzanilla and Mayaro; the calypso tents and the band at the Miramar, and the great, exhausted shuffle on the last lap of Carnival jump-up.

In Jamaica, Spanish Town, with Rodney resplendent in toga and sandals; the drive up to Oracabessa, the river glinting like mercury, and back along the banana-hung ravines that wind from Port Maria down to Stony Hill; the light mellowing and fading on the Blue Mountains, and dinner by the rushing waters of Blue Mountain Inn.

In Antigua, Nelson's Dockyard at English Harbour, the blue-and-white weatherboarded houses of St. Johns. In British Guiana, our trip up the Demerara river and into the liana-strung reaches of the Kamuni.

BARBADOS. On the leeward side, on that part of St. James known as the 'platinum' coast, some of the bluest waters in the world lap the coral beaches and palatial villas of the migrant rich.

At Bathsheba, on the windward, empty Atlantic coast, the long rollers break up on tricky reefs, through which the flying-fish fleet has to pick its way.

BRIDGETOWN. The careenage, where inter-island sloops cluster alongside pink warehouses. Nelson, among cannon-ball trees and fountains, stands on his plinth in the middle of the traffic. The air smells of sacking and tar and ship-chandlers. This is the heart of Barbados, most of which is flat, and tall with sugar cane. One hopes the barber cuts hair better than he spells.

TRINIDAD. Immortelles, rust-pink over a country road, act as shade-trees to cocoa and coffee plantations

MARACAS BAY

PORT OF SPAIN

La Ro PHEBE

JAMAICA. In Montego Bay there's plen of time for sitting around outside nig clubs or gazing at the banana bo Tourists in Bermuda-shorts and seemin lined with dollars, provide good pickin most of the year round.

Spanish Tov the former ca tal, until placed by upstart, ugly, dustrial port Kingston.

At Round Hill, beyond Montego Bay, privacy is literally golden. The status-seeker or any claimant to membership of the international set cannot go wrong here.

A bamboo grove in western Jamaica. Roads are winding, driving lethal.

Traditional skills. By day, balancing produce from the citrus orchards; by night, going under the bar in the Limbo. The best Limbo dancers get the bar down to a mere eight inches.

ANTIGUA. Nelson's Dockyard, at English Harbour. Nelson, arriving as a young captain of 26, spent the years 1784-7 at this headquarters of the Leeward Islands station. The dockyard, a few years ago almost derelict, is to be completely restored.

BRITISH GUIA
Georgetown,
low sea-level
a city of d
and canals
weatherboard
white houses
Dutch gab
Mosques a
Hindu tem
gleam in the
lying subur
and the ca
dral is the
gest all-w
building in
world.

But I am conscious, too, of much else I should have liked to have seen in the Caribbean: Cuba and Haiti, the French islands of Martinique, Marie-Galante, and Guadeloupe; St. Lucia, St. Vincent and Grenada. The mixed worlds of Spanish music, of meringues and rumbas, of French Creole cooking and beguines, of Voodoo rituals; the fragrance of the spice islands, and, among them, the British sugar islands, some lying lightly moored to the Caribbean and much as they must have looked to Rodney and Nelson, others trinketed for tourists, or fighting their way up to the stormy surface of political independence.

That bow of Ulysses, Froude calls it, with British Honduras and Guiana at opposite ends of the curve and the arrow ready for aiming at the heart of Empire.

★   ★   ★

How much of these Tests will remain in the memory? The fast bowling of Hall and Watson, Trueman and Statham; Hall, in those giant bursts-through at Sabina Park and Bourda, Trueman in that thrilling morning at Port-of-Spain in the Second Test, and again on the last day at Sabina Park.

Sobers's three fine, but constrained hundreds; Kanhai's dogged fight to save the Second Test, ended by a full toss; Hunte's gallant flash of wings that could have brought West Indies victory at Kingston.

For England, the brilliant moments were Cowdrey's second innings of 97 at Sabina Park, the outstanding purple passage of the whole series. Dexter's two centuries, and his 77 in the Second Test, perhaps the most devastating innings of the three. Barrington's hundred under fire at Port-of-Spain.

Yet it is of Trueman, fielding at leg-slip with his trousers hitched up his thighs as if wearing bicycle clips, a floppy, butterfly-catcher's hat shoved on his head, that I shall think chiefly. He became increasingly exhibitionistic as the tour wore on, yet whenever the crowd got restive he was able, by such elementary gestures as cupping an ear to them, to calm and amuse at once.

He has rarely before looked a dangerous bowler on plumb wickets overseas, yet once he had trimmed his Barbados waistline he bowled with mounting pace and excellent control. His action became more beautifully rhythmic and flowing than ever, he used varying angles of approach very skilfully, especially against Sobers, and he developed the yorker to unnerving effect. After Barbados he never bowled short, but moved the ball off a fairly full length either way. Like Hall, with a wicket in his pocket he was able to produce a burst of speed that had the incoming batsman often ludicrously late. He was sparing with the bouncer, but it was there up his sleeve and the West Indians knew it.

Already, with one Test to go, he has taken more wickets in a Test series in the West Indies than any English bowler. Laker, with 18 in 1947/48, held the previous record; Trueman now has 19.

Statham as usual beat the bat with sickeningly little result. Yet only twice, for short periods in the first innings of the Second and Third Tests, did he rival Trueman in pace and general threat. He is never untidy; yet often that extra foot of pace, that annihilating whippiness, was absent. He plays a similar rôle to Trueman as in 1954/55 he did to Tyson, and that is much to be thankful for.

Dexter, we hoped, might develop enough as a bowler to take Bailey's place; he didn't. Instead, he has usurped May's. Here at last is the ideal number 3, magnificently combative from the start, correct in defence against pace, improved out of all recognition in his technique against spin.

If we have lost a bowler—which we have, unless he is prepared to start from scratch again, with left leg further across the stumps, the final stride lengthened and left shoulder shown more aggressively to the batsman—we look to have gained a potentially great batsman, and a vindictive cover point too.

Having no medium-pace stock bowler, we have had to drop straight from pace to off-spin (West Indies usually had Worrell). In England we shall need one in place of a second off-spinner. Barrington has helped out a lot with his leg-breaks, and in England he could develop into a top-class all-rounder.

He seems at the moment to have had the stuffing knocked out of him as a batsman—one can almost see the sawdust running out. His two centuries, made in much discomfort against Hall and Watson, brought about an increasing spate of short lifting balls on the leg stump and his faulty judgement of them got him a fearful pounding, as well as giving Hall a sadistic increase in hostility. But he will get a second wind shortly, and he was for two Tests a stout sea-wall against the initial onslaught.

Allen has come on beyond all expectations; he has fielded beautifully, his batting helped to save us two Tests, and on pitches that gave him no help he not only kept the West Indians quiet for long stretches but always looked likely to take—and did take—useful wickets.

Illingworth, though he played a key part in the process of curtailment, and improved all the time, never carried the same promise of wickets (though he was, in truth, unlucky with several decisions and a dropped catch or two). He tended to bowl a shade short, and the lowness of his arm and general position of the body at the moment of delivery seem to cost him something in both flight and nip.

We had expected runs from him and he played so well against Barbados that these seemed assured. But Ramadhin tied him up in all kinds of knots and only once—in his valuable second innings in the Second Test—has he been able to unravel them.

Pullar has been wonderfully consistent and phlegmatic, but curiously unable to put on steam after weathering the new ball. A fine player off his legs, he never quite times it through the covers or manages to give the offside half-volley a rich thump.

At one time he and Cowdrey seemed all at sixes and sevens as an opening pair. Yet they struggled through; Pullar's response to running sharpened, and the difference between

England's opening partnerships and West Indies' is significant. Before the Third Test Cowdrey was fatalistically gloomy about his own form and seemed to regard himself merely as a sacrificial victim. His objections to openings were, he knew, irrational; he realized the challenge and must have been aware that technically he was the best equipped. Yet it was not until, towards the end of his first long innings in the Third Test, that he successfully made up his mind to hook Hall, that he broke out of the spell. Thereon in he was the master and Hall gazed at him as if he had suddenly grown an extra arm—which, in a way, he had. From Jamaica on, he has dominated the bowlers, as only in fits and starts at home and overseas has he felt inclined to do.

His great innings stick out in the memory: I remember his 145 for Oxford in the University match, his bat as sweetly tuned and melodious as a mandolin. Then that wonderful, match-saving hundred at Melbourne in 1955, followed by another there four years later. His 150 against West Indies when he and Peter May snuffed out Ramadhin at his moment of triumph. His hundred at Cape Town, when he laboured to eighty, then, with the last man in, literally soared in a matter of minutes, with off-drives skimming over mid-off and past extra cover, to his century.

There must have been many others: but only now do I see him commanding the bowlers with lofty, if kindly disdain. Hitherto some gentleness of character, a humility almost approaching inhibition, seems to have got in the way. But, watching him these past weeks, my feeling is that, without loss of charm, he can become a great captain as well as a great batsman.

May, not for the first time alas, has been a sad disappointment, greater even than in South Africa, when he passed fifty once in ten Test innings. One must doubt now whether his doctors were wise to let him come on tour at all. In South Africa he was a benevolent slayer in state matches. Here he has scored one solitary hundred. Yet what is strange is that in his last two Test innings in Jamaica he looked more like himself than before. My feeling is that he would have scored heavily at Georgetown, where the ball lifted less than anywhere. It has been the lifting ball, throughout his career, that has always troubled him: Miller, Heine, now Hall and Watson. Against anything else, he has been the most imposing batsman of the last decade: a magnificent straight driver of fast, as well as of slow bowling, especially in his early Test days, a crasher of the half-volley, a powerful back-foot hitter wide of mid-on, a savage square-cutter. He has been the destroyer of the second rate, and often of the first rate too.

Only against such as Heine, Hall and Miller, big men who get the length ball up sharply, has he appeared vulnerable, playing too far from the body, too much inside the line of the ball.

He has been a dedicated, determined captain, somewhat rigid of idea, rather over-loyal to old colleagues, to a degree that militated against desirable changes. I'm not sure that in crucial encounters he had enough daring or imagination: nor that he showed the responsiveness, as well as firmness of command that can get the best out of both worlds.

With Subba Row, Greenhough, Andrew and Moss one has felt much sympathy. Subba Row's eventual opportunity, and his admirable taking of it, has therefore given us all particular pleasure. Indeed, he looked so safe at Georgetown, and played so fluently, that he could settle in the England team for some while now. To make sure, though, I want to see how he bats against Ramadhin in this final Test.

Greenhough's disappointment must have been the most acute, for it seemed a possibility that he might be the spearhead of our attack. Yet what with the slowness of the wickets, Allen's batting and ability to seal up an end, his number was soon up. He and Andrew, accepting their fate, were reduced to playing their own private Test matches in the nets.

Andrew and Moss, very likeable and engaging companions, were virtually signed up for Colony matches; a less pleasing prospect than it may seem. Moss, it is true, has a great chance next week and if he can grasp it half as well as Subba Row did, we shall have cause to be grateful to him.

Swetman, with many of Evans's mannerisms and a natural friendliness, never managed to get a sight of the fast bowlers: his constant scuffling against Ramadhin, too, got him into difficulties. One feels he ought to have his right leg pegged, as schoolboys once used to, so that he is forced to play a stroke cleanly and from a stable mooring.

Unfortunately, as he lost confidence batting, so did his wicket-keeping grow edgy and untidy. His faults here seem similar in origin; he moves about too much, and too uneconomically, yet lacks Evans's agility and hard brilliance.

Yet he is always alert, and the routine of coming quickly up to the stumps after each shot, even when the fast bowlers are on, has helped to give England their splendid appearance in the field.

★   ★   ★

So Cowdrey is captain, Subba Row vice-captain, Fred Trueman senior professional. I understand Fred's first remark, on learning of this rise in situation, was: 'Well, they can all cut out the bloody swearing for a start.'

★   ★   ★

The news has come through that Frank Worrell has been appointed captain of West Indies in Australia this winter. Gerry Alexander, who, it appears, declined a nominal invitation, will be vice-captain. It was a pity that politics muddied the issues, for Worrell's experience of Australian conditions, his maturity and charm, as well as his greatness as a player, made him a natural choice. Gerry Gomez is to be manager. It should be a good combination.

All the same, Alexander, in four series as captain, has served West Indies well. He plays hard certainly, and I fear there is not much love lost between the sides in the present series. But wicket-keeper is a nerve-racking post for any Test captain. Already, Alexander, who I think has taken nineteen catches or stumpings, has equalled the West Indian record. The world record for a series is 23, by John Waite of South Africa.

He can beat this too. He is a tremendous performer to the quicks; standing up, not so certain. His failure as a captain—though perhaps lack of success is a better word—has been two-fold. He never managed, largely because he drew too much, too early, on Hall and Watson's stamina, to devise a means of rolling up the last three England wickets; and he seemed unable to inculcate the proper daring into his major batsmen, Sobers and Kanhai included. Having lost the Second Test, Alexander's obvious course was to hasten, in the field and when batting. He failed to do either. The fear generated by Trueman and Statham against the long West Indies tail had a decisive influence over the tactics of the front-line batsmen. This, more than anything, has left West Indies one down, with one to play. They have nothing to lose now by going all out, since they may as well be two down as one. Only a victory in the Fifth Test should interest them.

★   ★   ★

What can one say about the umpiring? By Test standards it has not been good, and England particularly have had to put a good face on some painful disappointments. They have taken them well. One would not presume to write this on press-box evidence alone. But the consensus of on-the-field opinion, even adding a pinch of salt, makes it undeniable. The umpires had an unenviable task: the heat, the pressure of the crowds, the basic difficulty of the job, added to their own inexperience, made it a thankless business at the best of times. It was brave of them to stand at all. Yet wickets, on these diabolical pitches, are at such a premium that a wrong decision usually means the difference of a hundred runs, to say nothing about morale.

At the moment, with Lee Kow intimating that three times is enough to stand in one series (who can blame him?), we have only one umpire, Cortez Jordan, for the last Test. Pay is inadequate, and one of the nominees from Jamaica, Perry Burke, has turned it down. In view of the Second Test, it's not altogether surprising.

*   *   *

The scores in British Guiana: Berbice 387 for 2 declared. M.C.C. 641 for 6 (Parks 183, Barrington 103, Illingworth 101). Parks's 183, scored in 4 hours 20 minutes, is M.C.C.'s highest of the tour. He hit five sixes, twenty-one fours, and with Barrington put on 283 for the third wicket, beating the previous best stand of 281 by Pullar and Cowdrey against British Guiana. M.C.C. on the third day scored 438 runs, an average of 85 runs an hour.

I understand the agreement was to be that each side batted for a day, with the last day shared to make a match of it. But Berbice batted well on into the second day, so something must have gone wrong. If Solomon broke the agreement, he got more than he can have bargained for.

I see that the *Trinidad Guardian* reports an interview with Jeffrey Stollmeyer, the former West Indian captain. In answer to a question about Cowdrey's captaincy at Bourda, he is quoted as replying that he could see no unusually delaying tactics, and that England played good defensive cricket.

*   *   *

It has been unsettled the past few days, the sea windless but rough—the aftermath of an Atlantic gale. At night it roars on the reef, and the coconuts thud down outside my window. When it's like this, the undertow is fierce and one gets painfully cut about by loose stone and coral.

*   *   *

Buccoo reef. Though less than a mile from shore, as against the Great Barrier Outer Reef's eighteen miles, Buccoo is not dissimilar. A circle of unnaturally flat, blue water a quarter of a mile in diameter, and seaward the swell arching up on the verge of the reef and crashing in endless breakers. Navigation is tricky, but having slid through the channel at the lowest possible tide you get out and swim with masks over the waist-deep coral.

The Great Barrier, microscopic in the Pacific, with hissing giant clams that can take your leg off, anemones, sea-serpents and marauding sharks beyond the shelf, gives off an air of murder as well as orgy. Buccoo is neatly suburban and polite: a stray moray or green eel streaks into its hole, but mostly there are well-bred and demure angel-fish and parrot, queen mullet and blue tang, parrot-tailed chub and squirrel-fish, doctors and sergeant-majors. Take up position over a jutting coral edge, paddle against the strong rip to keep station, and wait. Perhaps you will spot the angels first: a pair of black ones, eyes yellow-rimmed as if after a night out, the scales flickering with gold; or a Blue Angel in sequined cobalt, as glamorous as Miss Dietrich; or a school of striped angels, a whole team going by in Newcastle United shirts.

The angels, very properly, are ethereal, pure colour rather than substance. The parrot-fish are extravagantly got-up, often overdoing it like showgirls in a night-club floor-show: one may be iridescent blue-green with scarlet, luminous blue, and jade green sashes; another has vertical red, yellow and blue stripes like a national flag.

In an hour's lurking before the tide turns you will see creatures of every colour in the spectrum, often half a dozen colours together, slatted or spotted or striped, sometimes with scales in pink and gold against a cobalt or emerald or ultramarine background. Dior or Balenciaga never contrived such elegance, nor Ziegfeld or Cochran such dazzle.

You can dry out on the way back, swinging round by one of the sandbars, packed as Victoria Station on a Bank Holiday with sea-gulls, boobies, and the odd bowl-billed, dark-suited pelican gazing superciliously about with a ticket-collector's self-importance. Between the sandbars, half a mile out to sea but in your depth, you can swim again through a blue-green sand-pool of fabulous clarity and brilliance. The sea-bed is flawless white sand, and the sun, hitting the water above it, achieves a sheer nylon-like texture of surface. Of the shore you can see nothing but coconut-palms swerving along white bays, with the distant outline of Pigeon Peak to the north-east. The hills of the Northern Range of Trinidad, running through the Morne Bleu Pass above Blanchisseuse to Toco, are like intensifications of cloud on the horizon.

★   ★   ★

Living in Tobago it would be impossible not to become a naturalist. Flowers, fish, shell, birds, animals: in what would one specialize?

In the high woods are agouti and manicou, sloths and wild hog; on the river-banks to the north-west caymans sun themselves, as spendthrift of time as tourists.

To see these requires effort and cunning. But the birds are as sociable as they are voluble. The hooting mot-mot, with pendulum flight, and tail as long as its tailored, green-gold body and reddish waistcoat, haunts our windows in the search for food. The jacamar, a smaller, six-inch version of the mot-mot, makes a noise like a referee's whistle. Walking through the estate here, you can hear and see mocking-birds and keskedees, tanagers and emerald humming-birds, grackles and golden-eyed thrushes. Farther north, cocoa-birds and parrots, spinetails and trogons fly in and out of the woods with the twittering restlessness of women at a cocktail party.

The island of Little Tobago, a mile or so off the north-east corner, is the only place outside central New Guinea where birds of paradise live wild. In 1909 Sir William Ingram, the then owner of Little Tobago, imported twenty-six pairs from Dutch New Guinea and set them free. Water and their favourite trees were put down for them, and they thrived. On Ingram's death the island was given to the Government, on condition it remained a bird sanctuary, by his sons. The birds can only be seen at early morning and late afternoon, and not always then. The dance, when, before mating, the nar-cissistic male struts under his gold erect cloak, showing himself off to the female while crying out and performing a kind of quick-step, has had a mere handful of witnesses in half a century.

★   ★   ★

Yet as many people come to Tobago for the shells and wild flowers as for the coral reefs and birds of paradise. The flowering trees—immortelles, tamarinds, cassias, tulips, pouis —are much as in Trinidad; the narrow, twisting roads are hedged with hibiscus and bougainvillaea.

★   ★   ★

Travel about the island's fifty miles of coastline is tortuous and slow: though Tobago is only twenty-seven miles by seven, the journey from south to north and back is a whole day's drive, and an exhausting one at that. It is not difficult to understand why Tobago, whose population of 35,000 contains less than two hundred of European origin, was the most squabbled over of any Caribbean island. It was handily placed, strategically, between South America and the islands of the Spanish Main, it was out of the main hurricane lane, was more or less self-supporting, and in Man-o'-War Bay possessed as perfect a natural anchorage as anywhere in the West Indies.

Thus it changed hands between the British, Dutch and French a dozen times before Hood finally captured it from the French, a year after the Peace of Amiens, in 1803.

Ruined forts and overgrown gun-emplacements litter the island still, and scarcely a bay but whose name does not testify to some violent sea-battle.

★   ★   ★

A blue, rinsed day, the sea relaxed and clear. The long-prowed fishing-boats, with their curving bamboo rods raised like antennae, crunch up the beach with a catch of kingfish and dolphin. Over by the reef the angel-fish and red parrots glide over the coral waterfalls and along the sun-netted ravines. On the river-banks the angelina crabs, with their black goo-goo eyes on long stalks, and coach-and-pair sideways trot, bury themselves in the sand and feign nonexistence.

As do I.

12

THE FIFTH TEST MATCH

BACK in Port-of-Spain an excellent lunch, with a hock, a claret and a champagne of unusual quality for the Caribbean, was given at the Hotel Normandie by the Premier of Trinidad and Tobago. One of the pleasures of each Test was the seeing again of friends like John Goddard and Gerry Gomez, and this time I had on my right Jeffrey Stollmeyer, one of that select band of elegant, willowy players, with yet enough underlying steeliness to decorate the opening phases of a Test Match—C. F. Walters, Alan Melville, Mushtaq Ali, were others.

The teams, when they were announced, were much as we expected. West Indies kept Walcott, and brought in Griffith, the Barbados fast bowler, for Singh. Ramadhin's return to fitness disposed of Scarlett. Thus, for the first time in the series, West Indies were committed to three pace-bowlers.

In the England side, Moss took Statham's place, and Parks came in for Swetman. For Parks it was an astonishing piece of fortune that he could not, in his wildest dreams, have envisaged at Christmas. Yet there were precedents for this: George Gunn in Australia, H. W. Lee in South Africa, were lurking handily when reinforcements for M.C.C. had been needed.

Port-of-Spain had scarcely had a drop of rain for weeks. The head groundsman at Queen's Park vowed that whatever else the match might be, it wouldn't be a draw. There were those who thought that the pitch was bound to powder. Frank Worrell expressed the view that five days would be plenty. We should see.

*   *   *

FIRST DAY

A cloudy, breezy day and Cowdrey, calling right, saw to it that England made a clean sweep of the tosses. Alexander, with the traditional gesture, flung his coin into the crowd. It was more than justified. The pitch looked to have a shade more grass on it than usual and one felt the fast bowlers might fancy their morning's bowl.

Alexander began surprisingly, but not unshrewdly, with Griffith instead of Watson. Though Griffith, who had not played since Barbados, is some way the slower he is a more genuine seam-bowler and he was soon moving the ball off a thoughtful length, much at Bailey's speed. Hall produced three no-balls in succession, then a vast bouncer which Alexander rose to like a performing seal. Cowdrey, the batsman, applauded this piece of agility as if he'd been the trainer. Hall's field was four slips, gully, cover, and three short legs. Griffith had two slips less, with these at mid-off and mid-on.

At the end of half an hour, only five overs had been bowled. Griffith then pitched two demonstrably short to Pullar, the second flew up sheer and Sobers at first slip took a comfortable catch off Pullar's glove.

Hall, after three overs liberally extended by no-balls, gave way to Watson. Cowdrey drove his first ball to the mid-off boundary and Watson's drop in length was predictable and immediate. Three short, violent balls later Cowdrey flashed outside the off-stump and Sobers, at second slip, dived to his right. He got both hands there, but the force of it spun him round and it didn't stick. Cowdrey pursed his lips. Dexter played Griffith beautifully off his toes through the short legs and twice to the square-leg boundary, then in the same over hit him firmly under the saman-tree at extra cover.

The jerk in Watson's action looked more pronounced than usual. The sun emerged and Hall tried to find more favour at Griffith's end. But there were no-balls here too: it was as if the computer had got out of order. At the end of an hour, with eleven overs bowled, England were 46. At this rate, the time-overs-wickets machinery so necessary for Alexander to get oiled and smoothly flowing looked ominously in danger of rusting up early. Dexter off-drove Watson to send up the fifty and Watson dug the rest of the over in near his own toes. Cowdrey hooked a bouncer from Hall high over the square-leg umpire's white topee and sent the next ball—a no-ball—for four there too.

It was a nice contrast in styles: Cowdrey flowing, weighty, with an oceanic momentum and rhythm, Dexter wristy, angular, with harpoon-like thrust of stroke. Cowdrey mellow of tone, Dexter aggressive and strident.

Griffith, like Watson and Hall well over six foot and more heavily shouldered, replaced Hall; and before lunch Rama-dhin made his bow too. But the fifty for the partnership went up in well under the hour all the same. 70 for 1, Cowdrey 38, Dexter 20, was a handsome enough start in its own right for England: but still more so in relation to the 57 for 3, on the same strip, on the opening morning of the Second Test.

Hall got going again with a brutal over to Dexter, two heart-high, one head-high, one at lamp-post level. Ducking once, Dexter was struck on the back; Hall appealed and Dexter kicked the ball angrily into the covers. Hall's second over, wilfully short, was no improvement; only two were for the stumps rather than the body or the hornets that cruised the field in swarms. And they were mighty quick. Cowdrey, meanwhile, took ample runs at the other end, several times flicking Griffith off his legs, before cutting Hall and on-driving him with retaliatory power. He was past fifty now, though once, playing early to Hall, he looked to give a return catch. In this bounteous phase, taking in the half-hours before and after lunch, Cowdrey soared from 20 to 63, while Dexter, a target ship in choppier waters, managed no more than six. For Cowdrey, runs were clinking like doubloons in a pirate's haul, for Dexter it had become a matter of riding out the storm. The bowlers really had it in for him this time.

The hundred went up and at length Hall, downcast if not spent, was off after forty minutes at hurricane pace. Watson replaced him and struck Cowdrey three times in succession around the kidneys. Alexander, as if suddenly noticing the indignity of this spectacle, took Watson off. So Worrell, bowling spinners, joined Ramadhin, but still Dexter, an hour over ten, could not break free. Yet he was stoical, rather than fretful, in this unwonted captivity, and found partial appeasement by moving two paces into Ramadhin and precisely bisecting deep mid-off and deep mid-on.

The return to fluency, though, was effected by Cowdrey. He lay back to cut Worrell square through the covers and pushed Ramadhin for singles with complete certainty of timing. Dexter, too, became suddenly in spate. He hit Worrell off the back foot to the scoreboard, he pounced on Ramadhin and left mid-off happy to get clear: then he pulled a full-pitch from Sobers's first bounce into the stands at mid-wicket. His fifty, the hundred and fifty for the partnership, Cowdrey's hundred, were rung up now within minutes of each other. Cowdrey, whose last four Test scores had been 114, 97, 65, 27, was generously acclaimed at his hundred, made out of 177, five minutes before tea.

Soon the familiar pigeons were wheeling against the hills, the sun bleaching them. Cowdrey showed signs of weariness; Dexter, with drinks and salt tablets, struggled against cramp. The swift single became denied them. Then, in two overs, Sobers got rid of them both. He had already once drawn Cowdrey forward and had him perilously near stumped. Now he got Dexter to push towards mid-on against the spin, the ball took the outside edge, and Sobers, turning and racing back, just reached it. The second wicket had added 191. Cowdrey, in the next over, played back to Sobers, the ball, popping up, took the glove, and Alexander, swerving out from behind the stumps, dived on it.

So England, with the new ball due, were 215 for 3. For some reason Alexander kept Sobers and Walcott going for another half-dozen overs. Barrington, intent on making hay, drove Sobers twice beautifully through the covers and by the time Hall got his hands on the new ball at 228 he had made himself at home. He thrust Hall for three to mid-wicket, and making room for the strokes, hit Griffith for smacking boundaries either side of mid-wicket. Subba Row was scarcely less busy and a good deal sounder: for by now Hall was getting Barrington to give his customary display of mingled aggression and nervous distaste. They scampered singles with fine judgement, too, so that the last forty minutes, far from being barren, saw another forty runs onto England's score.

Then, in the last over of the day, Hall truly let fly, and Barrington, struck twice painfully on the knuckles, flung his bat down and, in mid-over, decided to retire hurt.

Yet, at 256 for 3—the biggest daily score of the series—England could feel a just glow of satisfaction. They had played strokes from first to last and they had got away with minor indiscretions. Cowdrey, at 11 and 50, had been let off, one that scorching chance to Sobers at second slip, the other through the off-balance Hall's hands as he followed through, and Dexter, at 20, was dropped in front of first slip by Alexander off Griffith. The ground fielding, after a brilliant start, had acquired all manner of blemishes.

It seemed, ironically, that this might turn out a spinner's wicket after all. Sobers got his customary bounce out of it, but it looked ominously dry, with the outfield parched as a desert. The toss—this was the first time since 1905 that England had won all five in a series—could again prove crucial.

ENGLAND

First Innings

Pullar, c. Sobers, b. Griffith	...	...	...	...	...	10
*M. C. Cowdrey, c. Alexander, b. Sobers		...	...	...	119
E. R. Dexter, c. and b. Sobers	...	...	...	...	...	76
R. Subba Row, not out	...	...	...	...	...	...	18
Barrington, not out	...	...	...	...	...	...	23
Extras	...	...	...	...	...	...	10
Total (for 3 wkts.) ...	...	...	...	...	...	256

M. J. K. Smith, Parks, Illingworth, Allen, Trueman and Moss to go in.

FALL OF WICKETS—1–19, 2–210, 3–215.

BOWLING (to date)—Hall, 14.5–1–54–0; Griffith, 11–0–47–1; Watson, 13–2–33–0; Ramadhin, 18–4–47–0; Worrell, 8–1–29–0; Sobers, 7–0–33–2; Walcott, 4–2–3–0.

WEST INDIES—*F. C. M. Alexander, C. L. Walcott, E. McMorris, C. C. Hunte, R. Kanhai, G. Sobers, F. M. Worrell, K. T. Ramadhin, W. Hall, C. Watson, C. Griffith.

SECOND DAY

There had been a sharp shower at ten o'clock, and Hall and Griffith found themselves with a heavy, steamy atmosphere for their second attempt with the new ball. The umpires had ruled that Barrington must await the fall of a wicket before continuing his innings, so Smith, fortified by a long spell at the nets, came out with Subba Row. He got off lightly with a full toss from Griffith and some over-eager, wide ones from Hall. To Subba Row, Hall pitched consistently short; once Subba Row steered him for four through the slips, twice he fended him just in front of Hunte at backward short-leg. But the second time Hunte, a wonderful virtuoso fielder in any position, dived forward and scooped it up. Barrington was welcomed with three fliers in his first over but he was sensibly combative and went for the hook each time. The spirit was right, if the strokes somewhat perilous. Alexander brought Watson on and Barrington, with left leg straight down the wicket, crashed him past extra cover. He was going to get after the bowlers before they got him, that was plain enough.

He had retired hurt four times in this series already, so some lightheadedness was pardonable. He swished now at Watson, jerked him twice just out of the bowler's reach, and then played two lovely strokes off the back foot to pierce the covers. Hall, though, soon had him squatting and once Watson flicked his forehead, but desperation was giving way to a genuine flourish. Twice in an over he savagely cut lifting balls from Griffith for four past gully; the first took England into the three hundreds, the second Barrington to his own fifty. Smith, meanwhile, was playing his strokes with all the time in the world, so much so that the first hour brought England 52, all off the quick bowlers.

Clouds that had been gathering steadily broke now on the tent-shaped hills, so that was all England had time for before lunch.

It was Ramadhin and Hall in the afternoon, and Ramadhin soon cut one from leg to hit the top of Smith's off-stump. Hall had Barrington on his behind so often that it seemed almost worthwhile his bringing a cushion in with him. Parks, however, kept the short ones from Hall down well enough for Alexander to bring Sobers on after three overs to him. This was a critical period for Parks, perhaps the decisive one of his career. He took a good, long look at Ramadhin, then pulled him high into the stands at mid-wicket. Next he cut him late and it seemed now that England would cruise happily along towards five hundred. But Ramadhin, who had bowled beautifully since lunch, struck two capsizing blows. Barrington played late to his low-slung faster one and was caught at the wicket. Then Illingworth, who must have nightmares about Ramadhin, stabbed a sharply turning one to Sobers at backward short-leg.

Ramadhin's blandly secretive mingling of off-spinners, leg-breaks and leg-cutters had brought him 3 for 14 in 9 overs, 6 of them maidens. Parks at length went down the pitch to him and hit him twice in an over soaringly high to the sight-screen. Alexander, for the first time, was forced to drop two men out, and singles in consequence were two a penny. But Ramadhin beat Allen in the flight with his leg-break and Nurse, substituting for Kanhai at slip, took a slick, left-handed and going-away catch. Trueman wore his opening batsman's scowl, reserved for those occasions when sentry duty denies the pleasure of profligacy, and he looked there for the day. But Parks hit a half-volley back at Sobers, and a moment later Watson rattled Moss's leg-stump. The last six wickets had fallen since lunch for 83, of which Parks's share was 43. Ramadhin, in fifteen overs, had got four of them for 23.

So Trueman, shaking his head over the unexpended runs in his bat, had to bowl instead. 393, in all conscience, seemed a reasonable enough score; yet England, with Smith and Barrington losing their way against Ramadhin when comfortably installed, had missed a great opportunity of setting West Indies an impossible target. As it was, West Indies needed to score 500 at fifty an hour if they were to get England scuffling against Ramadhin on a dusty pitch. That, even without Statham, would take some doing, especially if Allen and Illingworth could turn the ball before Ramadhin got at it again.

West Indies made a heartening start. Trueman took some time to work up pace and Moss, after having his first ball cut for four, was if anything the steadier of the two. Twenty-four runs came in half an hour; then one of the accidents that had been threatening from the first ball of the series happened. Trueman, who was having trouble with his run, pitched one short and Hunte, hooking too early at it, took the ball on the right of the forehead. Blood spurted out as he fell, and it was five minutes before he could be led from the field to be stitched up. It might have been a lot worse, and it was one of the miracles of these Tests that no one had been permanently damaged. Alexander chose to come in now and Trueman set four short legs for him, two of them right forward and in pickpocketing range. Alexander drove one back at him, Trueman stuck out a despairing foot, and McMorris, backing well up, was run out as the ball veered at great speed onto the stumps. He had been run out off a no-ball at Bridgetown and he departed looking about as fed up and dumbfounded as anyone can look.

The spinners bowled the last half-dozen overs of the evening, but Alexander and Sobers, with wary care, kept them out. One or two turned, not quickly, but enough to set one dreaming of Laker.

ENGLAND

First Innings

Pullar, c. Sobers, b. Griffith	10
*M. C. Cowdrey, c. Alexander, b. Sobers	119
E. R. Dexter, c. and b. Sobers	76
R. Subba Row, c. Hunte, b. Hall	22
Barrington, c. Alexander, b. Ramadhin	69
M. J. K. Smith, b. Ramadhin	20
Parks, c. and b. Sobers	43
Illingworth, c. Sobers, b. Ramadhin	0
Allen, c. sub., b. Ramadhin	7
Trueman, not out	10
Moss, b. Watson	1
Extras (b.7 n.b.9)	16
Total	393

Fall of Wickets—1–19, 2–210, 3–215, 4–268, 5–317, 6–350, 8–374, 9–388, 10–393.

Bowling—Hall, 24–3–83–1; Griffith, 15–2–62–1; Watson, 18.2–3–52–1; Ramadhin, 34–13–73–4; Worrell, 8–1–29–0; Sobers, 20–1–75–3; Walcott, 4–2–3–0.

WEST INDIES

First Innings

C. C. Hunte, retired hurt	...	...	...	...	...	...	12
E. McMorris, run out	...	...	...	...	...	...	13
*F. C. M. Alexander, not out	...	...	...	...	...	...	15
G. Sobers, not out	...	...	...	...	...	...	9
Extras	...	...	...	...	...	...	0
Total (for 1 wkt.)		...	...	...	...	...	49

C. L. Walcott, R. Kanhai, F. M. Worrell, K. T. Ramadhin, W. Hall, C. Watson and C. Griffith to go in.

FALL OF WICKETS—1–26.

BOWLING (to date)—Trueman, 7–0–21–0; Moss, 5–0–11–0; Allen, 4–0–11–0; Illingworth, 3-2-6-0.

THIRD DAY

By breakfast the hills were under mist and it was raining hard. At half-past eleven the covers still lay on the wicket and yellow smudges of blossom on pouis that had turned overnight were almost all that could be seen of the northern range. Then, in the twinkling of an eye, the sun was out, the drizzle had gone, the covers were off. But West Indies had lost forty, ill-spared minutes in the process.

They could have lost Sobers in the first over too; Alexander pushed Moss's third ball a few yards towards cover, Dexter was quickly in, and had he thrown under-arm at the stumps Sobers must have been comfortably out. But his throw was over-arm and wide.

For the remaining fifty minutes of the morning Alexander and Sobers managed only the occasional single. Moss once had a promising shout for l.b.w. against Sobers, the ball coming back at him and keeping low, but it must have pitched outside the leg-stump. Moss pinned both batsmen down admirably: he attacked Sobers on the off-stump, Alexander on the leg, and his direction, at a shade, no more, short of a length, was immaculate. Trueman was not at his quickest, but he kept pitching on the spot he wanted and neither batsmen showed the slightest inclination to go through with the stroke. The result was twelve singles in twelve overs, ten to Sobers, two to Alexander. It was self-interment, no less.

Sobers behaved as if he might have spent the interval on a psychiatrist's couch. He twice snicked Moss fine of slip, hooked Trueman to mid-wicket where Smith, diving, came near to taking the catch of the series, and, hooking next at Allen, found another savage hit cut off by Smith. Alexander, though once he picked Moss off his toes, remained a liability: and while England wanted wickets all right, the sudden removal of Alexander, bowled by a good-length ball from Allen, was something of a mixed blessing.

Walcott got off the mark with five overthrows, but Allen, making him play forward, kept him unusually quiet. Sobers, too, was unable to force Illingworth away off the back foot, so that Alexander's departure turned out to have caused a drop in the scoring rate, rather than the contrary. In forty minutes Walcott made 11, Sobers 8. Cowdrey was allowing deep singles, but a square third man on the boundary cut off any steady flow of runs. As Parks demonstrated against Ramadhin, the way to the boundary is straight and over, not square and through. Without the risk that this entails, the batsman is hard pressed by a cordon of fieldsmen, two of whom ought to be on the long-on and long-off boundaries.

Soon after three o'clock the hills were lost under thick mist that quickly turned to heavy drizzle. It was five before they could come out again, and when they did Trueman, after the best part of two hours with his feet up, looked a yard faster in the sweetened air. But he was no quicker back to his mark, which he reached with the resigned air of a shackled bear undergoing detention. Moss optimistically tried to bounce one at Walcott and Walcott hooked with the economy and force of a piston. Then he drove to the sight-screen, with disarming impassivity, first Moss, then Trueman, whose second wind had been oddly short-lived.

Off the last ball of the day West Indies reached 150—half what, over the weekend, they must reasonably have hoped for. At least this time it was their own weather they had to blame. As consolation Walcott, for half an hour, had looked a great master, casting his huge shadow even over Sobers. Laker, once, would get him monotonously often, pitching centimetres wider to him with high-precision accuracy, varying flight and pace, until Walcott, edging away to make room, cut under him and was caught by Evans. But that was in another country, at another time.

ENGLAND

First Innings

Pullar, c. Sobers, b. Griffith	10
*M. C. Cowdrey, c. Alexander, b. Sobers	119
E. R. Dexter, c. and b. Sobers	76
R. Subba Row, c. Hunte, b. Hall	22
Barrington, c. Alexander, b. Ramadhin	69
M. J. K. Smith, b. Ramadhin	20
Parks, c. and b. Sobers	43
Illingworth, c. Sobers, b. Ramadhin	0
Allen, c. sub., b. Ramadhin	7
Trueman, not out	10
Moss, b. Watson	1
Extras (b.7 n.b.9)	16
Total	393

FALL OF WICKETS—1–19, 2–210, 3–215, 4–268, 5–317, 6–350, 8–374, 9–388, 10–393.

BOWLING—Hall, 24–3–83–1; Griffith, 15–2–62–1; Watson, 18.2–3–52–1; Ramadhin, 34–13–73–4; Worrell, 8–1–29–0; Sobers, 20–1–75–3; Walcott, 4–2–3–0.

WEST INDIES

First Innings

C. C. Hunte, retired hurt	12
E. McMorris, run out	13
*F. C. M. Alexander, c. Barrington, b. Allen	26
G. Sobers, not out	61
C. L. Walcott, not out	34
Extras	4
Total (for 2 wkts.)	150

R. Kanhai, F. M. Worrell, K. T. Ramadhin, W. Hall, C. Watson and C. Griffith to go in.

FALL OF WICKETS—1–26, 2–103.

BOWLING (to date)—Trueman, 20–5–47–0; Moss, 20–1–59–0; Allen, 13–1–30–1; Illingworth, 6–2–10–0.

FOURTH DAY

Again West Indies looked anxiously at the clouds that spat, threatened, and finally drifted away indifferently during lunch. There was need now for a real move on, but although England were quicker through their overs, Sobers and Walcott were kept to 17 in half an hour, 37 in the hour. There was scarcely a stroke of note: an off-drive by Sobers off Trueman, a few tucks to leg by Walcott. Trueman finished his spell with a languid bouncer and Walcott, hooking at it, was dropped by Parks. It was not important. Allen came on, beat Walcott in the flight as he came down the pitch, and Parks had the bails off with Walcott scarcely bothering to look back. Walcott's share of the 87 partnership was 53: Sobers, it appeared, meant to see another day through. But his inability to pace an innings and to impose his own tempo remained odd in one so variously gifted; and, in an ironical way, his long innings cost West Indies dear.

The new ball had been due some overs before lunch but Cowdrey hung on until afterwards. Worrell, then, was late on Trueman's first ball, which came into him, and he chopped it hard on to his stumps. 216–4–15.

Trueman, despite the new ball, set two of his three short legs forward rather than backward, and Kanhai, as if to underline the eccentricity of this, nudged him waist-high between the three. An over later he chopped Moss, in not dissimilar fashion to Worrell, into his off-stump. This was Moss's first Test wicket of the tour and it had cost him 190 runs; 26 l.b.w. appeals had been turned down at various times off Moss and if he got one allowed in this match he had promised to do a lap of honour round the boundary.

Instead, with the last ball of the same over, he hit Sobers's middle stump. Perhaps it came in to him, but Sobers seemed outside and a shade over it. This was better than any lap of honour. Sobers's 92 had taken him five and a quarter hours, and his departure was as disconcerting to lovers of routine as a Rolex Oyster suddenly stopping in mid-afternoon. These wickets effected some physiological crisis in the bowler, who had been unwell since breakfast, and he left the field a moment or two later.

Ramadhin, having played several overs from Trueman with becoming modesty, carted Allen with offspinners' licence to the fence. He was on view for the best part of an hour, all told, before he steered Dexter to Cowdrey at slip. Now Dexter accomplished the neatest trick of the day: he got one to lift sharply off little short of a length to Hall, and Hall, cowering as if to a hand-grenade, nearly sat on his stumps. Barrington, forgivably, smirked. Otherwise Hall, though lurching, lunging and swaying precariously, was not discountenanced. Trueman found the edge but it was a thick edge and it only cost runs. Constantly admonished by Hunte, who, with sticking plaster protruding from his right ear like a cigarette, was back in full possession at the other end, Hall pushed forward to Allen, nose to the handle. Barrington, without a bowl so far, was finally given a try just before tea. He beat Hunte first ball with his googly and all but bowled him. He should have come on earlier. Nevertheless, the afternoon had brought England four good wickets for 87, and it was indifferent bowling that had cost the major part of those runs.

Hunte's refusal of the long single was almost wifely in its wayward inconsistency, and Hall, regardless of whether it was the first or last ball in the over, had to keep his wits about him. This he did, and his head too, scotching anything on the wicket, swatting with pent-up violence at everything off it. 300 went up, the fifty for the partnership; Moss and Trueman were treated like medium pacers, and the slowness, both in chase and throw, of the outfielders—Subba Row, Smith, Moss, Illingworth—grew depressingly marked as ones were turned into twos, twos into threes. Now Statham, not least as fieldsman, was really missed. At last Trueman found a fast yorker and Hall, his confidence twelve foot tall, swished and was bowled. He walked out to a sustained Derby-winner's welcome and one half-expected Alexander to come out and lead him in, followed by the loudspeaker announcement of 'weighed in'.

Small progress was made by either side after this, dilatory batting and dilatory bowling about cancelling each other out. So Alexander, 55 runs behind and with 20 minutes of the day left, declared. It was his last chance.

Hall, unsaddled, bowled a fearsome first ball to Pullar and it disabled him. His second ball, to Cowdrey, was almost a wide and Hall, holding his side, intimated his undoing. Alexander, with suitable readjustments to the field, let him go through the motions of finishing the over. He produced an ambling, slow half-volley outside the leg-stump and Cowdrey, with almost charitable gentleness, flicked it to Worrell at backward short leg.

Allen came out as night watchman, and Pullar and he kept Watson, despite an array of short legs and rat-tat-tat of short balls at head-height, safely at bay. At bay, anyway.

ENGLAND

First Innings		Second Innings	
Pullar, c. Sobers, b. Griffith ...	10	not out	12
*M. C. Cowdrey, c. Alexander, b. Sobers	119	c. Worrell, b. Hall ...	0
E. R. Dexter, c. and b. Sobers ...	76		
R. Subba Row, c. Hunte, b. Hall	22		
Barrington, c. Alexander, b. Ramadhin	69		
M. J. K. Smith, b. Ramadhin ...	20		
Parks, c. and b. Sobers	43		
Illingworth, c. Sobers, b. Ramadhin	0		
Allen, c. sub., b. Ramadhin ...	7	not out	5
Trueman, not out	10		
Moss, b. Watson	1		
Extras (b.7 n.b.9)	16	Extras (n.b.1) ...	1
Total	393	Total (for 1 wkt.) ...	18

FALL OF WICKETS—*First Innings*—1–19, 2–210, 3–215, 4–268, 5–317, 6–350, 7–350, 8–374, 9–388, 10–393. *Second Innings*—1–3.

BOWLING—*First Innings*—Hall, 24–3–83–1; Griffith, 15–2–62–1; Watson, 18.2–3–52–1; Ramadhin, 34–13–73–4; Worrell, 8–1–29–0; Sobers, 20–1–75–3; Walcott, 4–2–3–0. *Second Innings* (to date)—Hall, 1–0–3–1; Griffith, 2–0–10–0; Watson, 2–0–4–0.

WEST INDIES

First Innings

C. C. Hunte, not out		72
E. McMorris, run out		13
*F. C. M. Alexander, c. Barrington, b. Allen		26
G. Sobers, b. Moss		92
C. L. Walcott, st. Parks, b. Allen		53
F. M. Worrell, b. Trueman		15
R. Kanhai, b. Moss		6
K. T. Ramadhin, c. Cowdrey, b. Dexter		13
W. Hall, b. Trueman		29
C. Griffith, not out		5
Extras (b.6 l.b.4 n.b.4)		14
Total (for 8 wkts. dec.)		338

C. Watson did not go in.

Fall of Wickets — 1–26, 2–103, 3–190, 4–216, 5–227, 6–230, 7–263, 8–328.

Bowling—Trueman, 37.3–6–103–2; Moss, 34–3–94–2; Allen, 24–1–61–2; Illingworth, 12–4–25–0; Dexter, 4–1–20–1; Barrington, 8–0–21–0.

FIFTH DAY

The clouds were still hanging around, and altogether this was well on its way to being one of the most sunless of Caribbean Tests. Hall, after massage and heat treatment, tried himself out, but it was no good. This must have been a cruel blow to Alexander, for without Hall his pace attack was as Samson shorn of his hair. And the Philistines, in the shape of Pullar and Allen, prospered to an extent that they added 50 in under an hour. Pullar, under these Old Trafford skies, blossomed: he drove Griffith through the covers, Watson past mid-off, and his front foot moved into the line with more alacrity than for some time. Allen was no slouch either: he got firmly behind Watson, he played Griffith nicely off his legs, and when Sobers came on he pulled him sharply. Ramadhin, with a three short-leg bluff, found immediate length but got scant respect. The running was stealthy, almost mouse-like; and Ramadhin had much fielding of his own to do. It was all the more trying that Allen, going late for a definite but brisk single should find himself run out. Yet he had seen 3 turned into 69, and without indignity to the first-wicket down position.

Dexter drove Ramadhin to the extra-cover boundary first ball, swept him to the saman-tree at long leg in the same over, with the result that Ramadhin, empty-handed for 23 in seven overs, gave way to Worrell. Dexter next tickled Sobers for four, and struck him majestically wide of mid-on. The recoup from Allen's loss was so rapid that within ten minutes it had been turned to profit. Pullar reached 50 before lunch, his best-looking innings since the Bridgetown test, and then, in the last over of the morning, was caught-and-bowled, with dolphin-like dive, by Sobers. 102–3–54; and two wickets gone to charity.

Dexter was quickly at Worrell afterwards, flicking him to square leg, and crashing him past mid-off in the first over. But he should have gone in the second, McMorris at mid-wicket putting down a comfortable chance. Hunte at cover made thrilling stops from Dexter, and for a long time Subba Row could do nothing with Worrell, pitching at medium pace in the rough outside his off-stump. This rough—Trueman's footmarks—caused one or two to stop to Dexter as well, and Dexter, at 32, stabbed back the simplest of catches which Worrell, bending to almost casually, dropped. It could only have been too easy; the fielders averted their heads in mingled disappointment and pity. Worrell aimed at Dexter's leg-stump with a leg-slip, long leg, and an arc of three between midwicket and deep mid-on; his length and direction were exact, the odd one straightened and kept low. It was relaxed and beautiful bowling. Ramadhin at the other end threw the ball up, but his deep-set field scarcely encouraged the lofted drive. Subba Row got himself into some difficulties against Ramadhin, mainly by playing so late. He edged him just short of Walcott at slip; then he let one from Ramadhin, bowling round the wicket, hit him on the pads and was given out. Sobers relieved Worrell, and Barrington, jumpy as a cat on hot bricks, turned his first ball straight into McMorris's hands at forward short leg. 145 for 5, or England 200 runs on.

Three runs later Dexter drove Sobers hard to wide mid-off, where Hunte, pouncing one-handed, seemed to stumble; but as Dexter came on he regained control and threw the wicket down from an acute angle.

Three wickets had fallen for 12, and now West Indies, with spinners on at both ends, and the whites of the short leg's eyes showing, were almost through. Ramadhin, using Tayfield's tactic of two short mid-ons, baited Smith with high flight; but Smith denied himself as deliberately as one refusing poisoned chocolates. Sobers set a silly mid-off for him and Smith leaned the ball even farther into the ground. This was psychological warfare by the bowler, with only the slowest of pitches in support. Sobers's length slipped, and Smith stroked him through the covers. Two full-pitches cost him only a single apiece, and then Hall, diving late at cover, failed to scoop up Parks on the half-volley.

England, at tea, were 168 for 6. Parks pulled a long hop from Sobers, cut him late; each run now was of consequence, and batsmen and bowlers knew it. Smith had drizzle on his glasses to contend with, but soon it thickened and he was allowed proper reprieve in the dressing-room. The minutes lost must have made of the West Indian section a dentist's waiting-room: there were twenty-five wasted, and Alexander would probably have settled to have a tooth out instead.

There was evident humming and hawing about whether to take the new ball when they came back, with three-quarters of an hour to go. Alexander, after consulting with Worrell, decided on it, and strangely, gave it to Hall; though after one ball it was evident he could manage only an ambling, looping delivery, with swerve but without pace. Parks took five off his first over, then edged Griffith for four and two wide of second slip. Watson replaced Hall, and Parks, turning him off his legs, sent up fifty for the stand, then the 200. Watson bounced three at him and Parks hooked the middle one off the lower edge for four. He placed Griffith to the square-leg boundary, and now Smith was left in his dust. The new ball had gone for 35 runs in 22 minutes.

Worrell bowled, and Smith hit him gorgeously through the covers, before doing the same to Watson. Then Parks, off the back foot, rippled Watson away to the cover boundary. In the next over he reached fifty, in just an hour and a half, and it must, after so much disappointment so long waiting, have been the sweetest music. Watson pitched consistently short to him, but when once he pitched up Parks drove him all along the grass to the fence. By the end England, at 238, were 293 on: the forty minutes since the new ball had brought England 60 runs. Since three o'clock, when Parks joined Smith, 90 had been added. These were significant figures, and after a day of somersaulting fortune, few could but think that the series was finally in England's pocket. But it had been a desperately near thing.

For Alexander there was the frustration of two dropped catches that gave Dexter lives, and time, if not many runs; for Cowdrey, an agony of apprehension, and then, in the rinsed, evening sky, a growing, beguiling serenity.

ENGLAND

First Innings		Second Innings	
Pullar, c. Sobers, b. Griffith ...	10	c. and b. Sobers ...	54
*M. C. Cowdrey, c. Alexander, b. Sobers	119	c. Worrell, b. Hall ...	0
E. R. Dexter, c. and b. Sobers ...	76	run out	47
R. Subba Row, c. Hunte, b. Hall	22	l.b.w., b. Ramadhin ...	13
Barrington, c. Alexander, b. Ramadhin	69	c. McMorris, b. Sobers	6
M. J. K. Smith, b. Ramadhin ...	20	not out	35
Parks, c. and b. Sobers	43	not out	55
Illingworth, c. Sobers, b. Ramadhin	0		
Allen, c. sub., b. Ramadhin ...	7	run out	25
Trueman, not out	10		
Moss, b. Watson	1		
Extras (b.7 n.b.9)	16	Extras	3
Total	393	Total (for 6 wkts.) ...	238

FALL OF WICKETS—*First Innings*—1–19, 2–210, 3–215, 4–268, 5–317, 6–350, 7–350, 8–374, 9–388, 10–393. *Second Innings*—1–3, 2–69, 3–102, 4–136, 5–145, 6–148.

BOWLING—*First Innings*—Hall, 24–3–83–1; Griffith, 15–2–62–1; Watson, 18.2–3–52–1; Ramadhin, 34–13–73–4; Worrell, 8–1–29–0; Sobers, 20–1–75–3; Walcott, 4–2–3–0. *Second Innings* (to date)—Hall, 4–0–16–1; Griffith, 9–1–40–0; Watson, 10–0–41–0; Ramadhin, 23–6–43–1; Sobers, 24–5–64–2; Worrell, 17–0–31–0; Walcott, 1–1–0–0.

WEST INDIES

First Innings

C. C. Hunte, not out	72
E. McMorris, run out	13
*F. C. M. Alexander, c. Barrington, b. Allen	26
G. Sobers, b. Moss	92
C. L. Walcott, st. Parks, b. Allen	53
F. M. Worrell, b. Trueman	15
R. Kanhai, b. Moss	6
K. T. Ramadhin, c. Cowdrey, b. Dexter	13
W. Hall, b. Trueman	29
C. Griffith, not out	5
Extras (b.6 l.b.4 n.b.4)	14
Total (for 8 wkts. dec.)	338

C. Watson did not go in.

FALL OF WICKETS—1–26, 2–103, 3–190, 4–216, 5–227, 6–230, 7–263, 8–328.

BOWLING—Trueman, 37.3–6–103–2; Moss, 34–3–94–2; Allen, 24–1–61–2; Illingworth, 12–4–25–0; Dexter, 4–1–20–1; Barrington, 8–0–21–0.

SIXTH DAY

The obsequies, as far as West Indies were concerned, were painlessly over. Alexander, who had received a good drubbing in the local press for taking the new ball after the rain the evening before, used Ramadhin with Watson first thing. Watson was twice beautifully stroked to the boundary by Parks in his opening over and after that he concentrated on bouncers until Alexander bored of him. Parks next pulled Ramadhin to the fence, then danced out to loft him between long-on and long-off. Having flexed his muscles, he contented himself with a sequence of a dozen gentle singles, taken with rather over-leisurely ease. Smith, after staring at the bowling with the concentrated effort of a myopic reading the small print in *The Times*, drove Sobers over his head and struck Walcott for six. At one point it was Parks 75, Smith 37; by lunch it was Parks 91, Smith 76; then Smith 96, Parks 97.

The seventh wicket record Test partnership for England—
174 by Cowdrey and Evans against West Indies in 1957—
went by the board comfortably, and with it the last dregs of
hope for the West Indians. They had only a charitable declaration to look to, and they didn't get it. Nor, in truth, did
they deserve it. Instead Parks went to a handsome, if latterly
languid century, and Smith, caught at the wicket for 96,
allowed Alexander to reach 23 and equal Waite's world
wicket-keeping record for a Test series.

At 350 for 7 Cowdrey declared. Some would have liked
him to have given West Indies an outside chance earlier, but
there was precious little point in squandering 29 days' hard
graft on a spree for a sprinkling of spectators. The only regret
was that the runs came, not slowly—for 100 were added in
under two hours—but as if the mechanism was running
down.

Had the series been all square, it could have been a great
day. As it was, England held safely on to what they had
struggled so long and so hard to wrest. A first victory in the
Caribbean! Not Raleigh or 'Bloody Morgan' or any other
pirateer of the Spanish Main had borne home so elusive or so
rich a plunder.

The last couple of hours or so produced a mellow innings
by Frank Worrell, including a sweep, made with the right
knee on the ground, that went for six—a copy-book stroke by
a batsman whom no photographer has ever caught in an un-
graceful position. Nor is likely to. In the last moments Fred
Trueman nonchalantly caught him one-handed on the boundary off what would have been another six. It was a just exit.

Among the traditional tomfoolery of the final overs, the
pigeons came out for their final swoop, the sun catching their
wings as they circled against the yellow poui, the blue sky and
the hills.

Then it was all over. The England team, justly happy, had
almost to drag themselves off the field. Trueman had gone in
both legs, Moss had barely eaten for four days, Allen's spinning fingers were in Laker-like condition.

An earlier declaration in such circumstances could only have been nominal, if not downright foolish. Yet, on what should have been an afternoon of celebration, the manager chose to rebuke the England captain in unnecessarily crude terms before his team and to dissociate himself from the whole proceedings. I hope he has repented, though I doubt whether repentance comes easily to him. Robins was an admirable manager from a Public Relations viewpoint, and he consequently got the best press any touring manager has ever had. He had a young, determined side to handle, not yet blasé nor cut off from one another by their individual haloes, and in this he was lucky. He was sparing of praise, and he kept aloof from his players, believing that they would be happier in their off-duty moments without him. He was probably right. They belonged to different generations, they had a different outlook. Yet the evident lack of warmth and sympathy between them was not all to the good. Cricketers are not machines, they have human failings and they sometimes need jollying along rather than criticism. The path between aloofness and familiarity is not an easy one to tread, but the best leaders command both respect and affection.

Robins wanted England always to do the right thing; I think he would always put the spirit of the game before the result. That is a proper and necessary corrective to much of the meanness and grudging behaviour that is shown on first-class grounds today. He himself as a player was a fine embodiment of the spirit of adventure: keen, mercurial, quick to the attack. He was a natural enemy of sloth, timidity and boredom.

Yet I think that on this occasion he was a good deal less than fair to Cowdrey. Did he want England, with three crocks as the main bowlers, to risk losing without a shadow of a chance of winning? Cowdrey could have set West Indies to score 80 an hour and have been defeated. It was unlikely, but possible. And to what end? For some shallow publicity, and the undiscriminating pleasure of a few spectators.

It would have been quite unrealistic. West Indies, if they

wanted to salvage the series, had to bowl England out. They had every chance to do so and they failed. At the last hurdle they were thwarted by Parks, and Cowdrey, quite justifiably and with an eye to the future, put a priority on Parks's maiden Test century. We all hoped Parks would have reached it by lunch; but he didn't, though he and Smith scored their 197 together as quickly as anyone had scored in the series.

That was about all there was to it.

★   ★   ★

ENGLAND

First Innings		Second Innings	
Pullar, c. Sobers, b. Griffith ...	10	c. and b. Sobers ...	54
*M. C. Cowdrey, c. Alexander, b. Sobers	119	c. Worrell, b. Hall ...	0
E. R. Dexter, c. and b. Sobers ...	76	run out	47
R. Subba Row, c. Hunte, b. Hall	22	l.b.w., b. Ramadhin ...	13
Barrington, c. Alexander, b. Ramadhin	69	c. McMorris, b. Sobers	6
M. J. K. Smith, b. Ramadhin ...	20	c. Alexander, b. Hunte	96
Parks, c. and b. Sobers ...	43	not out	101
Illingworth, c. Sobers, b. Ramadhin	0		
Allen, c. sub., b. Ramadhin ...	7	run out	25
Trueman, not out	10	not out	2
Moss, b. Watson	1		
Extras (b.7 n.b.9)	16	Extras (b.2 l.b.3 n.b.1)	6
Total	393	Total (for 7 wkts. dec)	350

FALL OF WICKETS—*First Innings*—1–19, 2–210, 3–215, 4–268, 5–317, 6–350, 7–350, 8–374, 9–388, 10–393. *Second Innings*—1–3, 2–69, 3–102, 4–136, 5–145, 6–148, 7–345.

BOWLING—*First Innings*—Hall, 24–3–83–1; Griffith, 15–2–62–1; Watson, 18.2–3–52–1; Ramadhin, 34–13–73–4; Worrell, 8–1–29–0; Sobers, 20–1–75–3; Walcott, 4–2–3–0. *Second Innings*—Hall, 4–0–16–1; Griffith, 9–1–40–1; Watson, 14–1–52–0; Ramadhin, 34–9–67–1; Sobers, 29–6–84–2; Worrell, 22–5–44–0; Walcott, 7–2–24–0; Hunte, 5–1–17–1.

WEST INDIES

First Innings		Second Innings	
C. C. Hunte, not out	72	st. Parks, b. Illingworth	36
E. McMorris, run out	13	l.b.w., b. Moss ...	2
*F. C. M. Alexander, b. Allen ...	26	not out	4
G. Sobers, b. Moss	92	not out	49
C. L. Walcott, st. Parks, b. Allen	53	c. Parks, b. Barrington	22
F. M. Worrell, b. Trueman ...	15	c. Trueman, b. Pullar	61
R. Kanhai, b. Moss	6	c. Trueman, b. Illing-	
		worth	34
K. T. Ramadhin, c. Cowdrey, b. Dexter	13		
W. Hall, b. Trueman	29		
C. Griffith, not out	5		
Extras (b.6 l.b.4 n.b.4) ...	14	Extras (l.b.1)	1
Total (for 8 wkts. dec.) ...	338	Total (for 5 wkts.) ...	209

C. Watson did not go in.

Fall of Wickets—*First Innings*—1–26, 2–103, 3–190, 4–216, 5–227, 6–230, 7–263, 8–328. *Second Innings*—1–11, 2–72, 3–75, 4–107, 5–194.

Bowling—*First Innings*—Trueman, 37.3–6–103–2; Moss, 34–3–94–2; Allen, 24–1–61–2; Illingworth, 12–4–25–0; Dexter, 4–1–20–1; Barrington, 8–0–21–0. *Second Innings*—Trueman, 5–1–22–0; Moss, 4–0–16–1; Illingworth, 16–3–53–2; Allen, 15–2–57–0; Barrington, 8–2–27–1; Subba Row, 1–0–2–0; Smith, 1–0–15–0; Pullar, 1–0–1–1; Cowdrey, 1–0–15–0.

On the wall of the Miramar, dimly discernible through the smoke layers that partially conceal the steel band, two painted hands—a black one and a white one—grasp one another fraternally. Under them the boldly lettered words UNITY IS OUR STRENGTH flank a map of Trinidad. Derek Walcott, a St. Lucian and the most talented poet in the Caribbean, has written in his beautiful poem *A Map of the Antilles*:

> On maps to Federalists the Antilles may seem
> A single chain, in the bright geography
> Of shoals and bays like emeralds in a book
> For children; to scholars, they are seas
> Of simple tongues and customs, in the dream

Of ageing transients, the Hesperides.
Nothing which I assert can prove them fools
Since men invent those truths which they
    discover,

Mariner or minister, I am none of these,
My compass keeps avoiding all the facts
To find that South is its magnetic mover;
By force of separation it directs
All active interest towards your shores,
    moreover,
As a true governor it approves its acts.

'A single chain'? Alas, they are not that. It is their separate-ness, the uniqueness of each island, that, first and last, strike one. Allegiances here are local, not federal; and with thousands of miles of water isolating island from island it is scarcely surprising.

Yet the emblem of the black hand grasping the white hand—and, quite as important, of a Jamaican hand grasping a Barbadian and a Trinidadian—must be made a reality if the federal idea is not to disintegrate through self-interest and distrust. At this initial stage, when certain islands, like Jamaica and Trinidad, must expect to put more into Federation than they can hope to get out from it, patience and good-will and tolerance must be made to override minor irritations. It may be that Jamaicans and Trinidadians, with their superior economies, justly see Federation as a brake on their own development. But for the smaller islands—for Antigua, St. Kitts, Grenada, Barbados and St. Lucia—it is a life-belt to which they must all cling.

At present, Federation, despite the best efforts of its administrators, remains a concept rather than a belief. Politicians, with a prime responsibility to their own islands, tend, for political reasons, to stress the disadvantages of union. They seek for loop-holes, not necessarily because they disown their federal allegiance, but because they are bargainers by nature, by habit and by trade.

There are, unfortunately, white people to whom the Miramar emblem is repugnant, except in terms of master and slave. Should the West Indies ever go the way of South Africa it is they who will be responsible. Because of them, there are negroes who, acquiring power, will wish to make extreme use of it. It is a natural reaction.

A period of emergent nationalism rarely shows a people at their most attractive, any more than does repressive colonialism: the agents of oppression suffer equally with its victims. It would be odd if the contemporary West Indian did not sometimes look bitterly back into his past, and smarting under the humiliations and injustices of slavery, vow retribution. He has still colour prejudice to contend with, often more in his own island than in any other. At the same time there are real basic backwardnesses that lead Europeans to a dismissive impatience at some of the more arrogant West Indian aspirations. A correct assessment of the speed at which power can most happily be transferred is not easy to make; and even when it is made it rarely finds favour on all sides. Politics is an art of vocal dissatisfaction.

Despite these difficulties, despite the hierarchies of colour that among West Indians themselves lead to wasteful discriminations—often unconsciously—there has been since the war a marked breakdown in racial hostility. The great hope for these green, lovely, rather sad islands is that colour will cease to have meaning either way, and that to be a West Indian, negro, Indian, or of European descent, will be sufficient passport to each others' goodwill. The British in the West Indies have as great a part to play, economically, as once they had administratively, and when the day comes, as it will, that the black hand is the one that has to be thrust forward in welcome first, one must hope that it will be proffered and grasped with an equal warmth.

POSTSCRIPT

THE island swung under us for the last time: the fresh green of the Northern Range, the breaking surf on the beaches of Toco and Blanchisseuse, the coconut curve of Mayaro. Climbing with the rising sun, the Trinidad of canefield and rice, of oil and pasture, contracted into contour and then was gone. After four months of living in and out of suitcases, of packing and unpacking in hotel rooms, of eating dreary food, of being separated from our families, we were longing to get home. Yet, as always on leaving, one was struck by nostalgia, for faces, for places, for the routine that had become part of one's life. Soon we were free of the brown mud halter that yokes Trinidad to the Orinoco and to South America. Tobago, a blob of green lapped by cobalt, slid away with its tether of islets; somewhere beneath, the parrot-fish cruised the coral and the birds of paradise fluttered among their hills.

We landed at Barbados, and Garfield Sobers, baby-faced and gum-chewing, who seemed in one's mind's eye to have been batting non-stop right through the series, left us. Liners stood out to sea off Bridgetown and through the palms schooners looked like models mounted on glass.

Then we were up to 19,000 feet again, making for Antigua. On board were Colin Cowdrey, returning early to see his week-old son, and Fred Trueman, whose first child was due any day. The rest of M.C.C. were flying later that day to play two one-day games in British Honduras. The correspondents had split up too, some returning by sea, others by different airlines. Only John Woodcock and Ron Roberts were travelling with me.

We were returning to English spring. Already the daffodils were out in the orchard at home. That was something extra to look forward to. In a fortnight the South Africans would be with us. We had learned a lot on this tour, and almost all the pieces were complete for the Tests ahead of us, and for the Australians in 1961. In Dexter, who would never have come as a batsman alone, we had looked for an all-rounder;

instead we had found a successor to the luckless Peter May (who was that day undergoing a second operation in London). In Allen, picked as an apprentice off-spinner, we had fished up a genuine Test all-rounder. Pullar had come to stay. Parks, without help from the selectors, had made his point (and mine, I'm glad to say) as finally as anyone could. An England side with him at No. 7 was not going to be beaten easily, by the Australians or anyone else.

There were those who thought Barrington's confidence may have been dented irreparably. Yet I very much hoped not, for he is not only an unaffected, agreeable man, but an all-rounder of great potential. A brilliant field anywhere; an unusually accurate leg-spinner who could develop into a Benaud. Mike Smith alone remained a mystery. After ten minutes at the wicket he played even the quickest bowling at leisure. He was a killer to the on, and latterly his range of off-side strokes had extended noticeably. Yet during those first ten minutes the most modest of quick bowlers seemed able to get him out.

We discussed all these things over gin and tonics, then lunch, between Antigua and Bermuda. A left-hand spinner; a seam-bowler who could bat a bit; those were the only missing pieces before we had a side of ideal balance and with great punishing powers. After 1961 we should need to have found a pair of fast bowlers to replace Statham and Trueman, but these two ought to last us until then. It was a happy prospect.

In Bermuda it was raining, a grey, obliterating downpour. Half-way to New York, admiring the sunset, we noticed one of the propellers feathering. Seconds later we were tilting over and aiming south again. A pump had failed. Sonny Ramadhin, on his way to England for his usual league engagement, came down the aisle. 'I don't like it,' he said. A New York negro, homeward bound after visiting relatives in his island of birth, Antigua, nudged me and said he'd had premonitions during the night that something would go wrong. 'I'm psychic,' he explained seriously, 'deeply psychic.'

I thought at first he'd said 'sick', and began to sympathize with suitably concerned expression.

We circled Bermuda for half an hour using up fuel; our landing was of gossamer lightness. Two hours later we were headed back for New York, and this time, premonitions or no premonitions, we got there. At Idlewild we exchanged our Viscount for a Britannia; then were high over the Atlantic, travelling against the sun, with the night whisked away from us almost as soon as it had started.

SCOREBOOK

M.C.C. v WINDWARD ISLANDS
At Grenada, December 21, 22 and 23. M.C.C. won by 10 wickets

WINDWARD ISLANDS

First Innings		*Second Innings*	
J. Steele, c. Subba Row, b. Trueman	8	c. Swetman, b. Trueman	8
E. Bramble, l.b.w., b. Greenhough	16	b. Moss	12
E. Gresham, run out	18	c. Barrington, b. Trueman	2
A. Roberts, l.b.w., b. Greenhough	1	b. Moss	0
O. Jackson, c. Subba Row, b. Barington	24	st. Swetman, b. Illingworth	25
T. Walker, b. Greenhough	4	c. Cowdrey, b. Moss ...	0
G. Brisbane, l.b.w., b. Greenhough	1	l.b.w., b. Trueman ...	2
T. Redhead, c. Trueman, b. Greenhough	12	not out	19
G. Niles, b. Greenhough	0	c. Trueman, b. Greenhough ...	1
O. F. Mason, c. Pullar, b. Barrington	3	b. Trueman ...	0
V. Eli, not out	0	b. Trueman ...	0
Extras (n.b.2)	2	Extras	0
Total	89	Total	69

FALL OF WICKETS—*First Innings*—1–10, 2–37, 3–39, 4–57, 5–63, 6–70, 7–86, 8–86, 9–87, 10–89. *Second Innings*—1–16, 2–18, 3–21, 4–26, 5–26, 6–48, 7–49, 8–69, 9–69, 10–69.

BOWLING—First Innings—Trueman, 8–0–27–1; Moss, 10–1–14–0; Greenhough, 16–7–32–6; Illingworth, 5–0–8–0; Barrington 5.2–3–6–2. *Second Innings*—Trueman, 8–1–22–5; Moss, 8–2–21–3; Greenhough, 5–1–25–1; Illingworth, 6–5–1–1.

M.C.C.

First Innings		Second Innings	
Pullar, not out	7		
M. C. Cowdrey, b. Redhead ...	4	not out	17
Swetman, b. Mason	1		
R. Subbar Row, l.b.w., b. Gresham	23	not out	14
*P. B. H. May, c. Steele, b. Gresham	38		
M. J. K. Smith, c. Robers, b. Gresham	1		
Barrington, b. Redhead	9		
Illingworth, c. Mason, b. Gresham	12		
Trueman, b. Redhead	16		
Moss, b. Redhead	5		
Greenhough, c. Brisbane, b. Redhead	3		
Extras (l.b.2)	2	Extras (b.8)	8
Total	121	Total (for 0 wkt.) ...	39

FALL OF WICKETS—1–8, 2–16, 3–68, 4–75, 5–75, 6–93, 7–105, 8–114, 9–117, 10–121.

BOWLING—*First Innings*—Mason, 7–1–16–1; Redhead, 14.5–2–39–5; Eli, 8–0–24–4; Brisbane, 12–2–27–0; Gresham, 12–6–13–4. *Second Innings*—Mason, 3–0–7–0; Redhead, 3–0–15–0; Eli, 1.5–0–7–0; Jackson, 1–0–2–0.

M.C.C. v BARBADOS COLTS

At Bridgetown, December 26 and 28. Drawn

M.C.C.

Pullar, l.b.w., b. White	28
M. C. Cowdrey, st. Gill, b. White	56
R. Subba Row, c. Gill, b. White	28
M. J. K. Smith, l.b.w., b. Rock	102
Barrington, c. Bethel, b. Foster	55
E. R. Dexter, run out	24
Illingworth, c. Bethel, b. Foster	4
Swetman, not out	19
Extras (l.b.7 w.1 n.b.1)	9
Total (for 7 wkts. dec.)	323

Allen, Statham and Moss did not bat.

FALL OF WICKETS—1–61, 2–98, 3–147, 4–248, 5–287, 6–297, 7–323.

BOWLING—Walker, 5–0–26–0; Greenidge, 12–1–68–0; Rock, 15–1–65–1; White, 17–7–50–3; Brancker, 4–0–12–0; Holford, 11–1–45–0; Foster, 14.3–3–48–2.

BARBADOS COLTS

L. Yearwood, run out	5
R. Brancker, c. Cowdrey, b. Moss	33
W. Greenidge, c. Smith, b. Barrington	61
D. Holford, c. Cowdrey, b. Allen	19
O. Broome, b. Moss	0
A. Bethel, run out	0
G. Foster, c. Smith, b. Subba Row	36
G. Rock, l.b.w., b. Barrington	0
A. White, b. Illingworth	25
C. O. Gill, st. Swetman, b. Subba Row	29
R. Walker, not out	1
Extras (b.3 n.b.10)	13
Total	222

FALL OF WICKETS—1–8, 2–104, 3–125, 4–128, 5–128, 6–129, 7–130, 8–157, 9–217, 10–222

BOWLING—Statham, 14–5–29–0; Moss, 18–7–58–2; Barrington, 21–10–31–2; Dexter, 14–3–36–0; Allen, 15–7–24–1; Illingworth, 18–11–25–1; Subba Row, 3–0–6–2.

M.C.C. v BARBADOS

At Bridgetown, December 30, 31, January 1 and 2.
Barbados won by 10 wickets.

BARBADOS

First Innings		Second Innings	
C. C. Hunte, c. Smith, b. Illing-			
worth	69	not out	14
M. R. Bynoe, c. Swetman, b. Ill-			
ingworth	34		
S. Nurse, b. Barrington	213		
G. Sobers, c. and b. Greenhough	154		
P. Lashley, c. Swetman, b. Dexter	45		
C. Smith, not out	4	not out	40
A. White, not out	6		
Extras (l.b.2 w.3 n.b.3) ...	8	Extras (b.2 l.b.2) ...	4
Total (for 5 wkts. dec.) ...	533	Total (for 0 wkt.) ...	58

E. D. Weekes, D. Atkinson, C. Griffith and D. Allan did not bat.

FALL OF WICKETS—1–87, 2–116, 3–422, 4–520, 5–522.

BOWLING—*First Innings*—Trueman, 24–1–110–0; Statham, 19–4–34–0; Greenhough, 30–2–125–1; Dexter, 23–1–105–1; Illingworth, 29–2–93–2; Barrington, 17–2–58–1. *Second Innings*—Trueman, 3–0–16–0; Statham, 3.2–0–38–0.

M.C.C.

First Innings		Second Innings	
Pullar, b. Lashley	46	c. and b. White ...	20
M. C. Cowdrey, l.b.w., b. Griffith	16	c. Griffith, b. White ...	40
M. J. K. Smith, b. Griffith ...	o	b. Griffith	4
P. B. H. May, c. Lashley, b. Griffith	2	b. Atkinson	69
Barrington, b. Griffith	79	l.b.w., b. Weekes ...	79
E. R. Dexter, run out	33	c. and b. Griffith ...	26
Illingworth, l.b.w., b. White ...	1	c. Nurse, b. Weekes ...	72
Swetman, c. Allan, b. White ...	33	c. Sobers, b. Weekes ...	13
Trueman, b. Atkinson	13	c. Atkinson, b. White	7
Statham, b. Atkinson	4	c. Allan, b. Weekes ...	12
Greenhough, not out	4	not out	o
Extras (l.b.6 w.1)	7	Extras (b.4 l.b.3 w3) ...	10
Total	238	Total	352

FALL OF WICKETS—*First Innings*—1–21, 2–21, 3–23, 4–113, 5–171, 6–177, 7–204, 8–227, 9–233, 10–238. *Second Innings*—1–30, 2–34, 3–84, 4–165, 5–212, 6–281, 7–307, 8–328, 9–352, 10–352.

BOWLING—*First Innings*—Griffith, 21–4–64–4; Atkinson, 25.1–12–27–2; White, 27–6–76–2; Sobers, 18–5–39–0; Lashley, 4–1–17–1; Smith, 2–0–8–0. *Second Innings*—Griffith, 23–4–66–2; Atkinson, 31–18–38–1; White, 32–10–80–3; Sobers, 23–4–77–0; Lashley, 9–1–27–0; Smith, 1–0–5–0; Weekes 14.3–2–38–4; Bynoe, 4–0–11–0.

M.C.C. v TRINIDAD

At Port-of-Spain, January 15, 16, 18, 19.
M.C.C. won by 6 wickets.

TRINIDAD

First Innings		*Second Innings*	
A. Corneal, c. Barrington, b. Trueman	54	l.b.w., b. Greenhough	39
B. Davis, run out	62	c. Dexter, b. Illingworth	18
N. Asgarali, c. Barrington, b. Illingworth	9	c. Illingworth, b. Barrington	10
K. Furlonge, c. and b. Trueman	29	st. Andrew, b. Barrington	19
M. Carew, not out	102	c. Andrew, b. Greenhough	7
W. Rodriguez, l.b.w., b. Statham	0	run out	25
M. Minshall, c. Andrew, b. Illingworth	22	not out	7
O. Corbie, b. Greenhough	2		
C. Singh, b. Statham	0		
J. Taylor, b. Statham	1		
B. Peters, not out	12		
Extras (b.2 l.b.6)	8	Extras (l.b.5 n.b.1)	6
Total (for 9 wkts. dec.)	301	Total (for 6 wkts. dec.)	131

FALL OF WICKETS—*First Innings*—1–88, 2–107, 3–137, 4–183, 5–190, 6–257, 7–264, 8–271, 9–281. *Second Innings*—1–33, 2–46, 3–76, 4–80, 5–111, 6–131.

BOWLING—*First Innings*—Statham, 30–5–75–3; Trueman, 23–6–40–2; Dexter, 10–3–18–0; Greenhough, 20–4–76–1; Illingworth, 24–5–57–2; Barrington, 7–1–17–0; Subba Row, 5–1–10–0. *Second Innings*—Statham, 8–2–21–0; Trueman, 4–2–3–0; Greenhough, 13–1–53–2; Illingworth, 11–2–25–1, Barrington, 10.1–3–23–2.

M.C.C.

First Innings			*Second Innings*	
Pullar, c. Peters, b. Singh	...	24	c. Furlonge, b. Corbie	21
R. Subba Row, c. Minshall b. Singh		49	c. Minshall, b. Taylor	73
Barrington, c. Corneal, b. Corbie		1	st. Minshall, b. Singh	16
P. B. H. May, c. Corneal, b. Peters		24	c. Peters, b. Asgarali	24
M. J. K. Smith, c. Peters, b. Singh		9	not out	47
E. R. Dexter, l.b.w., b. Singh	...	0	not out	69
Illingworth, st. Minshall, b. Corbie		7		
Trueman, c. Furlonge, b. Corbie		21		
Andrew, b. Singh	... ...	4		
Statham, not out	... ...	12		
Greenhough, not out	... ...	8		
Extras (b.10 l.b.2)	... ...	12	Extras (b.8 l.b.3 n.b.1)	12
Total (for 9 wkts. dec.)	...	171	Total (for 4 wkts.) ...	262

FALL OF WICKETS—*First Innings*—1–53, 2–64, 3–104, 4–118, 5–118, 6–119, 7–143, 8–147, 9–151. *Second Innings*—1–44, 2–73, 3–121, 4–156.

BOWLING—*First Innings*—Taylor, 20–6–31–0; Peters, 17–4–37–1; Singh, 34–11–57–5; Corbie, 19–6–34–3. *Second Innings*—Taylor, 12.5–0–54–1; Peters, 4–1–20–0; Singh, 14–0–70–1; Corbie, 14–1–48–1; Asgarali, 12–0–58–1.

M.C.C. v TRINIDAD

At Pointe à Pierre, January 21, 22, 23 and 25.

M.C.C. won by 10 wickets

M.C.C.

First Innings			Second Innings		
Pullar, c. Carew, b. Corbie ...	68				
M. C. Cowdrey, c. Caesar, b. Corbie	173				
R. Subba Row, l.b.w., b. Caesar	1		not out		0
P. B. H. May, c. Minshall, b. Aleong	25				
Barrington, c. Carew, b. Aleong ...	8		not out		2
M. J. K. Smith, b. Aleong ...	1				
E. R. Dexter, c. Charles, b. Corbie	17				
Swetman, st. Minshall, b. Rodriguez	28				
Allen, l.b.w., b. Corbie	1				
Statham, not out	4				
Moss, not out	5				
Extras (b.5 w.1)	6				
Total (for 9 wkts. dec.) ...	337		Total (for 0 wkt.) ...		2

FALL OF WICKETS—1–174, 2–184, 3–242, 4–267, 5–270, 6–278, 7–307, 8–325, 9–325.

BOWLING—*First Innings*—Caesar, 10–2–39–1; Charles, 16–2–55–0; Olton, 3–0–26–0; Aleong, 18–2–71–3; Corbie, 38–8–107–4; Rodriguez, 7–2–33–1. *Second Innings*—Rodriguez, 0.2–0–2–0.

TRINIDAD

First Innings			*Second Innings*	
A. Corneal, c. Barrington, b. Allen		13	run out	7
B. A. Davis, b. Barrington	...	38	c. Smith, b. Barrington	24
K. Furlonge, b. Moss ...	...	45	b. Dexter	4
M. C. Carew, l.b.w., b. Allen	...	6	hit wkt. b. Statham ...	70
W. Rodriguez, c. Subba Row, b. Allen		0	c. Subba Row, b. Moss	5
M. Minshall, b. Allen ...	...	2	c. Dexter, b. Allen ...	14
E. Aleong, b. Allen ...	...	4	b. Allen	0
M. Olton, b. Allen ...	...	24	c. May, b. Barrington	15
O. Corbie, l.b.w., b. Allen	...	15	l.b.w., b. Barrington ...	2
S. Charles, not out ...	...	13	b. Allen	7
S. Caesar, b. Statham ...	...	0	not out	0
Extras (b5 l.b.1) ...	...	6	Extras (b.7 l.b.13 n.b.4)	24
Total	...	166	Total	172

FALL OF WICKETS—*First Innings*—1–41, 2–55, 3–68, 4–74, 5–78, 6–86, 7–130, 8–138, 9–163, 10–166. *Second Innings*—1–28, 2–37, 3–57, 4–62, 5–143, 6–143, 7–145, 8–159, 9–170, 10–172.

BOWLING—*First Innings*—Statham, 7–1–23–1; Moss, 10–2–38–1; Allen, 22–8–33–7; Barrington, 15–1–63–1; Subba Row, 3–1–3–0. *Second Innings*—Statham, 15–3–16–1; Moss, 10–2–30–1; Allen, 27–12–30–3; Barrington, 14.4–4–42–3; Dexter, 7–1–30–1.

M.C.C. v JAMAICA COLTS

At Kingston, February 6 and 8. Drawn

M.C.C.

Pullar, b. Scarlett	84
M. C. Cowdrey, c. Wellington, b. Charvis	24
R. Subba Row, c. Nangle, b. King	23
Swetman, c. Taylor, b. Wellington	100
Barrington, b. Scarlett	1
M. J. K. Smith, b. Griffith	34
Allen, b. King	31
Andrew, l.b.w., b. Wellington	0
Statham, st. Nangle, b. Wellington	6
Greenhough, not out	0
Extras (l.b.2 w.1)	3
Total (for 9 wkts. dec.)	306

Moss did not bat.

FALL OF WICKETS—1–56, 2–111, 3–141, 4–143, 5–230, 6–292, 7–296, 8–298, 9–306.

BOWLING—King, 21–5–72–2; Griffith, 10–0–49–1; Charvis, 10–0–51–1; Wellington, 11.3–0–57–3; Scarlett, 12–2–40–2; Williams 2–0–34–0.

JAMAICA COLTS

P. Taylor, b. Allen	56
E. Griffith, c. Moss, b. Greenhough	177
F. Harvey, l.b.w., b. Greenhough	8
A. Charvis, c. and b. Barrington	11
G. Daniels, c. Swetman, b. Greenhough	0
F. Nangle, c. Andrew, b. Greenhough	11
R. Scarlett, b. Barrington	4
H. Bennett, c. Subba Row, b. Barrington	7
B. Wellington, c. Swetman, b. Greenhough	8
L. Williams, not out	0
L. King, c. Moss, b. Barrington	0
Extras (b.9 l.b.4)	13
Total	295

FALL OF WICKETS—1–171, 2–199, 3–242, 4–243, 5–255, 6–262, 7–276, 8–294, 9–295, 10–295.

BOWLING—Statham, 11–4–30–0; Moss, 15–3–42–0; Greenhough, 25–3–91–5; Allen, 20–8–42–1; Subba Row, 1–0–1–0; Barrington 21.1–2–72–4; Swetman, 1–0–4–0.

M.C.C. v JAMAICA

At Melbourne Park, Kingston, February 10, 11, 12 and 13. Drawn

JAMAICA

First Innings		Second Innings	
J. K. Holt, c. Andrew, b. Trueman	6	b. Trueman	o
E. McMorris, c. Andrew, b. True-man	104	b. Greenhough ...	74
V. Lumsden, b. Greenhough ...	46	l.b.w., b. Trueman ...	o
F. M. Worrell, c. Barrington, b. Trueman	75		
E. Griffith, b. Dexter	18	b. Trueman ...	15
J. Hendricks, l.b.w., b. Trueman	20	st. Andrew, b. Subba Row	23
R. Scarlett, not out	72	b. Greenhough ...	59
A. F. Rae, c. Andrew, b. Green-hough	12	c. Trueman, b. Illing worth	6
L. Mullings, l.b.w., b. Barrington	4	not out	6
A. L. Valentine, c. Andrew, b. Greenhough	o		
C. Watson, st. Andrew, b. Barring-ton	8		
Extras (l.b.2 n.b.7)	9	Extras (b.4 l.b.8 w.1 n.b.6)	19
Total	374	Total (for 7 wkts.) ...	202

FALL OF WICKETS—*First Innings*—1–10, 2–103, 3–237, 4–254, 5–263, 6–322, 7–353, 8–360, 9–365, 10–374. *Second Innings*—1–0, 2–7, 3–27 4–63, 5–172, 6–183, 7–202.

BOWLING—*First Innings*—Trueman, 21–3–54–4; Moss, 24–4–82–0; Dexter, 18–4–59–1; Greenhough, 23–5–58–3; Illingworth, 21–4–56–0; Barrington, 9.5–0–44–2; Subba Row, 3–0–12–0. *Second Innings*—Trueman, 11–4–27–3; Moss, 8–4–14–0; Dexter, 3–1–13–0; Green-hough, 21–10–54–2; Illingworth, 11–6–21–1; Barrington, 14–4–48–0; Subba Row, 3–1–6–1.

M.C.C.

M. C. Cowdrey, b. Scarlett	...	...	...	...	...	19
R. Subba Row, c. Watson, b. Valentine		...	...	...	92
Barrington, c. Lumsden, b. Valentine	...	...	...	...	30
P. B. H. May, b. Mullings	...	...	...	...	...	124
E. R. Dexter, c. McMorris, b. Scarlett	...	...	...	...	75
M. J. K. Smith, l.b.w., b. Scarlett	...	...	...	...	111
Illingworth, not out	...	...	...	...	...	60
Extras (b.7 l.b.2 w.1 n.b.4)	...	...	...	...	...	14
Total (for 6 wkts. dec.)	...	...	...	...	...	525

Andrew, Trueman, Moss and Greenhough did not bat.

FALL OF WICKETS—1–56, 2–109, 3–177, 4–332, 5–382, 6–525.

BOWLING—Watson, 27–3–94–0; Worrell, 4–0–19–0; Valentine, 44–10–108–2; Griffith, 14–1–63–0; Scarlett, 33.3–9–113–3; Mullins, 23–3–101–1; Lumsden, 3–0–13–0.

M.C.C. v LEEWARD ISLANDS

At Antigua, February 25, 26 and 27. Drawn.

LEEWARD ISLANDS

First Innings		*Second Innings*	
O. Williams, st. Andrew, b. Subba Row	84		
P. Evanson, b. Greenhough	45	b. Dexter	8
L. Harris, c. Cowdrey, b. Subba Row	16	not out	89
K. Rock, run out	1	b. Greenhough ...	28
F. Edwards, b. Greenhough ...	0	st. Andrew, b. Subba Row	5
D. Michael, c. Andrew, b. Moss.	64	not out	55
E. Matthew, b. Moss	33		
R. Buchanan, b. Moss	0		
H. Turner, b. Barrington ...	35		
H. Anthonyson, c. Cowdrey, b. Greenhough	10		
A. Freeland, not out	0		
Extras (b.2 l.b.1 w.1 n.b.1) ...	8	Extras (b.6 l.b.4 w.1 n.b.3)	14
Total	296	Total (for 3 wkts.) ...	199

FALL OF WICKETS—*First Innings*—1–63, 2–111, 3–118, 4–118, 5–183, 6–235, 7–235, 8–264, 9–296, 10–296. *Second Innings*—1–11, 2–83, 3–92.

BOWLING—*First Innings*—Moss, 21–9–55–3; Dexter, 11–2–38–0; Illingworth, 6–1–14–0; Greenhough, 24–9–46–3; Barrington, 24.4–4–56–1; Allen, 9–2–29–0; Subba Row, 16–4–50–2. *Second Innings*—Moss, 9–2–31–0; Dexter, 9–1–22–1; Ilingworth, 2–1–2–0; Greenhough, 8–2–25–1; Barrington, 8–1–27–0; Allen, 2–0–21–0; Subba Row, 8–0–26–1; Swetman, 1–0–10–0; Smith, 1–0–4–0; Cowdrey, 1–0–17–0.

M.C.C.

M. C. Cowdrey, c. Anthonyson, b. Turner	115
R. Subba Row, c. Williams, b. Freeland	110
Barrington, l.b.w., b. Matthew	83
E. R. Dexter, st. Buchanan, b. Matthew	107
M. J. K. Smith, not out	21
R. Illingworth, l.b.w., b. Freeland	8
Extras (b.9 l.b.3)	12
Total (for 5 wkts. dec.)	456

FALL OF WICKETS—1–210, 2–258, 3–426, 4–426, 5–456.

BOWLING—Freeland, 22.1–0–108–2; Turner, 18–1–67–1; Anthonyson, 11–0–71–0; Matthew, 26–2–94–2; Williams 6–0–36–0; Harris, 2–0–15–0; Michael, 2–0–19–0; Rock, 2–0–34–0.

M.C.C. v BRITISH GUIANA

At Georgetown, March 6, 7, 8, 9. Drawn.

BRITISH GUIANA

First Innings		Second Innings		
G. Gibbs, b. Trueman	78	c. Illingworth, b. Dexter ...	4
J. Solomon, c. and b. Allen ...	37	not out	28
R. Kanhai, c. Trueman, b. Allen	14		
B. Butcher, b. Allen	122	b. Dexter	0
C. L. Walcott, c. Allen, b. Moss ...	83		
C. Stayers, not out	19		
W. Edun, b. Moss	0		
I. Mendonza, not out	7	not out	31
Extras (b.6 l.b.2 n.b.6) ...	14	Extras (l.b.1 n.b.3) ...	4
Total (for 6 wkts. dec.) ...	375	Total (for 2 wkts.) ...	67

L. Gibbs, E. Mohamed and P. Legall did not bat .

FALL OF WICKETS — 1–77, 2–102, 3–186, 4–327, 5–365, 6–366.

BOWLING — Trueman, 20–7–35–1; Moss, 34–11–65–2; Dexter, 22–2–80–0; Illingworth, 32–12–74–0; Allen, 30–10–64–3; Subba Row, 11–0–43–0.

M.C.C.

Pullar, c. Mendonza, b. Legall	141
M. C. Cowdrey, b. Mohamed	139
E. R. Dexter, b. Gibbs	1
M. J. K. Smith, b. Stayers	97
Allen, c. Legall, b. Mohamed	27
R. Subba Row, c. Mendonza, b. Mohamed	1
Swetman, not out	44
Trueman, c. Mendonza, b. Legall	10
Moss, c. L. Gibbs, b. Mohamed	0
P. B. H. May, absent ill	0
Extras (b.1 l.b.8 w.6 n.b.3)	18
Total	494

FALL OF WICKETS — 1–281, 2–286, 3–292, 4–360, 5–398, 6–409, 7–477, 8–491, 9–494.

BOWLING — Stayers, 29–4–114–1; Legall, 28–9–56–3; Edun, 15–2–47–0; L. Gibbs, 55–17–105–1; Mohamed, 45.2–14–114–4; Solomon 4–0–28–0; Walcott 5–1–12–0.

M.C.C. v BERBICE
At Blairmont. Drawn.

Berbice, 387–2 dec. (J. Solomon 201*, B. F. Butcher 131*)
M.C.C. 641–6 (Pullar 65, Smith 50, Parks 183, Barrington 103, Illingworth 100, Dexter, 54, Subba Row 58*.)

BELIZE, BRITISH HONDURAS—M.C.C., 278 for 8 wkts. dec.
(Allen, 55 not out, Barrington 48); Governor's XI, 60 (Swetman 3 for 9,
Greenhough 3 for 13). M.C.C. won by 218 runs.

TEST MATCH AVERAGES

ENGLAND

BATTING

	Innings	Times not out	Runs	Highest score	Avge.
E. R. Dexter	... 9	1	526	136*	65·75
M. C. Cowdrey	... 10	1	491	119	54·55
Barrington	... 9	0	420	128	46·66
Pullar	... 10	1	385	66	42·77
R. Subba Row	... 4	0	162	100	40·50
M. J. K. Smith	... 9	0	308	108	34·22
Allen	... 9	4	171	55	34·20
P. B. H. May	... 5	0	83	45	16·60
Statham	... 4	1	46	20*	15·33
Trueman	... 8	2	86	37	14·33
Illingworth	... 8	1	92	41*	13·14
Swetman	... 7	0	58	45	8·28
Moss	... 2	0	5	4	2·50

Also batted—Parks, 43 and 101*.

* Not out.

BOWLING

	Overs	Maidens	Runs	Wickets	Avge.
Trueman	... 220·3	62	549	21	26·14
Statham	... 130·4	42	286	10	28·60
E. R. Dexter	... 64·4	18	170	5	34·00
Barrington	... 106·5	41	217	5	43·40
Allen	... 197	53	417	9	46·33
Moss	... 85	17	226	3	75·33
Illingworth	... 196	61	383	4	95·75

Also bowled—M. C. Cowdrey, 2–0–19–0; R. Subba Row, 1–0–2–0;
M. J. K. Smith, 1–0–15–0; Pullar, 1–0–1–1.

WEST INDIES

BATTING

	Innings	Times not out	Runs	Highest score	Avge.
G. Sobers	8	1	709	226	101·28
F. M. Worrell ...	6	1	320	197*	64·00
C. C. Hunte ...	8	1	291	72*	41·57
R. Kanhai ...	8	0	325	110	40·62
C. L. Walcott ...	3	0	84	53	28·00
E. McMorris ...	6	0	124	73	20·66
F. C. M. Alexander ...	8	2	108	33	18·00
R. Scarlett ...	4	1	54	29*	18·00
J. Solomon ...	4	1	50	23	16·66
W. Hall	6	3	48	29	16·00
B. Butcher	3	0	31	13	10·33
K. T. Ramadhin ...	4	0	41	23	10·25
C. Singh	3	0	11	11	3·66
C. Watson	3	1	3	3	1·50

Also batted—S. Nurse, 70 and 11; C. Griffith, 5*.

* Not out.

BOWLING

	Overs	Maidens	Runs	Wickets	Avge.
K.T.Ramadhin ...	248·3	83	491	17	28·88
W. Hall ...	236·2	49	679	22	30·86
C. Singh ...	84·2	35	165	5	33·00
C. Watson ...	199	39	593	16	37·06
F. M. Worrell ...	115·5	37	233	6	38·83
G. Sobers ...	114	14	356	9	39·55
R. Scarlett ...	134	53	209	2	104·50

Also bowled—C. C. Hunte, 13–3–26–1; R. Kanhai, 4–3–2–0; J. Soloman, 17–2–51–1; C. L. Walcott, 20–4–70–1; C. Griffith, 24–3–102–1.

M.C.C. TOUR AVERAGES

ALL FIRST-CLASS GAMES

BATTING

	Innings	Times not out	Runs	Highest score	Avge.
M. C. Cowdrey	... 18	2	1,014	173	63·37
E. R. Dexter	... 18	2	908	136*	56·75
R. Subba Row	... 14	3	598	110	54·36
Pullar	... 18	2	777	141	48·56
Barrington	... 19	1	830	128	46·11
M. J. K. Smith	... 19	2	649	111	38·17
P. B. H. May	... 12	0	389	124	32·41
Allen	... 12	5	199	55	28·42
Illingworth	... 16	2	353	100	25·21
Swetman	... 12	1	177	45	16·09
Statham	... 8	3	78	20*	15·60
Greenhough	... 4	3	15	8*	15·00
Trueman	... 13	2	153	37	13·90
Andrew	... 1	0	4	4	4·00
Moss	... 5	1	15	5*	3·75

Also batted—Parks, 183, 43 and 101*.

* Not out.

BOWLING

	Overs	Maidens	Runs	Wickets	Avge.
Trueman	... 342·3	86	883	37	23·86
Allen	... 305	94	639	23	27·78
Greenhough	... 182	43	590	21	28·09
Statham	... 213	57	493	15	32·86
Barrington	... 237·3	64	619	17	36·41
R. Subba Row	... 53	7	169	4	42·25
Moss	... 251	56	687	13	52·84
E. R. Dexter	... 192·4	36	637	11	57·90
Illingworth	... 365	107	781	11	71·00

Also bowled—M. C. Cowdrey, 3–0–36–0; M. J. K. Smith, 2–0–22–0; Swetman, 1–0–10–0; Pullar, 1–0–1–1.